T0328628

EXPLAINING MANAGEMENT PHENOMENA

One key objective of management research is to explain business phenomena. Yet understanding the nature of explanation is essentially a topic in philosophy. This is the first book that bridges the gap between a technical, philosophical treatment of the topic and the more practical needs of management scholars, as well as others across the social sciences. It explores how management phenomena can be explained from a philosophical perspective and renders sophisticated philosophical arguments understandable by readers without specialized training. Covering virtually all the major aspects of the nature of explanation, this work will enhance empirical and theoretical research, as well as approaches combining the two. With many examples from management literature and business news, this study helps scholars in those fields to improve their research outcomes.

ERIC W. K. TSANG is the Dallas World Salute Distinguished Professor at the University of Texas at Dallas and a fellow of the Academy of International Business. He is a leading management scholar in applying philosophy to tackle methodological problems. In 2017, he published *The Philosophy of Management Research*.

EXPLAINING MANAGEMENT PHENOMENA

A Philosophical Treatise

ERIC W. K. TSANG

CAMBRIDGE
UNIVERSITY PRESS

Shaftesbury Road, Cambridge CB2 8EA, United Kingdom

One Liberty Plaza, 20th Floor, New York, NY 10006, USA

477 Williamstown Road, Port Melbourne, VIC 3207, Australia

314–321, 3rd Floor, Plot 3, Splendor Forum, Jasola District Centre, New Delhi – 110025, India

103 Penang Road, #05–06/07, Visioncrest Commercial, Singapore 238467

Cambridge University Press is part of Cambridge University Press & Assessment,
a department of the University of Cambridge.

We share the University's mission to contribute to society through the pursuit of
education, learning and research at the highest international levels of excellence.

www.cambridge.org
Information on this title: www.cambridge.org/9781009323116

DOI: 10.1017/9781009323109

First published 2023
First paperback edition 2024

A catalogue record for this publication is available from the British Library

ISBN   978-1-009-32313-0   Hardback
ISBN   978-1-009-32311-6   Paperback

Contents

Figures and Tables

Figures

Tables

Preface

In the summer of 2018, I attended a management conference in Wuhan, China, where I had a casual conversation with an ethnic Chinese scholar whom I had known for some years. He was an enthusiast of the theory of yin (陰) and yang (陽) rooted in Chinese philosophy and he tried to persuade me that this theory could explain virtually all phenomena, whether natural or social. I expressed some serious reservations about his claim because if a theory is said to be able to explain everything, it probably explains nothing. However, so as not to jeopardize our friendship, I refrained from challenging his argument. The way he described how yin–yang theory explained a certain phenomenon also indicated that he had a problematic conception of explanation. What does it really mean anyway when one claims that a theory has explained a phenomenon?

Fast forward to 2021. The whole world had been in "lockdown" for close to a year because of the Covid-19 pandemic that had originated in Wuhan (coincidentally the same city where the management conference mentioned above was held). Since I was born and grew up in Hong Kong and many of my friends and relatives lived there, I paid particular attention to news about infection and vaccination in the city. Not long after the vaccination program started there in early 2021, several people died within a few days of receiving the first dose of the vaccine. However, each time this happened, the Hong Kong government announced — after an investigation by a team of medical experts — that it had found no direct relationship between vaccination and the death of the unfortunate person; that is, it could not be scientifically established that the vaccination had caused death and so vaccination was ruled out as an explanation of the death. I wondered how the team of experts determined whether a causal relationship existed or not. Was it that only if a person died within, say, thirty minutes of receiving a vaccine that vaccination would be considered to be the cause of death? How should the post-vaccination death of people be explained?

The above two incidents reminded me of the theories of explanation and causation that I read in philosophy, in particular the philosophy of science, decades ago. Given the critical role played by explanation in not only science but also our daily lives, it is natural that explanation has long been a key topic of philosophical discourse. In fact, the literature has grown voluminously, especially so after the publication in 1942 of Carl Hempel's landmark paper "The Function of General Laws in History," which presents the deductive-nomological model of scientific explanation.

The act of explaining is something most people seem to have an intuitive grasp of. Yet many may be caught off guard by a question like "When we say that this is an explanation for an event or a phenomenon, what exactly do we mean?" Although I wrote a chapter on explanation in my previous book *The Philosophy of Management Research*, a single chapter does not do justice to this complex and important subject matter. My search of the extant literature failed to identify even one book that bridged the gap between a technical, philosophical treatment of the subject and the more practical needs of management as well as other social science scholars. This omission in the literature gave rise to my idea to write this book.

The main objective of this book is to deepen management scholars' understanding of various issues associated with explanation. Such under-standing in turn will improve the quality of their research both conceptu-ally and empirically. This objective has determined the book's practice orientation and selection of materials. For instance, I skipped Philip Kitcher's unification theory of explanation, which is so technical that few management researchers would likely find it useful. Similarly, my presen-tation of Aristotle's doctrine of the four causes in Chapter 3 is relatively brief despite the doctrine's significant position in philosophy and its complicated nature; it is less relevant to management research than the other modes of explanation discussed in that chapter. I drew examples mostly from management literature and business news but also used examples from natural science and daily life if I judged that these examples would illustrate more clearly my arguments. Needless to say, I repeated some of the common examples used by philosophers, such as the barom-eter, the birth-control pill and the flagpole counterexamples to illustrate the problems of the covering law model of explanation. Given that one of the basic objectives of scientific research is to explain phenomena, scholars in social science disciplines other than management will also find this book useful. In addition to providing knowledge about explanation, I also hope that readers will appreciate and benefit from the philosophical arguments presented in the book. These arguments, in my opinion, are generally more rigorous and sophisticated than those that usually appear in management literature.

I tried to strike a balance between breadth and depth of coverage within given space constraints. The coverage is broad enough that management scholars should be able to find in this book a great deal of what they need to know about explanation for the benefit of their own research, whether qualitative or quantitative. Owing to the broad coverage of topics, depth is sometimes sacrificed; each of the highly technical issues included in this book could have easily taken up the space of a journal article or even an entire book. My treatment is presented necessarily in a simplified manner. Readers may refer to the cited references if they wish to go into details. To help readers in this respect, I have included in this book most of the classic references for each topic discussed.

Although this book has a stronger philosophical flavor than most academic management texts, as indicated by the phrase "A Philosophical Treatise" in its title, I sometimes sacrificed the rigor of argument typically found in philosophy by avoiding pedantic and technical philosophical issues. While some background knowledge of philosophy would surely be helpful to readers, my writing is pitched at a level such that in-depth knowledge of philosophy is not required to understand most of the discussion. Philosophical concepts and arguments – especially complicated ones – are as far as possible introduced with clarity and elaboration. That said, I hope readers will be willing to exert more effort to understand this book than they would employ when reading an average management text and that they are prepared to consult philosophical texts where necessary to understand particularly technical points. I also won't explain commonly used terms like ontology, epistemology, metaphysics, positivism, realism, induction and deduction, the meanings of which can be easily found via the Internet.

The process of writing this book was, for my part, a learning journey. I started to delve into the literature about three years ago and soon noticed that the number of references had snowballed quickly to an unmanageable scale. I therefore had to be more selective in my review. Moreover, my routine (and sometimes unexpected) research, teaching and administrative duties as well as family issues interrupted my progress from time to time. This book was really a side-project, partly because none of my doctoral students at that time were working on anything remotely related to the topic of the book. Since most of the examples appearing in the literature were from the natural sciences, I faced occasionally the challenge of finding appropriate management examples to illustrate my arguments. A consolation, however, was that I not only got to know more about the subject of explanation but was also able to sort out conceptual issues that had previously puzzled me. On the whole, the process of researching and writing this book was an enjoyable, albeit strenuous, intellectual experience.

I wish to pay special thanks to Professors Florian Ellsaesser and Jochen Runde, my coauthors on a journal paper, extracts of which were incorporated into Chapter 2. I learned a great deal from working with them. Miss Valerie Appleby and Mr. Toby Ginsberg of Cambridge University Press gave me generous assistance without which the publication of this book would be delayed. Last but not least, I thank my younger son, Boris, who let me use his photo as the cover of the book.

Articles

Articles partially incorporated into this book

Ellsaesser, F., Tsang, E. W. K. and Runde, J. 2014. Models of causal inference: Imperfect but applicable is better than perfect but inapplicable. *Strategic Management Journal*, 35: 1541–1551.

Tsang, E. W. K. 2021. Multi-theoretical approaches to studying international business strategy. In K. Mellahi, K. Meyer, R. Narula, I. Surdu and A. Verbeke (Eds.), *The Oxford handbook of international business strategy*: 153–172. Oxford: Oxford University Press.

CHAPTER I

The Nature of Explanation

In our daily lives, the practice of giving explanations is ubiquitous; we often want to explain or obtain an explanation for certain events we encounter. Using more formal language, "explanandum" refers to the event to be explained while "explanans" refers to that which does the explaining. The example of deaths (explanandum) following Covid-19 vaccination (a possible explanans) mentioned in the Preface belongs to the domain of scientific explanations, which this book focuses on.[1] Yet there are explanations that fall outside this domain; one example might be an explanation for why our friend, Mary, got married last year. Scientific explanations and explanations in everyday life appear to be distinct. The former tend to be more objective, systematic, precise and rigorous than the latter, but the distinction may be more apparent than real. This notwithstanding, explanation should be a unified notion in the sense that explanations in everyday life are more or less continuous with scientific explanations (McCain 2015); that is, the differences between the two types of explanation are a matter of degree rather than a distinction in kind (Woodward 2003) and "no argument has ever proved that the logic of explanation in everyday life differs from that of explanation in science" (Faye 1999: 61). In response to a query about her recent marriage, Mary may reply, "I was already thirty years old last year. As you know, in our society, people expect a woman to settle down around that age." Mary's casual everyday-life explanation contains an implicit scientific flavor, revealing a first-person reaction to a social norm concerning the socially desirable marital age for women. Her explanation points to a legitimate research topic in sociology, psychology, or even anthropology. It goes without saying that the structure and very nature of explanations may depend on the explanandum (i.e., what sort of thing is being explained) (Wilson and Keil 1998); explaining why Mary got married last year is very different from explaining why the Hunga Tonga-Hunga Ha'apai volcano erupted in January 2022 or why a jetliner of China Eastern Airlines crashed on March 21, 2022, resulting in 132 deaths.

Explanations, whether scientific or otherwise, are answers to why-questions, as put forward forcefully by Hempel and Oppenheim (1948: 135):[2]

> To explain the phenomena in the world of our experience, to answer the question "why?" rather than only the question "what?", is one of the foremost objectives of all rational inquiry; and especially, scientific research in its various branches strives to go beyond a mere description of its subject matter by providing an explanation of the phenomena it investigates.

The act of explaining should be distinguished from explanation. Explaining is an action that we take to communicate verbally or non-verbally an explanation to others (McCain 2015), while an explanation is "something one grasps or understands that makes things more intelligible" (Harman 1986: 67). Here the thing we grasp refers to a set of propositions; that is, "an explanation is a set of propositions with a certain structure" (Strevens 2013: 510). According to this view, explanations assume the form of arguments. Put simply, when we explain, we communicate verbally or non-verbally a set of propositions to others. As such, explaining is an intentional act of communication bounded by context, directed at the questioner and potentially persuasive (Faye 1999). This view of explanation belongs to the epistemic conception of explanation discussed in the next section.

The Epistemic versus Ontic Conception of Explanation

In the second half of the twentieth century, philosophers of science set for themselves the task of answering questions related to the nature of explanation, such as "What are the essential features of an explanation?" or "Do different science disciplines have different methods of explaining their research results?" Although the twentieth century closed with no real consensus on the nature of explanation, at the very least, most philosophers of science presumed that explanations belong to a special class of representations (Wright and van Eck 2018). A typical example is Hempel and Oppenheim's (1948: 136–137) description of the relationship between the explanandum and the explanans: "By the explanandum, we understand the sentence describing the phenomenon to be explained (not that phenomenon itself); by the explanans, the class of those sentences which are adduced to account for the phenomenon." Providing an explanation is an attempt to account for a phenomenon and such an account necessarily represents matters in a certain way but not in another way. In other words, explanations explain by subsuming a phenomenon under a general representation.

The above is essentially the epistemic conception of explanation, according to which "explanations are complexes of representations of entities in the physical world" (Wright and van Eck 2018: 998). Explanation is concerned with understanding and the cognitive abilities of human beings. Ruben (1990: 6) argues that "the analysis of explanation belongs to general epistemology, in the same way as the analysis of knowledge does, and not just to the philosophy of science, narrowly conceived. Scientific explanation, like scientific knowledge, has a special importance and pride of place in a general theory of knowledge." Scientific explanations are texts or descriptions that aim to increase our knowledge about phenomena. For the epistemic conception, it is the text or description that explains (Illari 2013).

At the beginning of the twenty-first century, some philosophers of science challenged the epistemic conception by proposing the ontic conception, according to which "the term *explanation* denotes a class of non-representational, mind-independent entities that are located within reality among its other extant spatiotemporal parts" (Wright 2015: 20). The key difference between the two conceptions concerns "whether explanations are representations of entities in the world or the worldly entities so represented" (Wright and van Eck 2018: 1001). Instead of being representations, ontic explanations are physical entities that reside and participate in the causal structure of the world. In his study of how the brain functions, Craver (2007: 27) provides a definitive description of the ontic conception:

> the term explanation refers to an objective portion of the causal structure of the world, to the set of factors that bring about or sustain a phenomenon (call them objective explanations) . . . . Objective explanations are not texts; they are full-bodied things. They are facts, not representations. They are the kinds of things that are discovered and described. There is no question of objective explanations being "right" or "wrong," or "good" or "bad." They just are.

Mechanismic explanation, which is discussed in Chapter 3, has become the key battlefield where the debate between the epistemic conception and the ontic conception is located. For proponents of the epistemic conception, "since explanation is itself an epistemic activity, what figures in it are not the mechanisms in the world, but representations of them"

(Bechtel 2005: 425). In contrast, the ontic conception maintains that "mechanisms explain the phenomena they explain by being responsible for them" (Illari and Williamson 2011: 821). As such, the mechanisms involved in an explanation might sometimes be beyond our cognitive capacity to comprehend.

Following most philosophers of science, in this book I adopt the epistemic conception of explanation. In addition to the fact that "explanation has traditionally been taken to be squarely in the realm of epistemology" (Humphreys 1989: 3), there are some problems with the ontic conception. For instance, since explanations are a portion of the mind-independent causal structure of the world, explanations do not have any unnecessary or irrelevant parts and "scientists can discover, dissect, disrupt, depict, and describe — but, ironically, not explain" (Wright 2015: 20–21). Since explanations are not arguments, multiple competing good or bad explanations for a given phenomenon do not exist (Waskan 2006). Finally, the ontic conception focuses on the occurrence of an event "explained" by a singular causal interaction (Wright and van Eck 2018). Salmon (1975), however, argues that explanations of particular events seldom have genuine scientific import (as opposed to practical value) and that explanations which deserve serious attention are almost always explanations of categories of events.

The Influence of Ontology

The debate between the epistemic conception and the ontic conception is concerned with the ontological nature of explanation. Ontology in fact also affects how one explains certain phenomena. The current heated debate concerning entrepreneurial opportunities is an excellent illustration. In our daily conversations, a business opportunity is something that can be identified, spotted, seen, seized, or discovered, as shown in the following passage from a *Forbes* article written by the CEO and founder of a technology company dedicated to simplifying digital security for consumers: "Endless business opportunities await those who can spot the openings. Think about the challenges you have faced, services you use regularly and the frustrations you might have had. You might just identify your next big opportunity" (Ravichandran 2021). When an entrepreneur is asked why she set up a new company, a standard answer is something like, "I just discovered an opportunity to provide a new product (or service) that serves a certain market niche." The validity of the explanation hinges on whether an opportunity is something that can be discovered, leading to the question: "In what mode does an opportunity exist?" This is squarely an ontological problem.

The debate concerning the ontological nature of entrepreneurial opportunities was initiated more than two decades ago by Shane and Venkataraman's (2000) seminal paper "The Promise of Entrepreneurship as a Field of Research," in which they maintained that the defining feature of entrepreneurial phenomena is "the discovery and exploitation of profitable opportunities" (217) and that the objective existence of entrepreneurial opportunities offers a solid foundation for entrepreneurship as a distinctive subject of study. They defined entrepreneurial opportunities as "those situations in which new goods, services, raw materials, and organizing methods can be introduced and sold at greater than their cost of production" (220). That is, entrepreneurial opportunities have to be profitable, in line with people's usual conception of business opportunities. After all, it is nonsensical to say that one has discovered (or created) an opportunity to lose money.[3]

This discovery view of opportunities has been challenged increasingly by scholars expressing their dissatisfaction with the idea that opportunities exist objectively "out there" in ways visible to potential entrepreneurs (McMullen et al. 2007; Davidsson and Wiklund 2009; Alvarez et al. 2014). Challenging the ontological shallowness of Shane and Venkataraman's conceptualization, Görling and Rehn (2008: 101) commented that "opportunities are assumed to simply exist ... without any real clarity as to what this would mean." Some scholars even denied categorically that opportunities are preexisting entities in the external world, arguing that opportunities are created endogenously through entrepreneurial agency (Wood and McKinley 2010; Korsgaard 2011). The core idea is that "opportunities do not exist until entrepreneurs create them through a process of enactment" (Alvarez et al. 2013: 307). This creation approach places more emphasis on human agency in entrepreneurial activities.

Both the discovery and the creation approaches have obvious fatal flaws. In the case of the former, suppose that a business executive claims to have discovered an entrepreneurial opportunity and then exploits it by establishing a new company. Since the opportunity, by definition, must be profitable, this profitability attribute of the outcome is known with certainty at the moment of "discovery" even before the exercise of entrepreneurial action during exploitation (Ramoglou and Tsang 2016). This is an impossible situation. However, the creation approach does not fare any better. The statement that "opportunities do not exist until entrepreneurs create them through a process of enactment" (Alvarez et al. 2013: 307) is a universal statement. As such, a single counter-example is good enough to overturn the statement. In fact, one can easily think of many cases where the business opportunity was not created by the entrepreneur but emerged from certain structural changes in the economy. For instance, although many businesses were hit hard by the Covid-19 pandemic, some new business opportunities did emerge because of the structural changes brought about by the pandemic (Colvin 2020). Alvarez et al. (2013) may abandon the universal statement and concede that some opportunities are created whereas others aren't. Yet this is anything but a solution because they will then face the uphill task of distinguishing clearly between these two types of opportunities and delineating their relationship, as well as dealing with the fatal flaws associated with the discovery approach (Ramoglou and Tsang 2017).

As a remedy, Stratos Ramoglou and I proposed the actualization approach. Based on a realist philosophy of science, we rehabilitated ontologically the objectivity of entrepreneurial opportunities by elucidating their propensity mode of existence. We defined entrepreneurial opportunity as "the propensity of market demand to be actualized into profits through the introduction of novel products or services" (Ramoglou and Tsang 2016: 411). Opportunities exist akin to a flower seed's propensity to germinate into a flower versus the flower itself. There are three ways individuals might have cognitive contact with opportunities: (1) imagining the state of the world where one makes profits by engaging in an entrepreneurial course of action; (2) believing that this state of the world is ontologically possible; and (3) after the realization of profits, knowing retrospectively that the opportunity in question was truly there. That is to say, the only occasion where we can know the existence of an opportunity is at the realization of profits; in the case of failure, we are agnostic. Our approach provides an intuitive and paradox-free understanding of what it means for opportunities to exist objectively.

The fatal flaws of the discovery and creation approaches are also reflected in the different explanatory efficacies of the three approaches. This can be illustrated by the case of Theranos – a high-flying but ultimately failed biotech start-up that promised to revolutionize blood testing by inexpensively performing dozens of tests based on a single finger-prick. Theranos is said to have been Silicon Valley's greatest disaster in recent years. The trial of Theranos's former CEO and founder, Elizabeth Holmes, ended in early January 2022 and drew a great deal of media attention; Holmes was found guilty on four charges of defrauding investors. Let's conduct a thought experiment. Rewind to 2013 when Theranos was at its peak, valued at about US$9 billion, with Holmes not only an entrepreneur but also a celebrity. Suppose that in an entrepreneurship course, a student asks the professor somewhat naively, "Why did Elizabeth Holmes establish Theranos?" How would the professor reply?

If the professor is a follower of the discovery approach, he would probably reply, "Holmes discovered a business opportunity that will revolutionize blood testing. She set up Theranos to exploit the opportunity." If he subscribes to the creation approach, his answer would be something like: "Holmes created an opportunity to revolutionize blood testing and is exploiting the opportunity through Theranos." With the benefit of hindsight, both answers are problematic. Given the current state of blood testing technology, it can be concluded safely that the entrepreneurial opportunity that Holmes came up with simply didn't and still doesn't exist. Since the opportunity never existed, there was nothing to be discovered, period. As to the creation-based answer, it was simply impossible for Holmes to have created the so-called opportunity. Note that an entrepreneurial opportunity has to be profitable and, in this case, the opportunity in question could not be profitable. Rather, what she had in fact created was Theranos, nothing more, nothing less.

If the professor buys our argument that opportunities exist objectively as propensities, he would have replied, "Since Theranos hasn't been profitable, we are not sure whether Holmes's *imagined* business opportunity exists. At this moment, what we can say is only that she seems to *believe* that the opportunity does exist and so established Theranos to exploit it." In 2015, John Carreyrou, who at that time was working for the *Wall Street Journal*, began writing a series of investigative articles on Theranos that questioned the firm's blood testing claims and exposed its alleged fraudulent activities. His book, *Bad Blood: Secrets and Lies in a Silicon Valley Startup*, provides a detailed account of the Theranos case. The book, as well as media reports of the case, indicate that Holmes's coming up with the idea of performing dozens of blood tests based on a single finger-prick and her belief that her idea would work are consistent with the first two ways of cognitive contact with opportunities, namely, imagining and believing. (It's just that in this case, her imagined opportunity did not exist.) Holmes had little relevant technical knowledge when she conjured up her revolutionary idea of blood testing. It is not an exaggeration to say that her idea was born out of passion and pure imagination:

> She quoted Jane Austen by heart and referred to a letter that she had written
> to her father when she was nine years old insisting, "What I really want out
> of life is to discover something new, something that mankind didn't know
> was possible to do." And it was this instinct, she said, coupled with a
> childhood fear of needles, that led her to come up with her
> revolutionary company. (Bilton 2016)

Despite her idea lacking any scientific foundation, the following description indicates Holmes's strong belief in the idea's feasibility:

> Phyllis Gardner, an expert in clinical pharmacology at Stanford, recalled
> discussing Holmes's skin patch idea and telling her it "wouldn't work."
> "She just stared through me," Dr Gardner told the BBC.
> "And she just seemed absolutely confident of her own brilliance. She
> wasn't interested in my expertise and it was upsetting." (Thomas 2022)

Such a belief propelled Holmes through the obstacles encountered in
growing Theranos until its fraud was exposed by people like Carreyrou.
In brief, the actualization approach provides the best answer to the
student's why-question in 2013 without the benefit of hindsight.

Explanation involves relationships between entities. As demonstrated by
the above example, ontology plays a significant role when an entity's mode
of existence is ambiguous. Such ambiguities are not rare in the social
sciences, given the complexity of social ontology, which are concerned
with the reality of money, government, property, marriage and so on
(Searle 2006).

Understanding

The above distinction between explaining and explanation can also be
framed in cognitive terms. Explaining is a cognitive process that, when
carried out successfully by the initiator, yields a particular cognitive outcome — explanation — that in turn promotes understanding (McCain
2015) and is sometimes accompanied by an "aha" feeling or "Eureka!"
moment. Wilkenfeld (2014: 3368) argues that "explanations just ARE
those sorts of things that, under the right circumstances and in the right
sort of way, bring about understanding." In other words, an explanation
must be capable of "making clear something not previously clear" (Scriven
1962: 175), or "relating (or reducing) unfamiliar phenomena to familiar
ones" (Friedman 1974: 9). Metaphorically describing the distinctive cognitive experience of explanatory understanding, Peirce (1908: 100) says
that a good explanation "is turned back and forth like a key in a lock."

Since a phenomenon is inextricably bound up with others, a given explanation usually has implications for phenomena associated with the one it initially attempts to explain. Therefore, explanation increases understanding not just for its target but also for a larger domain of related affairs (Wilson and Keil 1998). Explanation is like detective work, in which the researcher meticulously pieces together otherwise disparate facts into a coherent, understandable picture.

To understand why an event occurs is a cognitive achievement greater than simply knowing that the event occurs (Lipton 2009). For example, in early 2010, there was news reporting that Toyota had recalled millions of vehicles in the United States. Knowing that this event had occurred is one thing; understanding why it occurred is another. Here, it is useful to distinguish between description and explanation. Put simply, "description tells us what is there, explanation why it is there" (Bergmann 1957: 79). News reporting provided a description of the Toyota recall, usually with an explanation: the recall was due to a problem with the gas pedal. This explanation promoted understanding of the event, leading to a greater epistemic gain than simply knowing of its occurrence through reading the related description.

Another example is in natural science. Robert Brown in 1827 discovered the continuous movement of small particles suspended in a fluid. He announced the following year this discovery – later termed Brownian motion – only by describing it. At the close of the century, Gouy's research convinced him that Brownian motion was a clear demonstration of the existence of molecules in continuous movement. Nevertheless, he failed to work out any mathematized theory that could be subjected to quantitative confirmation or falsification. In 1905, Einstein formulated the mathematical laws governing the movements of particles based on the principles of kinetic-molecular theory, thus providing an explanation for Brownian motion (Maiocchi 1990). The explanation renders the movement of such small particles intelligible. This is why understanding is said to be "a mental state with positive epistemic status" (McCain 2015: 833).

An explanation "fills in a particular gap in the understanding of the person or people to whom the explanation is directed" (Scriven 1962: 175). As a cognitive achievement, understanding necessitates the exercising of cognitive ability and can be an effortful activity; it "requires the grasping of explanatory and other coherence-making relationships in a large and comprehensive body of information" and "is achieved only when informational items are pieced together by the subject in question"

(Kvanvig 2003: 192). As such, understanding of complicated matters often comes in degrees (Elgin 2007). Suppose that immediately after its massive vehicle recall in 2010, Toyota releases a detailed and rather technical report of the gas pedal problem that explains how that problem was related to the scale of the recall. Individuals' cognitive ability, as reflected in their relevant background knowledge, affects the depth of their understanding promoted by Toyota's explanation. In other words, the same explanation may lead to different degrees of understanding by different individuals. The quality of an explanation is thus audience-relative.

Explanations should be based on facts: we want explanations to be truth-tracking (Faye 1999). However, citing that a fact in question is an instance of a generalization is not an explanation because it provides no additional understanding beyond the generalization (Bunge 1997). Suppose someone asked, "Why did Peter die last month?" The answer "Peter was human and all humans are bound to die eventually" is not an explanation for Peter's death, presuming that we already know Peter was a person. Rather, the answer merely identifies Peter as a member of the human race and so supplies no understanding at all. In contrast, the answer "Peter was hit by a car and died instantly" is a valid explanation, promoting our understanding of his death.

The cognitive sense of understanding is derived from the intellectual satisfaction that a research question has been answered adequately. This sense of satisfaction often increases one's confidence that the related explanation is true; that is, the explanation is an accurate description of the underlying causal factors that bring about the phenomenon in question. A helpful example is Jean Perrin's work on molecules. At the turn of the twentieth century, there was heated debate among scientists about the reality of molecules. Perrin proposed a lucid argument in favor of molecules' existence. His argument was based on the experimental determination of Avogadro's number, N, which is the number of molecules in a mole of any substance. Perrin performed a spectacular set of experiments on Brownian motion of colloidal particles. Using an ultramicroscope, he was able to determine N based on observations of the vertical distribution of these particles in suspension. A number of distinct experimental techniques were developed in the science community to determine N. Perrin counted thirteen different techniques, including those with a basis in Brownian motion, alpha decay, X-ray diffraction, blackbody radiation, or electrochemistry (Jenson 2015). All these methods produced practically the same number, enabling Perrin to comment with confidence concerning the validity of his molecular hypothesis as an explanation for the striking agreement among the methods:

> Our wonder is aroused at the very remarkable agreement found between values derived from the consideration of such widely different phenomena. Seeing that not only is the same magnitude obtained by each method when the conditions under which it is applied are varied as much as possible, but that the numbers thus established also agree among themselves, without discrepancy, for all methods employed, the real existence of the molecule is given a probability bordering on certainty. (Perrin 1913 [1923: 215–216])

Perrin's confidence is natural in the sense that his explanation contributes significantly toward the understanding of the agreement among the widely different methods.

One caveat is that it is possible for a sense or feeling of understanding to come from two well-documented psychological biases – hindsight and overconfidence. For the former, explanation accounts for events that have happened. When we construct an explanation, we may not be aware of the extent to which we are affected by outcome information, such as the extinction of a species, the explosion of an aircraft or the bankruptcy of a company. We tend to conceptualize the outcome as inevitable and may claim that it was fairly predictable all along. This hindsight bias leads us to believe that we have a rather thorough understanding of an effect and thus regard the search for an explanation as complete (Trout 2002). As to overconfidence bias, it exists among both laymen and experts, such as chief financial officers of large corporations predicting the Standard & Poor Index for the following year and physicians providing a diagnosis (Kahneman 2011). Similar to the case of hindsight bias, the subjective, "settled" feeling of understanding associated with overconfidence may prompt a "stopping rule" that sees us cease considering alternative explanations of an event on the grounds that we have understood the relevant causes (Trout 2002). After completing the DNA model, the intrinsic elegance of the DNA structure seemed obvious to Crick and Watson from the start: "The idea was so simple that it had to be right . . . . A structure this pretty just had to exist" (Watson 1968: 131). Their claim reflects both hindsight bias (the DNA structure had to exist) and overconfidence (the structure had to be right).

The fact that an explanation conveys a sense of understanding seems to offer a reason for thinking it is also a true explanation. Yet, a false explanation may convey a sense of understanding too. For instance, Aristotle created the well-known geocentric model of the planets, in which the earth is stationary and is the center of all other motions such as the circular movements of the sun and the moon around the earth. Claudius Ptolemy, who worked out the details of the model, claimed that if the earth did not lie in the center of the universe, the whole order of things that we observed concerning the increase and decrease in the length of daylight would be fundamentally upset (Toomer 1984). For centuries, the geocentric model surely contributed to people's understanding of the change between day and night and the movements of the planets. Explanation plays an objective, truth-tracking role (Faye 1999), which contrasts with the subjective feeling of understanding that explanation may generate. We have to be cautious about attributing an epistemic virtue to a sense of understanding when evaluating an explanation; an explanation that conveys a deep sense of understanding is not necessarily more accurate than one that conveys a shallower sense. The discussion of inference to the best explanation in Chapter 6 elaborates on the distinction between the understanding provided by an explanation and the truthfulness of the explanation.

Tautology

Explanation brings about understanding but tautological explanation does not. More than three centuries ago, Locke (1975) wrote about tautologies (or what he called "trifling propositions"), being of the opinion that this sort of proposition brought no increase in knowledge:

> What is this more than trifling with Words? It is but like a Monkey shifting his Oyster from one hand to the other; and had he had but Words, might, no doubt, have said, Oyster in right hand is *Subject*, and Oyster in left hand is *Predicate*: and so might have made a self-evident Proposition of *Oyster, i.e. Oyster is Oyster*; and yet, with all this, not have been one whit the wiser, or more knowing. (IV.viii.3)

Stated more formally, tautologies are propositional statements that "have the property of being true regardless of the truth values assigned to the constituent elements of the proposition" (Caplan 1977: 390). For instance, a proposition of the form "A is A," "A or not A" or "If A then A" is tautological because the proposition is true whether A is true or false.

Tautologies are not rare in our daily lives. The most famous of all tautologies is probably God's reply to Moses, "I am that I am." Emmet (1962) identifies seven uses of tautology and categorizes God's reply as a "shut up" tautology: "You mind your own business: I am that I am." (23).

None of Emmet's seven uses are about increasing our knowledge due to the very content of a tautology. Alleged or real tautologies encountered in research usually take a more complicated form than "Oyster is Oyster" or "I am that I am." An early challenge to evolutionary theory made by Scriven (1959) is the tautological nature of its well-known "survival of the fittest" thesis — if researchers define "the fittest" as those that survive, then it will lead to the empirically empty statement that evolution is concerned with the survival of the survivors.[4]

A well-known accusation of tautology in economics and management research is related to the attempt of transaction cost economics (TCE) to explain the size of a firm. Coase (1988: 19) provides a concise description of the accusation:

> The limit to the size of the firm would be set when the scope of its operations had expanded to the point at which the costs of organizing additional transactions within the firm exceeded the costs of carrying out the same transactions through the market or in another firm. This statement has been called a "tautology." It is the criticism people make of a proposition which is clearly right.

Peters (1976: 2) argues that "tautologies are not subject to empirical falsification"; so does Popper (1959). Thus, an acid test of whether a proposition is tautological is whether one can come up with a thought experiment that falsifies the proposition. It is not difficult to think of a situation where the proposition concerning the size of the firm is falsified. A major weakness of TCE, as argued by Zajac and Olsen (1993), is that the theory over-emphasizes cost minimization and neglects the value creation aspect of a transaction. A more comprehensive approach should take both cost minimization and value maximization aspects into account (Tsang 2000). As such, it is possible empirically for a firm to have expanded beyond the point at which "the costs of organizing additional transactions within the firm exceeded the costs of carrying out the same transactions through the market or in another firm" (Coase 1988: 19) if it created value that more than compensated for the extra costs incurred in the expansion. The alleged tautology thus does not exist and Coase (1988) rightly denies the accusation.

A more recent and well-known accusation of tautology in strategic management research is Priem and Butler's (2001a) critique of Barney's (1991) heavily-cited paper delineating the resource-based view. To explain why competitive advantage arises, Barney (1991: 107) maintains that "valuable and rare organizational resources can be a source of competitive advantage." This propositional statement is the foundation for his explanation of the generation of sustained competitive advantage. If the proposition is flawed, the explanation for sustained competitive advantage collapses too. Here, I provide a simpler version of Priem and Butler's challenge that Barney's proposition is tautological. In Barney's paper, firm resources refer to "firm attributes that may enable firms to conceive of and implement value-creating strategies" (101),[5] and "a firm is said to have a *competitive advantage* when it is implementing a value creating strategy not simultaneously being implemented by any current or potential competitors" (102). Substituting these definitions of firm resources and competitive advantage for the corresponding terms in the statement "Valuable and rare organizational resources can be a source of competitive advantage," we arrive at a revised statement: "Valuable and rare firm attributes that may enable firms to conceive of and implement value-creating strategies can be a source of implementing a value creating strategy not simultaneously being implemented by any current or potential competitors."[6] When elaborating the meaning of rare resources, Barney (1991: 106) maintains that "if a particular valuable firm resource is possessed by large numbers of firms, then each of these firms have the capability of exploiting that resource in the same way, thereby implementing a common strategy that gives no one firm a competitive advantage." Therefore, the word "rare" in the revised statement refers to the point that the value-creating strategy is "not simultaneously being implemented by any current or potential competitors." As a result, "competitive advantage is defined in terms of value and rarity, and the resource characteristics argued to lead to competitive advantage are value and rarity" (Priem and Butler 2001a: 28). In short, the statement "Valuable and rare organizational resources can be a source of competitive advantage" is tautological and thus unfalsifiable. As such, the statement does not increase our understanding of why competitive advantage arises.

The tautological nature of Barney's (1991: 107) statement "valuable and rare organizational resources can be a source of competitive advantage" is somewhat similar to that of Agassi's (1971) example of the law of diminishing returns used in his discussion of tautology and testability in economics. For example, the law says that if we have two production factors and if we increase one while keeping the other constant, a moment will come when it will be more profitable to start increasing the latter rather than to keep increasing the former. Suppose "a precondition for a factor to be a production factor rather than an initial investment — or overhead, for that matter! — is that it obeys the law of diminishing returns" (51). If that is the case, the law is a tautology because "a precondition of our attempting to apply it is our knowledge that it applies successfully" (51).

In response to Priem and Butler's (2001a) critique, Barney (2001: 41) makes a bold, sweeping claim that at the definitional level, "all strategic management theories are tautological in the way Priem and Butler describe." To support this claim, he uses the examples of TCE and Porter's (1980) five forces framework. For the latter, he argues that "Porter's (1980) assertions about the relationship between industry attractiveness and firm performance can be reduced to tautology by observing that firms in attractive industries will outperform firms in unattractive industries and by defining industry attractiveness in terms of the ability of firms to perform well" (41). Priem and Butler (2001b: 58) aptly rebut this as an inaccurate account of Porter's theory:

> Reading Porter's (1980) chapter on the structural analysis of industries shows that he *does not* claim that industry attractiveness is related to firm performance. He never mentions "industry attractiveness" at all. The only place where the term appears in Porter's 1980 book is in the appendix, concerning the GE/McKinsey matrix.

In other words, Barney distorts Porter's theory in order to make it tautological. Using the acid test mentioned above, the theory is obviously not tautological. Consider Barney's (2001: 42) own description of Porter's core proposition: "firms operating in industries characterized by high rivalry, high threat of substitutes, high threat of entry, high buyer power, and high supplier power will perform at a lower level than firms operating in industries without these attributes." It is surely possible that this proposition is falsified empirically; that is, firms operating in industries without those attributes perform at a lower or similar level than firms operating in industries with such attributes because the effects of the five factors (or forces) on firm performance are complicated and may not be consistent with Porter's prediction. As to the other example of TCE, Barney (2001: 41–42) restates its proposition as: "hierarchical forms of governance will replace market forms of governance when the costs of market governance are greater than the costs of hierarchical governance." Unlike the case of Porter's theory, this restatement does not make the proposition tautological because, as discussed, the proposition is falsifiable. Barney (2001: 42) further argues that "the critical issue is not whether a theory can be restated in such a way as to make it tautological – since this can always be done – but whether at least some of the elements of that theory have been parameterized in a way that makes it possible to generate testable empirical assertions." The above discussion has indicated that if a theory is not tautological, it can't (without serious distortion) be restated in a way that makes it tautological, period. If a theory is tautological, it is simply impossible to parameterize some of its elements so that testable empirical assertions are generated; otherwise, the theory is not tautological in the first place. For example, can anyone parameterize some elements of the statement "All bachelors are unmarried" so that the statement can be empirically tested?

Barney (2001: 42) attempts to justify tautologies in a footnote:

> Moreover, because a theory is tautological does not mean that it might not be insightful and even empirically fruitful. For example, all game theoretic models are tautological in the sense that the hypotheses they generate are completely determined by the assumptions adopted in the models and the laws of mathematics applied to these assumptions. However, these tautological models can sometimes generate quite counterintuitive insights that can, in principle, lead to important empirical research. Again, the issue is not tautology, per se, but, rather, whether the propositions derived from a tautology can be parametrized in a way that makes empirical testing possible.

Since Barney seems to have mixed up scientific theories with mathematical models, such as game theoretic models, we have to first distinguish between the two. Mathematical models are not created for the purpose of explaining empirical phenomena, although they may generate useful implications, as illustrated by Ramsey's (1925: 347) example:

> Thus we use "2x2 = 4" to infer from "I have two pennies in each of my two pockets" to "I have four pennies altogether in my pockets." "2x2 = 4" is not itself a genuine proposition in favour of which inductive evidence can be required, but a tautology which can be seen to be tautologous by anyone who can fully grasp its meaning.

Tautologies involve different levels of complexity, depending on the number of premises and the amount of logical manipulation performed on the premises (Peters 1976). The premises and analyses can be so complex that the validity of the conclusion is not immediately apparent. An excellent example of a complex tautological system is Euclidian geometry learned commonly in school. Some of this geometry's theorems require a strenuous reasoning process to deduce from axioms. Such tautologies can, as Barney (2001) maintains, generate counterintuitive insights.[7] Yet it makes absolutely no sense to talk about parametrizing mathematical theorems in a way that makes empirical testing possible;

does it make sense, say, to measure the three angles of a triangle in the empirical world to see whether they add up to 180 degrees? A key characteristic of mathematics is its separation from the empirical world: "Once the axioms and the rules are fully formulated, everything else is built up from them, without recourse to the outside world, or to intuition, or to experiment" (Lane 1981: 465). Thus, the issue of parametrizing is nonexistent.

In contrast to mathematics, the primary objective of scientific theories, which include management theories, is to explain empirical phenomena (McCain 2015). In searching for a criterion of demarcation between science and non-science, Popper (1959) argues that a theory is scientific if and only if it is testable. He then goes on to equate testability with falsifiability. In other words, the distinction between scientific and non-scientific theories is that the former are falsifiable whereas the latter are not. Although his argument has been criticized heavily (see Jones and Perry 1982), falsifiability remains one of the main criteria for judging whether a theory is scientific. Since tautologies are unfalsifiable, tautological theories do not belong to science. To conclude, if the explanation offered by a scientific theory is tautological, it won't increase our understanding of the phenomenon in question and is thus useless in this respect.

Explanatory Completeness

In mid-2020, it was reported that Samsung Electronics planned to shift much of its display production from China to Southern Vietnam in 2020 (Reuters 2020). This piece of short news quoted a Vietnamese state-run newspaper saying that "Samsung sees Vietnam as an important gateway to other Southeast Asian countries and a link in its global supply chain." The quote provides an explanation to *one* aspect of Samsung's action. Explanation completeness can be discussed from two dimensions: psychological and philosophical. Although this book focuses on the latter, it is worth discussing briefly the former.

When people read the above quote from the Vietnamese state-run newspaper, some may deem that the explanation is complete, whereas others may not. In Zemla et al.'s (2017) study of how people evaluate naturalistic, everyday explanations, they found that incompleteness (i.e., whether there are gaps in the explanation) was one of the six attributes associated with explanation quality. That is, "if an explanation suggests that A causes B, but it is not immediately clear *how* A causes B, participants will be sensitive to this omission" (1495). According to this finding, how Vietnam being an important gateway to other Southeast Asian countries and a link in Samsung's global supply chain would impact Samsung's relocation plan affects one's perception of explanatory completeness.

Korman and Khemlani (2020) propose a theory predicting that if there exists an unspecified causal relation – a gap – anywhere within an explanation, individuals have to use multiple models to handle the gap and will treat such explanations as less complete than those without such a gap. Korman and Khemlani conducted four experiments that provided participants with causal descriptions, some of which yielded one explanatory model (e.g., A causes B and B causes C) and some of which demanded multiple models (e.g., A causes C and B causes C). Participants generally preferred one-model descriptions to multiple-model ones on tasks that implicitly or explicitly required them to assess explanatory completeness. The results of these experiments corroborated Korman and Khemlani's theory, suggesting that an explanation is considered complete when it refers to a single, integrated mental model, but incomplete when referring to multiple models.

Going back to the Samsung example, suppose we receive a piece of additional information that due to Vietnam's strategic position as stated in the newspaper quote, Samsung decided to set up a production hub there. This decision led to the relocation of its display production from China to Southern Vietnam. That is, Vietnam's strategic position caused the setting up of the production hub, which in turn caused the relocation of display production. In contrast to this hypothetical explanation, suppose the additional information is that Samsung's concern about concentrating too much of its production activity in China was another cause of the relocation. In other words, both Vietnam's strategic position and Samsung's concern caused the relocation. According to Korman and Khemlani's (2020) theory, the first explanation would be considered more complete because it is contained within an integrated mental model. As to the second explanation, the relation between two separate causes of the relocation is unspecified. People would thus find it difficult to construct an integrated model to accommodate both causes and so would judge the explanation as less complete. However, this conclusion is counterintuitive in that because the second explanation provides two causes, as opposed to only one, of the same event, people should consider the second explanation to be more complete. Therefore, more research is needed to test Korman and Khemlani's theory.

Regardless of one's subjective evaluation of an explanation's completeness, the fact is that we do not explain the totality of an event, only certain aspects of it (Hempel 1965). Thus, explanation is necessarily incomplete in this sense. The idea of a complete explanation is, in fact, "foreign to science" (Scriven 1962: 201). The contrastive approach to explanation captures this intrinsic characteristic of explanation.[8] A basic tenet of the approach is that explanation-seeking questions often have an implicit or explicit contrastive form (Garfinkel 1981). There are two crucial elements of a contrastive question — (1) allomorph and (2) fact and foil.

Allomorph

Returning to Samsung's relocation of production, the newspaper quote answers the question as to why Samsung moved production to Vietnam rather than, say, Thailand. A request for an explanation of why a certain event occurred raises different questions, depending on which word or words in the description of the event are stressed (Dretske 1977). Samsung's relocation can be described in the following statement:

(S) Samsung Electronics planned to shift much of its display production from China to Southern Vietnam in 2020.

The statement may be given different embodiments, which Dretske (1977) calls allomorphs, depending on its contrastive focus. This seemingly simple statement in fact contains eight different allomorphs, stated in italics:

(S$_a$) *Samsung Electronics* planned to shift much of its display production from China to Southern Vietnam in 2020.

(S$_b$) Samsung Electronics *planned to shift* much of its display production from China to Southern Vietnam in 2020.

(S$_c$) Samsung Electronics planned to shift *much* of its display production from China to Southern Vietnam in 2020.

(S$_d$) Samsung Electronics planned to shift much of its *display production* from China to Southern Vietnam in 2020.

(S$_e$) Samsung Electronics planned to shift much of its display production from *China* to Southern Vietnam in 2020.

(S$_f$) Samsung Electronics planned to shift much of its display production from China to *Southern* Vietnam in 2020.

(S$_g$) Samsung Electronics planned to shift much of its display production from China to Southern *Vietnam* in 2020.

(S_h)   Samsung Electronics planned to shift much of its display production from China to Southern Vietnam in *2020*.

Each of the eight allomorphs refers to a different aspect of the event and suggests a distinct type of contrastive question. An allomorph reflects the interest of the questioner and invokes an answer that addresses that interest. Needless to say, an explanation associated with one allomorph is irrelevant with respect to other allomorphs. The abovementioned quote from the state-run newspaper is related to allomorph S_g, answering the question as to why Samsung planned to move to Vietnam, instead of another country. The difference between S_g and S_f is that the latter's focus is on the location within Vietnam, not Vietnam itself. The difference between S_b and S_c is less obvious and needs elaboration. A question related to S_b could be "Why did Samsung plan to shift its display production from China to in Southern Vietnam, instead of setting up a new display production factory in Southern Vietnam?" That is, the focus here is the way in which display production was to be set up in Southern Vietnam. S_c is concerned with the extent of production shifting. Note that some of the above allomorphs may not make sense in the real world. For example, S_e assumes that Samsung had display production in countries other than China; otherwise, the question about why the shift of production was from China instead of another country makes no sense.

An explanation is often incomplete in the sense that it only captures a slice of an event's causal history. As Lewis (1986: 217) well says, "to explain an event is to provide some information about its causal history," usually from someone who possesses the information to someone who does not. However, for every why-question, there is an almost infinite number of causes that could be cited. Every causal explanation may lead to a further explanation ad infinitum, with each of these earlier causes a part of the causal history of the event. If we want to answer the question of why Samsung moved its display production to Vietnam, we could go as far back as the big bang, if we believe the big bang theory. For those who do, without the big bang, Samsung would not have existed in the first place. Based on this line of argument, the big bang is part of the causal history of every event but explains only a few (Lipton 1990).

Better questions lead to better explanations (Mäki 2004). The question "Why did Samsung plan to shift its display production from China to Southern Vietnam?" is vague because it may refer to any of the above eight allomorphs. To render the task of explaining an event manageable, we need to indicate which aspect of the event is up for explanation by, for instance, paraphrasing the question as "Why did Samsung plan to shift its display production from China to Southern Vietnam, instead of Thailand?" The revision makes clear which aspect of Samsung's relocation needs to be explained. In this case, the focus is on the comparison between Southern Vietnam and Thailand as potential locations. As such, the contrastive form of questioning eliminates a vast number of elements and aspects of the causal history of an event that are explanatorily irrelevant to the explanation-seeking question (Ylikoski 2007) and so aids selection of appropriate explanantia from the causal history (Marchionni 2006). Many why-questions that scientists ask are in fact contrastive in nature (Weber et al. 2013) although, more often than not, the foil is not stated explicitly because it is understood in the context of the discussion.

Fact and Foil

The question "Why P?" may be construed as "Why P in contrast to (other members of) X?", where the contrast class X is a class of propositions including P together with alternatives to P (van Fraassen 1980). More specifically, a typical contrastive question is of the form "Why P rather than Q?" where P is the fact to be explained and Q is the foil, an alternative to P. Q can be either a single alternative or a set of alternatives. Consider the abovementioned question associated with S_b "Why did Samsung plan to shift much of its display production from China to Southern Vietnam, rather than setting up a new display production factory in Southern Vietnam, in 2020?" Shifting display production from China to Southern Vietnam is the fact and the single alternative – setting up a new display production factory in Southern Vietnam – is the foil. A contrastive question related to S_g "Why did Samsung plan to shift much of its display production from China to Southern Vietnam, rather than Thailand or India, in 2020?" has two alternatives as the foil. An explanation has to compare between Southern Vietnam and these two alternatives.

The idea is that a fact is often not specific enough and we need to include a foil to indicate which aspect of the fact is up for explanation. Hence, a contrastive explanation of a fact is just a partial explanation of that fact, focusing on one of its aspects. Note that a contrastive question of the form "Why P rather than not-P?" is problematic because the global foil – not-P – is usually too general to narrow down the scope of explanation (Lipton 1993). In fact, this contrastive question is effectively the same as the non-contrastive question "Why P?" (Day and Botterill 2008). Since the factors that explain a fact relative to one foil often do not explain it relative to another foil, a contrastive question imposes a constraint on explanation by allowing only some of the virtually infinite number of causes in the causal history of a fact to be explanatorily relevant.

The contrastive question "Why P rather than Q?" presupposes that it was not possible for both P and Q to occur, implying that the fact and the foil are incompatible in this sense. Yet it is a misconception that contrasts must be incompatible (Barnes 1994). Consider a contrastive question related to S_g "Why did Samsung plan to shift much of its display production from China to Southern Vietnam, rather than Thailand, in 2020?" If one interprets "much of" as "greater than 50 percent," the fact and the foil are incompatible; otherwise, they are compatible. As another example, the fact and the foil in the question "Why did Samsung plan to shift its display production from China to Southern Vietnam, rather than setting up a new display production factory in Southern Vietnam?" are compatible because Samsung could do both.

In terms of problem solving, the contrastive approach to explanation helps to identify the cause of a problem, as shown by Lipton's (1993: 53) example below:

> Suppose that my car is belching thick, black smoke. Wishing to correct the situation, I naturally ask why it is happening. Now imagine that God (or perhaps an evil genius) presents me with a full Deductive-Nomological explanation of the smoke. This may not be much help. The problem is that many of the causes of the smoke are also causes of the car's normal operation. Were I to eliminate one of these, I might only succeed in making the engine inoperable. By contrast, an explanation of why the car is smoking *rather than running normally* is far more likely to meet my diagnostic needs.

Compared to the deductive-nomological explanation, which is discussed in Chapter 3, focusing on the contrast between the fact (the car smoking) and foil (the car is running normally) helps to narrow down the set of factors that cause the smoke.

Explanatory Generality

In addition to completeness, explanations also vary in terms of generality. Some explanations are more general than others, depending on the nature of the explanandum in question. In natural science, "scientific explanations can be given for such particular occurrences as the appearance of Halley's comet in 1759 or the crash of a DC-10 jet airliner in Chicago in 1979, as well as such general features of the world as the nearly elliptical orbits of planets or the electrical conductivity of copper" (Salmon 1984: 3). In management research, the explanation of why multinational corporations (MNCs) planned to move their production facilities out of China in 2020 is more general than the explanation of why Samsung planned to move its display production from China to Southern Vietnam in 2020. This is because the latter includes more contextual details. Simply put, "context is the set of circumstances in which phenomena (e.g. events, processes or entities) are situated" (Griffin 2007: 860) and can explain some salient aspects of the phenomenon under investigation (Cappelli and Sherer 1991). The explanation of Samsung's move is less general (or more contextualized) in that it involves specific details of the circumstances in which the event is situated. Scientific research usually aims at more general explanations. As mentioned, explanations of particular events seldom have genuine scientific import and explanations that draw serious attention usually explain classes of events (Salmon 1975).

Some management researchers hold the mistaken view that explanations are necessarily general in nature and so contextualization may hurt the quality of an explanation. Welch et al. (2011), for example, construct a typology of theorizing from case studies based on the trade-off between causal explanation and contextualization and "consider how the case study generates causal explanations and how it incorporates context – two features of the case study that are often regarded as being incompatible" (740–741).[9] They use the term "trade-off" to refer to the incompatibility. Here, I interpret their meaning of trade-off to be similar to that used in Bartlett and Ghoshal's (1989) typology of MNCs' operating options – "a trade-off (or conflicting contingencies) between integration and respon-siveness" (Brock and Hydle 2018: 118). When an MNC attempts to achieve global efficiency through integrating its overseas subsidiaries, it often faces the challenge of simultaneously making these subsidiaries more responsive to the host countries in which they are located. In other words, a high level of integration can be achieved only at the expense of respon-siveness. Using the term "trade-off" with a similar meaning, Welch et al. (2011) state a growing concern that "in the pursuit of robust explanations, contextualization has suffered" (741). By "robust explanations," Welch et al. are, in fact, referring to explanations that are causal in nature.

A serious problem is that Welch et al.'s so-called trade-off simply doesn't exist; that is, causal explanation and contextualization are certainly compatible.[10] They define causal explanation as something that "makes claims about the capacities of objects and beings to make a difference to their world" (741). According to this definition, there are many explanations that are unequivocally causal and yet highly contextualized. Suppose a main reason for Samsung's relocation of its display production from China to Southern Vietnam was, as the abovementioned Vietnamese state-run newspaper claimed, the strategic location of Vietnam in Southeast Asia. The explanation is surely causal — the cause (or one of the major causes) being Vietnam's strategic location. At the same time, the explanation is highly contextualized — it is about the production relocation plan of a specific MNC in a specific year from one specific host country to another; it is not about production relocation by MNCs in general. Hence, there is simply no relationship between whether an explanation is causal and how far the explanation is contextualized. As mentioned, the extent to which an explanation is general depends a great deal on the nature of the explanandum. Welch et al.'s (2011) paper subsequently won the 2021 Journal of International Business Studies Decade Award. In their retrospective paper on the award, Welch et al. (2022) drop their "trade-off" claim but keep their typology. Unfortunately, there is little variation along the dimension of causal explanation because, as I show elsewhere (Tsang 2013, 2022a), few case studies provide weak causal explanation. As such, their typology is of little use in guiding case study research.

In the main, management researchers investigate three types of explanandum. The first type refers to phenomena that have few spatiotemporal constraints and so are more abstract. Such phenomena are often targets of explanation by theories and theories are necessarily general. This may be a reason for Welch et al.'s belief that explanations are general in nature. A good example of this type of explanandum is Coase's (1937) pioneering work on TCE. In fact, Coase asks not just the simple question "Why is there any organisation?" but a contrastive question: "Having regard to the fact that if production is regulated by price movements, production could be carried on without any organisation at all, well might we ask, why is there any organisation?" (388). His question can be paraphrased as: Why are some production activities organized in firms rather than markets? He does not impose any national boundary or other constraints on the kind of organizations TCE attempts to explain. Therefore, the corresponding explanation is general in the sense that it does not refer to a specific organization or group of organizations, neither does it refer to a specific period of time during which organizations operate. TCE is designed to have a high level of explanatory power, with its explanation intended to be applicable widely such that the theory can be used to explain the other two types of explananda.

The second type of explanandum refers to phenomena that have well-defined spatiotemporal boundaries. This is the most common kind of empirical study published in management journals. Researchers often face this type of explanandum when they attempt to explain the results of quantitative studies. One of my own empirical studies offers a good example. Su and Tsang's (2015) sample consisted of US Fortune 500 firms during the period from 1996 to 2003, which defined the spatiotemporal boundary of the study. Our results indicated that secondary stakeholders – as represented by various nonprofit or nongovernmental organizations – play a positive moderating role in the relationship between product diversification and financial performance. This is the explanandum in question. We proposed an explanation – maintaining relationships with secondary stakeholders through donations can help firms that pursue diversification mitigate the costs of external controls in their sociopolitical environments. The explanation applies to our sample within the specific period of time only and thus is less general than the kind of explanation attempted by Coase (1937) discussed above. In our statistical analysis, we had to include a number of control variables, such as firm performance, firm size, advertising intensity and R&D intensity, which reflected the contextual details of our sample. How far our explanation can be generalized to phenomena outside our sample's spatiotemporal boundary is a different question (see Tsang and Williams 2012 for a typology of generalization).

The last type of explanandum refers to specific events, such as Samsung's plan to relocate its display production; the associated explanations are less general (or more contextualized) than those of the above two types of explanandum. Intensive case studies investigating specific events belong to this domain. Quantitative studies, especially those that are based on cross-sectional data, mostly generate correlative rather than causal relationships, an issue discussed in Chapter 7. In contrast, "getting closer to constructs and being able to illustrate causal relationships more directly are among the key advantages of case research vis-à-vis large-sample empirical work" (Siggelkow 2007: 22). However, this does not imply that identifying causal relationships in a case study is a straightforward task. Using the "Honda Effect" – Honda's success in capturing a large share of the US motorcycle market soon after its initial entry in 1959 – as an illustrative example, Runde and de Rond (2010: 445) propose three broad criteria for evaluating causal explanations of specific events:

> (1) that the factors cited as causes were present in the run-up to the event in question; (2) that those factors were causally effective in contributing to that event, and (3) that, given an affirmative answer to (1) and (2), the causes actually cited in the explanation explain well, taking into account

various contextual and epistemic considerations relating to the intended audience for the explanation, and the interests and theoretical presuppositions of the person providing the explanation.

Since the explanation is often highly contextualized, the causes evaluated by the criteria are likely to be contextualized as well. Runde and de Rond (2010) admit that the criteria are rather general and may be insufficient for discriminating between competing explanations in some cases.

From time to time, case researchers develop propositions from their findings, often as a means of contributing to theory development. For example, Yan and Gray's (1994) comparative case study of four Sino–US joint ventures indicates that the bargaining power of potential partners affects the structure of management control in a joint venture, which in turn affects venture performance. Based on their case findings, they develop an integrative model regarding bargaining power, management control, performance and the dynamic aspects of international joint ventures. They then derive five propositions from the model, the first of which is: "The bargaining power of a potential joint venture partner will be positively related to the extent of its management control over the joint venture's operation" (1507). This and the other four propositions are more general than the explanations they provide for some of their findings, such as: "The pattern of parents' management control of IndusCon had not significantly shifted because changes in bargaining power occurred simultaneously to both parents and were relatively equal" (1504). Propositions should not be mixed up with explanations. One major purpose of propositions is to guide future research and thus propositions have to be general. Yet, propositions are not explanations and the explanations case researchers provide are necessarily contextualized, although they may employ theories in the explanatory process.

Explanatory Interestingness

Should researchers care about whether their explanation of a phenomenon is interesting? The answer is related to the current interesting research advocacy in the management field originating from Murray Davis's (1971) article "That's Interesting! Towards a Phenomenology of Sociology and a Sociology of Phenomenology," which promotes the idea that great theories need to be interesting in the sense that they put forward counterintuitive arguments: "What seems to be X is in reality non-X," or "What is accepted as X is actually non-X" (313). Davis uses a number of examples, mostly from sociology, to illustrate his idea of interestingness. One example associated with explanation is Max Weber's (1958) argument in *The Protestant Ethics and the Spirit of Capitalism* that "the religion of a society, which was considered at the time he wrote to be determined by the economy of the society, in fact determines the economy of the society" (Davis 1971: 326). Davis elaborates his point by discussing the nature of the causation involved in the phenomena:

> What seems to be a simple one way causal relation between phenomena is actually a complex mutual interaction between phenomena. Scholars who have read Max Weber's entire *Sociology of Religion* continually point out that he does *not* exclusively define either religion or economy as the independent or the dependent phenomenon, as dilettantes who have read only his *Protestant Ethic* assume; rather he actually shows how both the religion *and* the economy of a society reciprocally influence each other's development. (326)

According to Davis, what makes Weber's argument counterintuitive is that although people at Weber's time thought that there was one-way causation from the economy to the religion, Weber in fact showed that the causation was mutual.

As the title of Davis's article clearly indicates, his target audience was sociologists. Yet Davis probably did not foresee that his idea would be particularly influential among management researchers decades later.[11] For instance, the following remarks from four former editors of the *Academy of Management Journal* – a top journal in management – in their editorial essays show how much they appreciate Davis's idea:

- "Murray Davis's (1971) analysis showed that the most influential sociological theories become widely cited, not because they are necessarily 'accurate' or 'correct,' but rather, because they are 'interesting.' On the basis of an examination of the content and subsequent citation rates of various sociological theories, Davis concluded that in order to generate interest, a new theory had to violate at least some expectations of readers. If it did not, the readers' perception was that no value was added." (Eden and Rynes 2003: 680)
- "Davis's (1971) 'index of the interesting' is one useful way to describe how to arouse a reader's curiosity." (Colquitt and George 2011: 433)

Davis's article has also affected how management scholars train the next generation of researchers, as indicated by this glowing remark: "When taking a broader view of theoretical insights, Murray Davis's (1971) classic, *That's Interesting*, is an article I've read yearly since my graduate school days that provides a number of concrete ways that works can provide novel interest by establishing counterintuitive observations." (Short 2009: 1315). Similarly, Podsakoff et al. (2018) claim that their own experiences of working with doctoral students indicate that Davis's suggestions are useful for generating good research ideas. In sum, interesting research advocacy is in full force.

Davis's article was concerned with interesting theories or theoretical propositions. Management researchers subsequently expanded its core arguments to include empirical findings. After rehashing Davis's idea about interesting propositions, Salvato and Aldrich (2012: 127) argue that "in the case of *empirical* works, challenging established assumptions and theory through counterintuitive research questions is also regarded as central in making an article interesting." More specifically, Cornelissen and Durand (2012: 152–153) model their concept of interesting explanation on Davis's arguments: "A novel conceptualization or explanation is generally considered interesting depending on the degree to which it is analogically 'related' or 'connected' and, as such, plausible or informative while simultaneously being counterintuitive, surprising, or unexpected, given the novel parallel that is drawn between previously unconnected and disparate domains and modes of understanding." The characteristic of "being counterintuitive, surprising, or unexpected" reflects Davis's core idea.

A pertinent question here is: From the perspective of scientific research, what is the value of having interesting theories or explanations? The short answer is "nil." McMullin (2008) proposes a list of virtues of a good scientific theory. The two *primary virtues* are empirical fit and explanatory power. The former refers to the extent that a theory can "account for data already in hand" (501), while the latter is "the persuasiveness in general of the underlying causal structure postulated by the theory" (502). There are three categories of *complementary virtues*: internal, contextual and diachronic. Surprisingly, whether or to what extent a theory is interesting, counterintuitive or novel is not a complementary virtue. In other words, contrary to interesting research advocacy, the interestingness of a theory is regarded to be of little value in science. Since a major function of a theory is to explain certain phenomena, interesting explanations are also of little value. This outcome is somewhat expected by those who have some knowledge of philosophy of science. Nothing in the arguments of Thomas Kuhn and Karl Popper – unquestionably two of the most influential philosophers of science – "values novelty for its own sake" (Cohen 2017: 3). I also cannot recall any announcement made by the

Nobel Committee citing interestingness of a scientist's theories and/or research findings as a key reason for awarding the Nobel Prize.

The above conclusion concerning the value of interestingness is understandable if we consider that the two main objectives of scientific research are explaining and problem solving, which are associated with pure and applied science, respectively (Yaghmaie 2017). Researchers working in the domain of pure science attempt to find an explanation for a phenomenon that happens in the world, such as lunar eclipses. By contrast, applied science researchers focus on finding a solution to a problem that affects human life, such as creating a method of capturing and storing renewable energy as a solution to the problem of greenhouse gas emissions and air pollution. These two distinct objectives are sometimes closely related to one another. For example, explaining why Covid-19 spreads so fast between people helps the development of measures to prevent infection. It is obvious that both objectives are only related remotely to interestingness. Regarding the objective of explaining, even if the phenomenon in question is interesting, it does not imply that its explanation is also interesting (in the sense of being counterintuitive or novel) in and of itself. In fact, whether the explanation is interesting isn't even relevant; what *is* relevant is whether it is a true explanation. The objective of problem solving is completely unrelated to interestingness. For example, I have been following closely news concerning the development of Covid-19 vaccines and related medicines and have never seen any mention of whether these vaccines or medicines were based on interesting theories or empirical findings. In an emergency such as this, who has the luxury of bothering with interestingness? What people care about is how effective and safe a vaccine or medicine is, period.

An Overview of the Book

As stated in the Preface, the objective of this book is to bridge the gap between a technical, philosophical treatment of the subject of explanation and the more practical needs of management as well as other social science scholars. My approach is more descriptive than prescriptive. That is to say, I discuss the key topics in the domain of explanation that are relevant to management research, incorporating where relevant occasional commentary, such as the above critiques of Barney (2001), Davis (1971) and Welch et al. (2011). My intention is to enhance readers' understanding of, and hopefully also arouse their interest in, the subject matter. I expect that readers will choose their own method or approach for their research after

reading the information and analysis in this book. Although I propose
several heuristics in the last chapter, these heuristics are just suggestions for
readers to consider. Readers with a proclivity for a specific philosophical
perspective or research method may disagree with some of the heuristics.
Overall, this book consists of two parts: Chapters 1–4 present the conceptual foundation of explanation while Chapters 5–8 discuss the practical
issues researchers may encounter when they attempt to explain their
results. While readers will have to spend more effort on understanding
the first part, they will benefit from their effort when reading the
second part.

As Craik (1943: 46) well says, "most of the great hypotheses and
experiments of Newton, Maxwell, Rutherford, Darwin and the rest have
been inspired by the idea of tracing the action of causes in nature."
Chapter 2 presents the nature of causation, which is a highly technical
topic. I remove some of the technical details while maintaining a reasonably strong philosophical flavor. This chapter lays the foundation for the
discussion of the various modes of explanation in Chapter 3 because
explaining a phenomenon or event usually involves spelling out its cause.
While Chapter 3 introduces different modes of explanation, mechanismic
explanation is the one that I usually adopt in this book. These two chapters
form the backbone of the subsequent chapters that deal with
specific topics.

Chapter 4 discusses the recent microfoundations movement in management studies, which promotes the process of explaining a particular
phenomenon in terms of lower-level phenomena. I trace the movement
back to the heated debate in social science between methodological individualists and methodological holists that started more than a century ago.
While the microfoundations movement is a laudable attempt to generate
better quality explanations, I highlight the principle of emergence as one of
its serious limitations.

It is well known that leading management journals, such as the *Academy
of Management Journal,* place a great deal of emphasis on theory development. Chapter 5 shows that a good explanation does not necessarily invoke
any theory although many management journals have "contribution to
theory" as a key criterion for accepting a manuscript. The chapter illustrates how luck can provide a better explanation than any management
theory in some situations. As to theoretical explanations, they may involve
such complications as theory-ladenness of observation and incommensurability of theories. The role played by meta-theories in explaining phenomena or events poses another challenge.

Most management phenomena are the result of complex decisions. When managers make such decisions, they naturally consider a variety of factors that are at the individual, firm, industry, national and/or even international level. Yet a theory is limited in scope and level and therefore unable to cover most of these factors, implying that researchers often have to bring in multiple theories. However, multi-theoretical studies are seldom published in management journals. Chapter 6 identifies the reasons for the lack of such studies, discusses the functions of a multi-theoretical approach in empirical research and provides some suggestions for not only promoting the approach but also highlighting some precautions when researchers adopt it.

The common empirical research methods used by management researchers include analysis of archival data (longitudinal or cross-sectional), questionnaire survey, experiment and case study. While the saying "correlation does not imply causation" is well-known for statistical analysis, few researchers are aware that the nature of a research method affects the quality of explanation. In addition to discussing this issue, Chapter 7 discusses the differences between structural and reduced models of quantitative analysis, the practice of post-hoc hypothesis development and why replication can be a remedy for the practice. The chapter ends with a proposal for a multi-method approach, analogous to the multi-theoretical approach presented in Chapter 6.

Chapter 8 – the concluding chapter – discusses inference to the best explanation, which is concerned with selecting the best explanation among competing ones. I propose some heuristics to help management researchers formulate explanation. It argues that despite these and related rules governing logical inference, such as deduction, induction and abduction, explaining social phenomena in general and management phenomena in particular requires imagination (e.g., using counterfactuals) and intuition (e.g., drawing on experience). Thus, more often than not, the endeavor is not just a scientific activity but also an art.

CHAPTER 2

Causation

"Causation is a topic of perennial philosophical concern" (Hitchcock 1996: 267). The way nature operates is via causation: the processes unfolding around us are *causal* processes, with earlier processes linked to later ones by causal relationships (Beebee 2006). Although words related to causation pervade our everyday conversations, natural scientists are more cautious in using such vocabulary. Judea Pearl, a key founder of causal modeling that is discussed later in this chapter, laments such conservatism in scientific research:

> The word *cause* is not in the vocabulary of standard probability theory. It is an embarrassing yet inescapable fact that probability theory, the official mathematical language of many empirical sciences, does not permit us to express sentences such as "Mud does not cause rain"; all we can say is that two events are mutually correlated, or dependent – meaning that if we find one, we can expect to encounter the other. Scientists seeking causal explanations for complex phenomena or rationales for policy decisions must therefore supplement the language of probability with a vocabulary for causality, one in which the symbolic representation for the causal relationship "Mud does not cause rain" is distinct from the symbolic representation for "Mud is independent of rain." Oddly, such distinctions have not yet been incorporated into standard scientific analysis. (Pearl 1998: 226–227)

In contrast to their natural science colleagues, social scientists seem to be more cognizant of the fact that knowledge of causation affects their understanding of the social world (Gerring 2008). In particular, management researchers do not shy away from using causal language. For instance, case studies enable researchers to tease out ever-deepening layers of reality when searching for mechanisms and contingencies and to peer into the box of causality when identifying the factors connecting some critical cause with its purported effect (Gerring 2007). More specifically, a longitudinal case design allows researchers to collect data about how events of interest unfolded over time and thus provide stronger evidence for proposed causal relationships than a cross-sectional design would allow. In other words, a main objective of case studies is to figure out the causes of events.

Explanation and causation are intimately related. To explain an event is to cite a cause of the event (Hausman 1998) and the event "stands at the end of a long and complicated causal history" (Lewis 1986: 214). Explanation involves causation but not vice versa; we may observe a causal process unfolding without any intention to explain it. Explanation is epistemological and causation is metaphysical. Causation is objective in that it is a relationship between events out there. Many causal relationships would exist even if no one observed or thought of them. In contrast, explanation is a human activity affected by human interests. "The intimate bond between causation and explanation threatens the objectivity of causation" (Hausman 1998: 7). Before I present the major modes of explanation in Chapter 3, I will discuss here as a backdrop the concept of causation.

Regularity Theory of Causation

Although David Hume, one of the best-known scholars in Western philosophy, developed his concept of causation more than 200 years ago, its influence can be felt even in modern-day academic research. Mackie (1974: 3) considers that Hume made "the most significant and influential single contribution to the theory of causation." Hume is traditionally credited with creating the regularity theory of causation, according to which the causal relationship between two events consists merely in the fact that events of one kind are always followed by events of another kind.

Necessary Connection

Hume's argument begins with his favorite everyday case that clearly shows cause and effect — colliding billiard balls. Suppose we observe a red ball rolling toward a blue ball and the red ball coming into contact with the blue ball. Then we see the blue ball rolling away from the spot where it was struck. Of course, we also hear a noise when the balls come into contact. Do we see a connection or tie between the two events (i.e., the collision of the balls and the ensuing motion of the blue ball)? Hume's answer is a resounding "no." He generalizes from the billiard ball case that no individual case of causation involving objects that we perceive by our senses will provide any impression of necessary connection. To put it in his words:

> When we look about us toward external objects, and consider the operation of causes, we are never able, in a single instance, to discover any power or necessary connexion; any quality, which binds the effect to the cause, and renders the one an infallible consequence of the other. We only find, that the one does actually, in fact, follow the other. The impulse of one billiard-ball is attended with motion in the second. This is the whole that appears to the *outward* senses. The mind feels no sentiment or *inward* impression from this succession of objects: Consequently, there is not, in any single, particular instance of cause and effect, any thing which can suggest the idea of power or necessary connexion. (Hume 1999: 136)

In other words, the idea of necessary connection cannot be derived from observing any individual pair of events in the physical world and so must be derived from an internal impression:

> This, therefore, is the essence of necessity. Upon the whole, necessity is something that exists in the mind, not in objects; nor is it possible for us ever to form the most distant idea of it, considered as a quality in bodies. Either we have no idea of necessity, or necessity is nothing but that determination of the thought to pass from causes to effects, and from effects to causes, according to their experienc'd union. (Hume 2007: 112)

According to Hume, all simple ideas are copies of impressions. When we exercise our wills, we have an idea of power derived from an impression of power that we have. For example, if we force ourselves to lift a heavy object, we form, by introspection, an "impression" of power, which leads to our awareness of the power. Could this idea of power be what we have in mind when we assert that one billiard ball exerts power on another, or that there is a necessary connection between the collision and the movement of billiard balls? Definitely not, because a billiard ball is a material object and cannot have an impression of power similar to the one we have in voluntary action. The same argument applies to other material objects that enter into causal relationships. Therefore, even if we have an idea of power derived from human volition, this idea does not enable us to understand causation in material objects. Hume assumes that any idea of power or necessary connection between events worth taking seriously must be based on a *deductive* inference from one event to another; otherwise the idea is "vulgar" and "inaccurate" (Dicker 1998). He therefore arrives at the conclusion that the idea is nonexistent in this sense. The following passage summarizes his reasoning:

All events seem entirely loose and separate. One event follows another; but we never can observe any tie between them. They seem *conjoined*, but never *connected*. And as we can have no idea of any thing which never appeared to our outward sense or inward sentiment, the necessary conclusion *seems* to be, that we have no idea of connexion or power at all, and that these words are absolutely without any meaning, when employed either in philosophical reasonings, or common life. (Hume 1999: 144)

After establishing that our idea of necessary connection or power is derived from an internal impression, Hume examines how we infer, from the occurrence of one event, that some other event will occur. After we have observed that an event of a certain kind is always followed by an event of another kind, we begin to infer, upon observing an event of the first kind, that an event of the second kind will follow. It is only after we repeatedly experience events of kind A always being followed by events of kind B that we begin to *inductively* infer an event of kind B from observing an event of kind A. Consequently, we think there is some necessary connection between the two kinds of events, calling event A the "cause" and event B the "effect." The idea of necessary connection cannot represent any mind-independent relationship between causes and effects. Hume (2007: 61) uses the example of flame and heat to illustrate his point:

We remember to have had frequent instances of the existence of one species of objects; and also remember, that the individuals of another species of objects have always attended them, and have existed in a regular order of contiguity and succession with regard to them. Thus we remember to have seen that species of object we call *flame*, and to have felt that species of sensation we call *heat*. We likewise call to mind their constant conjunction in all past instances. Without any farther ceremony, we call the one *cause* and the other *effect*, and infer the existence of the one from that of the other.

In other words, the idea of necessary connection arises from the experience of constant conjunction through observing many similar pairs of events rather than any individual pairs. If, whenever we observe an event like the first member of the pair, an event like the second member follows, we develop a feeling of expectation or anticipation that is in our minds rather than in the events themselves. This feeling is "the *only* new ingredient added by having the experience of constant conjunction" (Dicker 1998: 107) and is the impression of necessary connection. This impression arises simply from the psychological principle of human nature, which Hume calls custom or habit. Once we have acquired the habit of inferring events B from events A, we come to *judge* that events A are causes of events B. Then events A and events B no longer *seem* entirely loose and separate (Beebee 2006).

Why do we have a notion of some necessary connection between events themselves if the necessary connection is just a feeling in our minds? To answer this question, Hume argues that "we *project* our own feeling of expectation or anticipation outward into the observed events, and thereby mistakenly come to think that we are aware of a necessary connection" (Dicker 1998: 107–108). In the words of Hume (2007: 112–113):

> the mind has a great propensity to spread itself on external objects, and to conjoin with them any internal impressions ... the same propensity is the reason, why we suppose necessity and power to lie in the objects we consider, not in our mind, that considers them.

Definitions of Causation

Hume offers two definitions of causation that have led subsequently to much debate among philosophers as to how the definitions should be interpreted consistently. The first definition is as follows:

> Similar objects are always conjoined with similar. Of this we have experience. Suitably to this experience, therefore, we may define a cause to be *an object, followed by another, and where all the objects similar to the first are followed by objects similar to the second.* Or in other words, *where, if the first object had not been, the second had never existed.* (Hume 1999: 146)

The second definition goes this way:

> The appearance of a cause always conveys the mind, by a customary transition, to the idea of the effect. Of this also we have experience. We may, therefore, suitably to this experience, form another definition of *cause*, and call it, *an object followed by another, and whose appearance always conveys the thought to that other.* (Hume 1999: 146)

Hume uses the example of vibration and sound to illustrate both definitions:

> We say, for instance, that the vibration of this string is the cause of this particular sound. But what do we mean by that affirmation? We either mean, *that this vibration is followed by this sound, and that all similar vibrations have been followed by similar sounds: Or, that this vibration is followed by this sound, and that, upon the appearance of the one the mind anticipates the senses, and forms immediately an idea of the other.* We may consider the relation of cause and effect in either of these two lights; but beyond these, we have no idea of it. (Hume 1999: 146)

Hume's definitions are written rather loosely. For example, "it is more accurate to regard causes and effects as events than as objects" (Dicker 1998: 112). When we observe that a red billiard ball – one object – hits a blue billiard ball – another object – and causes the blue ball to move, the cause is not just the red ball as such, but its collision with the blue ball, which is an event.

The two different definitions have led to controversy concerning Hume's intentions, such as whether he had two different theories of causation (Beauchamp and Rosenberg 1981). It is beyond the scope of this book to discuss this controversy. Suffice it to say that the first definition is concerned with causation occurring objectively in nature, regardless of whether there are any people observing, while the second definition refers to the triggering of expectations through observation of the cause's occurrence. Stroud (1977: 90) describes the relationship between the two definitions:

> Any events or objects observed to fulfil the conditions of the first "definition" are such that they will fulfil the conditions of the second "definition" also. That is to say that an observed constant conjunction between As and Bs establishes a "union in the imagination" such that the thought of an A naturally leads the mind to the thought of a B. That is just a fundamental, but contingent, principle of the human mind.

The first definition makes no reference to necessary connection between cause and effect because necessary connection *is* just the feeling of expectation mentioned in the second definition. Instead, the first definition involves only "constant conjunction" – one type of event being always followed by another type of event – and lays the foundation of the regularity theory of causation.

Causal Relationships versus Accidental Regularities

Mackie (1974: 196) argues that the problem of distinguishing causal from accidental regularities "is the great difficulty for any regularity theory of causation." The most common objection to the theory is that it cannot distinguish between genuine causal relationships – or what Lewis (1973: 556) calls "causal laws" – and regular but non-causal relationships (Dicker 1998). For the former, suppose that last year John reached the retirement age of the company that he worked for – Company X – and so started receiving the pension provided by that company. All retired employees of Company X have been receiving the pension. When an employee reaches the retirement age, other employees expect that person to receive the pension. According to the two definitions of causation discussed above, reaching the retirement age in Company X causes pension payouts, as embodied by Statement (a) "Whenever an employee of Company X reaches the retirement age, they start receiving pension." As to accidental regularities, consider Companies A and B whose fiscal years end on September 30 and December 31, respectively. Therefore every year, Statement (b) "Company A's annual financial reports are followed by B's" holds. After seeing A's reports, one expects to see B's. This regularity holds for all companies having September 30 as the fiscal year-end and those having December 31 as the fiscal year-end. Again, according to the two definitions of causation, one may conclude that A's financial reports cause B's. Of course, this time the causal inference is flawed.

The main difference between causal relationships and accidental regularities is that the former do, but the latter do not, support counterfactuals (Beebee 2006). A counterfactual statement says that if something that did not happen but is assumed, counter or contrary to the fact, to have happened, then something else would have happened. To illustrate how causal relationships support counterfactuals, we return to the above example of John's pension. Suppose that John in fact did not reach the retirement age last year. The causal relationships captured in Statement (a) supports the corresponding counterfactual in the sense that we can infer from Statement (a) that if John had reached the retirement age last year, he would have started receiving his pension. On the other hand, this is not true for accidental regularities. Suppose that in the current year, Company A changed its fiscal year-end such that it no longer fell on September 30. We cannot infer from Statement (b) that if Company A's fiscal year had ended on September 30 in the current year, Company A's annual financial reports would have been followed by B's. In fact, if Company A's new fiscal year-end is June 30, its financial reports are still followed by B's; that is, this contradicts the counterfactual condition that if something that did not happen but is assumed to have happened, then *something else* would have happened. In brief, Statement (b) does not support the counterfactual. We use genuine causal relationships, not accidental regularities, as a basis for prediction and counterfactual reasoning. Some philosophers argue that Statement (a) possesses a special necessity but Statement (b) does not. This difference shows that the problem faced by the regularity theory – to distinguish between causal relationships and accidental regularities – is insuperable (Dicker 1998).

Necessary and Sufficient Conditions

Immediately after giving the first definition, Hume (1999: 146) adds a remark: "Or in other words, *where, if the first object had not been, the second had never existed.*" The remark is puzzling in that it is different from and cannot be implied by the definition. Although Hume makes the remark only once, some philosophers do not dismiss it as a careless slip because they deem that "an adequate analysis of causation *should* imply that a cause is not just a sufficient condition for its effect, but also a necessary condition for its effect" (Dicker 1998: 125). Returning to the example of John's pension, reaching the retirement age caused the pension payouts; that is, reaching the retirement age is a sufficient condition for receiving the pension. But this does not imply that it is also a necessary condition – if John did not reach the retirement age last year, he would not receive the pension. The remark plays the role of specifying the necessary condition.

The expanded definition – that is, the first definition plus the remark – therefore specifies both the sufficient and necessary conditions for the effect to occur. However, a difficulty arises because in this case, if the cause occurs, the effect occurs and if the effect occurs, the cause occurs. In other words, the relationship between cause and effect is perfectly symmetrical and we can no longer distinguish between cause and effect. Yet it is well known that a causal relationship is asymmetrical: reaching the retirement age causes pension payouts but receiving pensions does not cause an employee to reach the retirement age. Hume's requirement that the cause must occur *before* the effect in time offers one way to deal with the difficulty; one must reach the retirement age *before* receiving pensions. This temporal condition would restore the asymmetry of the causal relationship.

As Dicker (1998: 128) points out, "the idea that a cause is a necessary condition for its effect is not wholly accurate. Rather, a cause is necessary for its effect only on the assumption that no other cause of that effect is operative." For example, it may not be accurate to hold that the statement "Reaching the retirement age caused pension payouts" implies that if an employee had not reached the retirement age, they would not have received pensions. The statement in fact implies that if the employee had not reached the retirement age and nothing else could enable them to receive pensions, then they would not have the pensions. Note that it is rather common among companies that employees have the option of early retirement after serving their company for a certain number of years. Early retirement also enables them to receive pensions.

The complexity of necessary and sufficient conditions was highlighted by John Stuart Mill, another prominent philosopher in the English-speaking world after Hume:

> It is not true, then, that one effect must be connected with only one cause, or assemblage of conditions; that each phenomenon can be produced only in one way. There are often several independent modes in which the same phenomenon could have originated. One fact may be the consequent in several invariable sequences; it may follow, with equal uniformity, any one of several antecedents, or collections of antecedents. Many causes may produce mechanical motion: many causes may produce some kinds of sensation: many causes may produce death. A given effect may really be produced by a certain cause, and yet be perfectly capable of being produced without it. (Mill 1973: 435)

The gist of the above passage is that individual causal factors are neither necessary nor sufficient. Rather, they constitute an overall combination that is sufficient for the outcome and alternative combinations are possible.

Mackie (1974) develops systematically Mill's idea and argues that a cause is at least an INUS condition for the effect. The INUS condition stands for an **i**nsufficient but **n**onredundant part of a condition that is itself **u**nnecessary but **s**ufficient for the occurrence of the effect. Bennett (1988) simplifies the term to NS conditions — *necessary* parts of *sufficient* conditions. To illustrate an INUS condition, which offers some insights to management research, we use the example of Samsung's relocation of its display production from China to Southern Vietnam discussed in Chapter 1. Let us assume that the cause given by the Vietnamese state-run newspaper — Vietnam being an important gateway to other Southeast Asian countries and a link in Samsung's global supply chain — is genuine. Suppose further that this particular relocation decision was triggered by the Covid-19 pandemic, which revealed the risk of concentrating production activities in one host country (i.e., China) and that there were other causes such as low land cost and abundant supply of labor force in Southern Vietnam. Together these causes constitute an *unnecessary* but *sufficient* condition for Samsung's decision. The condition is sufficient given the fact that Samsung made the decision, but it is unnecessary because other causes could have led to the same decision; for instance, a political conflict arising between South Korea and China and Samsung wanting to hedge against its political risk in China. Within the current set of causes, the cause cited by the Vietnamese newspaper is *insufficient* because the cause alone is not good enough to account for Samsung's decision. However, the cause is also *nonredundant* because without it, Samsung would not have considered moving to Vietnam; there are other Southeast Asian countries, such as Indonesia, that have low land costs and abundant labor supply but these countries are less well located than Vietnam. Hence, the cause is an INUS condition for Samsung's relocation.

A Counterfactual Analysis of Causation

Collins et al. (2004: 3) claim that "counterfactuals are fundamental to any philosophical understanding of causation." Referring to Hume's (1999: 146) abovementioned remark: "Or in other words, *where, if the first object had not been, the second had never existed*," Lewis (1973: 557) argues that the remark is a proposal for "a counterfactual analysis of causation," and he is the principal advocate of such an analysis. He rephrases Hume's remark with a caveat indicating the difficulty of his task:

> We think of a cause as something that makes a difference, and the difference it makes must be a difference from what would have happened without it. Had it been absent, its effects — some of them, at least, and usually all — would have been absent as well. Yet it is one thing to mention these platitudes now and again, and another thing to rest an analysis on them. That has not seemed worth while. We have learned all too well that counterfactuals are ill understood, wherefore it did not seem that much understanding could be gained by using them to analyze causation or anything else. (Lewis 1973: 557)

Possible Worlds

To deal with the difficulty concerning counterfactuals, Lewis brings in the concept of "possible worlds." The core idea is that in the world in which we live, things need not have been as they are and might have been different in countless ways. History, since the Big Bang, could have unfolded in a way different from what it did. In short, the actual world is only one among many *possible worlds*. Lewis (1973) assumes that possible worlds can be ordered with respect to their similarity to the actual world.

Given the complexity of Lewis's arguments and subsequent developments and debates among other scholars, here I follow Hausman's (1998: 112) exposition because of its clarity and conciseness. Lewis (1973) specifies that his analysis applies to particular events only and not general phenomena. For two distinct events, C and E, E is said to be *counterfactually dependent* on C if and only if both of the following counterfactual statements are true:

(1)   If C were to occur, then E would occur.
(2)   If C were not to occur, then E would not occur.

If both C and E occur, the first statement is automatically true because the closest possible world in which C occurs is the actual world and in that world E also occurs. As to the second counterfactual statement, we consider possible worlds in which C does not occur. Given that these possible worlds can be ordered with respect to their similarity to the actual world, some of them will be more similar to the actual world than others. The statement is true if a possible world without C (a "non-C possible world") in which E does not occur is more similar to the actual world than any other non-C possible world in which E occurs. This counterfactual argument lays the foundation for understanding causation.

Let's return once more to the example of John's pension. In the actual world, John reached the retirement age and received his pension, satisfying the first counterfactual statement. Among possible worlds in which John did not reach the retirement age, the one where he did not receive the pension is more similar to the actual world than the others. This satisfies the second counterfactual statement. That is to say, receiving the pension is counterfactually dependent on reaching the retirement age. Let's assume that John's company did not have the option of receiving the pension upon early retirement. Lewis (1979) argues that the non-C possible world that is most similar to the actual world should have exactly the same history as the actual world until shortly before the time when C occurs in the actual world, with the necessary adjustments that lead to C's non-occurrence. Suppose that in one of the possible worlds in which John did not reach the retirement age, he took early retirement and so received his pension. This possible world is less similar to the actual world than the one where he did not receive his pension although he took the initiative to have early retirement. It is because according to our assumption, John's company in the actual world did not offer the early retirement option.

Symmetrical Overdetermination

Needless to say, Lewis's counterfactual approach is not without problems. Consider the well-known example of window-shattering, in which a rock is thrown at a window and the window is broken. Saying that the striking of the window caused the shattering of the window is the same as saying that if the window had not been struck, it would not have shattered. In other words, the shattering was counterfactually dependent on the striking. Suppose Tom and Mary both threw rocks at a window at the same time with exactly the same force. The window shattered. Moreover, each rock was thrown with sufficient force to shatter the window all by itself. Intuitively speaking, both Tom's and Mary's throws were causes of the shattering. Yet a counterfactual analysis says otherwise. If Tom had not thrown his rock, the window would still be shattered (by Mary's rock); the same applies to Mary's throw. Therefore, the shattering was not counterfactually dependent on either Tom's or Mary's throw; neither throw was a cause of the shattering. This example shows that Lewis's analysis breaks down in the case of symmetrical overdetermination of an effect (Collins et al. 2004).

Cases of symmetrical overdetermination are not rare in business. Let's continue with the example of John's pension. Suppose that when John joined his current employer decades ago, he decided that if he continued to work there, he would, once he was eligible, take the company's early retirement option, which allowed employees to receive their pensions after serving the company for at least thirty years. At the time of making his decision, John was thirty years old and the company's mandatory retirement age was sixty-five. In other words, he planned to retire at sixty, not sixty-five. Suppose further that not long after his joining the company, the mandatory retirement age was changed to sixty. Last year John reached sixty. His pension payouts were overdetermined in the sense that either the mandatory age or his plan of early retirement would have caused it. Yet, the payouts were not counterfactually dependent on either.

A more straightforward example is in finance. Suppose a mutual fund manager programed a sell instruction on a particular stock in her portfolio such that if the price of the stock fell during the day to $90 or by 10 percent of the opening price, 15 percent of the stock would be sold immediately. Then on a particular day the opening price of the stock was $100. After about an hour, it fell to $90 (or, by 10 percent) and so triggered the sell instruction. The sale was caused by either of the two conditions of the sell instruction but was counterfactually dependent on neither.

Backtracking

The above cases of symmetrical overdetermination show that counterfactual dependence is not necessary for causation. Counterfactual statements are vague, at least with respect to the issue of backtracking. Lewis (1979: 456) borrows this example from Downing (1959):

Jim and Jack quarreled yesterday, and Jack is still hopping mad. We conclude that if Jim asked Jack for help today, Jack would not help him. But wait: Jim is a prideful fellow. He never would ask for help after such a quarrel; if Jim were to ask Jack for help today, there would have to have been no quarrel yesterday. In that case Jack would be his usual generous self. So if Jim asked Jack for help today, Jack would help him after all.

Hence, there are two different interpretations of the counterfactual statement "If Jim were to ask Jack for help, Jack would help him." According to the first interpretation stated in the above passage, the statement is false because Jack is in no mood to be helping Jim given that he is still hopping mad. On the other hand, the second interpretation views the statement as obviously true: Jim would not ask Jack for help unless there had been no quarrel between them and if there had been no quarrel, Jack would be generous in offering his assistance. The first interpretation is non-backtracking and the second is backtracking. Heller (1985: 77) makes a distinction that "a non-backtracking counterfactual is concerned with what the result would be of a certain antecedent's being true in a situation similar to the actual situation" whereas a backtracking counterfactual "takes into account how the world would have to have been different in order for the antecedent to get to be true."

Back to the example of Jim and Jack, the antecedent in question is that Jim were to ask Jack for help. The non-backtracking interpretation considers what the result would be in case the antecedent is true in possible worlds closest to the actual world, which is that Jack is still angry about the quarrel. Therefore, the result of Jim seeking help is that Jack would not help. In contrast, the backtracking interpretation considers the closest worlds in which Jim asks Jack for help to be those in which there has been no quarrel (given that Jim is a prideful fellow and would never ask Jack for help after such a quarrel). In all of these worlds Jack is not angry and so he would help Jim. Here the focus is on the result of the antecedent being true in a situation where there has been no quarrel because, if otherwise, the antecedent won't be true.

In discussing causal analysis of singular events in history, Reiss (2009: 713) examines the following three counterfactual claims related to historical events:

- Had the Greeks not won against the Persians at Salamis, Western civilization would not have become dominant in the world.
- Had Chamberlain confronted Hitler at Munich, World War II would have been no worse and probably better.

- Had Kennedy shown more resolve prior to the Cuban Missile Crisis, Khrushchev would not have deployed missiles.

He concludes that counterfactuals in history are backtracking, although in philosophy "it is a generally accepted pillar of truth that if counterfactuals are to be used as stand-ins for causal claims, they have to be nonbacktracking" (720). Consider, for example, the third counterfactual claim above. Lebow and Stein (1996) deem that to evaluate the counterfactual, we need to examine what conditions would have to have been present in order for Kennedy to show more resolve before the Cuban Missile Crisis. Since those conditions that would have made Kennedy show resolve were just not present during that historical period, Lebow and Stein regard the antecedent as inadmissible. The topic of counterfactuals is discussed further in Chapter 3 where historical explanation is introduced.

Probabilistic Causation

An obvious problem of the regularity theory of causality is that contrary to the constant-conjunction view, most causes in everyday life are not invariably followed by their effects and causal attributions are often nondeterministic. For example, while it is well known that smoking is a cause of lung cancer, some smokers never develop the cancer. Dropping a glass on the floor causes it to break, but occasionally a glass is dropped but does not break. People generally believe that college education increases an individual's earning potential, but this may not hold for certain individuals. Punishments should deter theft but the deterrence is not perfect. Such examples account for an indeterministic view of causation and motivate the development of probabilistic causation.

The central idea of probabilistic causation is that causes raise the probability of their effects. Suppose Event A_{t1} occurred at time t1 and Event B_{t2} at time t2. Suppes (1970) defines a cause as a probability-raising event:

A_{t1} is a *prima facie* cause of B_{t2} if and only if

(1) $t1 < t2$
(2) $P(A_{t1}) > 0$
(3) $P(B_{t2}/A_{t1}) > P(B_{t2})$

That is, A_{t1} is a cause of B_{t2} if and only if A_{t1} occurred before B_{t2} and the conditional probability of B_{t2} given A_{t1} is greater than the absolute probability of B_{t2}. Simply put, if the probability of an event given another event is higher than the probability of the first event alone, the two events are causally connected in some way. This definition addresses each of the four simple examples discussed above: smoking increases the probability of having lung cancer; dropping a glass on the floor increases the probability of its breaking; college graduates are likely to earn more than non-college graduates; and punishments increase the probability of having a lower level of theft incidents. According to the definition, a sufficient or determinate cause underlying the constant-conjunction view is one that produces its effect with certainty (i.e., a probability of one).

A well-known fact in statistics is that a correlation between two variables X and Y does not warrant the conclusion that X causes Y or vice versa. Suppose a study found that the extent of peak hour traffic in Dallas from 2000 to 2010 was correlated positively with sales of lipstick in the city. Without doubt, traffic conditions do not cause lipstick sales. Rather, a higher level of employment causes more peak hour traffic. Moreover, women constitute about half of the US workforce; when more women go to work, the demand for lipstick rises. Suppes (1970) considers several ways to address this issue by introducing the term "spurious cause." One solution is to define a spurious cause as:

A_{t1} is a spurious cause of B_{t2} if and only if A_{t1} is a *prima facie* cause of B_{t2} and there is a t3 $<$ t1 and an Event C_{t3} such that

(1) $P(A_{t1}\&C_{t3}) > 0$
(2) $P(B_{t2}/A_{t1}\&C_{t3}) = P(B_{t2}/C_{t3})$
(3) $P(B_{t2}/A_{t1}\&C_{t3}) \geq P(B_{t2}/A_{t1})$

The idea is that a spurious cause does not change the conditional probability of Event B_{t2} given C_{t3}. The addition of Event A_{t1} into the picture has no real effect upon the occurrence of B_{t2}; Event C_{t3} can account for Event B_{t2} at least as well as A_{t1} can. Returning to the above example, traffic conditions are a spurious cause of lipstick sales and level of employment is what Suppes (1970) calls a "genuine cause," defined as a prima facie cause that is not spurious. Level of employment alone can account for lipstick sales and peak hour traffic has no additional effect on lipstick sales once level of employment has been included into the calculation.

The above discussion shows some of the complexity involved in inferring causal relationships from probabilistic correlations. Scholars have developed a number of techniques for representing systems of causal relationships and inferring causal relationships from probabilities. As a result, an interdisciplinary field called "causal modeling" devoted to the study of methods of causal inference has emerged. Given the technicalities of the field and the space limitations of this book, in the following section I introduce briefly two major techniques – causal graph modeling and vector space modeling. Readers may skip the discussion if they find it too technical.

Causal Graph Modeling

Figures of causal models are found commonly in management research papers to represent relationships between constructs or variables, although the authors may not use the technique of causal graph modeling. To my knowledge, Durand and Vaara (2009) were the first to introduce systematically to management research causal graph modeling, using the relationship between firm resources and performance as an illustration. My discussion in this section is based on their paper and the section after, "Vector Space Modeling," presents an alternative causal modeling technique to address the problems of causal graph modeling. The discussion here focuses on some basic principles to illustrate the nature of causal graph modeling and skips the mathematical details involved.

The attraction of causal graph modeling is that, under certain conditions, it permits the determination of the causal relationships between types of events with logical necessity. Both Spirtes et al. (1993) and Pearl (2009) prove theorems that show how causes can be identified through the probabilistic analyses of causal graph modeling, as well as present the various methods of estimation. In particular, Pearl (2009: xv–xvi) distinguishes between probabilistic and causal relationships: "I now take causal relationships to be the fundamental building blocks both of physical reality and of human understanding of that reality, and I regard probabilistic relationships as but the surface phenomena of the causal machinery that underlies and propels our understanding of the world."

Figure 2.1 shows three *directed acyclic* graphs. Each graph includes a set of points with *directed* arrows connecting them. The graphs show causal or explanatory relationships, represented by directed arrows. A graph is *acyclic* if following a series of arrows will never bring one back to where one started. A dot in a graph can represent a trope, an event or a variable; for simplicity of discussion, I consider dots to represent variables. Figure 2.1a depicts a causal graph where the two arrows represent causal relationships between Z at the origin and the other two variables X and Y at the arrows' heads. Z is a *parent* of X (and X is a *descendant* of Z) since there is a directed path from Z to X. By the same token, Z is also a parent

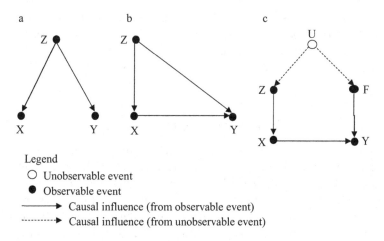

Notes:
1. Figures 2.1b and 2.1c are from Figures 2b and 2c, respectively, of Durand and Vaara (2009)
2. Figure 2b of Durand and Vaara on p. 1258 is inconsistent. Z is shown as an unobservable event, but the causal arrows from Z are not dotted. Thus, Z is taken to be an observable event here.

Figure 2.1   Back-door causal paths

of Y. Figure 2.1b shows that Z affects Y directly and also indirectly through X. Unlike Figure 2.1a and b, Figure 2.1c has a white dot, U, which represents an unobservable variable. The two dashed arrows represent causal influence from U on Z and F.

Back-door Paths

As Durand and Vaara (2009: 1257) well say, "the general principle of causal graph estimation is to eliminate 'back-door paths.'" A back-door path is constituted by any causal factor that influences the phenomenon to be explained through intermediate causes. Figure 2.1a illustrates a case in which Z affects X and Y directly and separately. There are no intermediate causes and therefore no back-door paths. The above example of lipstick sales in Dallas can be represented by this figure, with Z, X and Y standing for level of employment, peak hour traffic and lipstick sales, respectively. Figure 2.1b and c illustrate cases in which there is a back-door path from X to Y, assuming that these two variables constitute the cause-effect pair in question. The back-door path in Figure 2.1b is X ← Z → Y, while Figure 2.1c has a longer back-door path: X ← Z ← U → F → Y.

The logic of blocking a back-door path is based on the concept of "screening-off" introduced by Reichenbach (1956). Formally, if events X and Y are probabilistically *independent*, they display the following relationship:

$$P(X\&Y) = P(X) \times P(Y) \text{ (probabilistic independence)}$$

Events are probabilistically *dependent* if they occur together either more or less frequently than they would be expected to do by chance. This is the case when:

$$P(X\&Y) \neq P(X) \times P(Y) \text{ (probabilistic dependence)}$$

Screening-off occurs when there is a common cause of two events that are initially probabilistically dependent. Suppose there are three events X, Y and Z (see Figure 2.1a). Initially, there is a probabilistic dependence between events X and Y. Screening-off arises when a third event, Z, screens off the dependence between the first two events X and Y, rendering X and Y independent, that is:

$$P(X\&Y) \neq P(X) \, P(Y) \text{ (necessary condition)}$$
$$P(X\&Y/Z) = P(X/Z) \times P(Y/Z) \text{ (necessary condition)}$$

The above two conditions constitute a jointly sufficient screening-off condition. Therefore, Z must lie in the causal history of X and Y.

The logic of screening-off can be extended to eliminate any back-door path. Taking the situation depicted in Figure 2.1c, Z influences Y through a back-door path; hence, there is initially a dependence between Z and Y:

$$P(Z\&Y) \neq P(Z) \times P(Y)$$

However, once we condition for X and F (see the definition of "conditioning" below), Z becomes independent of Y:

$$P(Z\&Y/X\&F) = P(Z/X\&F) \times P(Y/X\&F)$$

Consequently, Z must lie in the causal history of either F, X, or both.

The first two strategies introduced by Durand and Vaara, conditioning (Figure 2.2a) and instrumenting (Figure 2.2b), are based on the back-door criterion. Conditioning involves accounting for all back-door paths ($C_1 \ldots C_n$) of one or more potential causal factors (X, Z). As shown in Figure 2.2a, C becomes independent of Y after taking into account X and Z. Hence, one can establish that there is a causal chain from the back-door factor C through X and Z to Y. In the case of instrumenting there is a controllable instrument (T) that influences directly X (Figure 2.2b). If T becomes independent of Y, given X, we know that

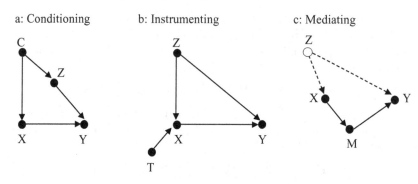

Note:
Figures 2.2b and 2.2c are from Figures 3b and 3c, respectively, of Durand and Vaara (2009)

Figure 2.2   Three strategies for causal effect estimation

there must be a causal chain from T through X to Y. Conditioning and instrumenting are thus both cases of the back-door path condition. While we are searching for a whole host of factors in the former, in the latter we know already of a factor, T, that triggers indirectly Y and with which the effect estimation can be carried out.

The third strategy presented by Durand and Vaara, mediating (Figure 2.2c), is based on the front-door condition. The front-door condition involves looking for a factor – M – that lies between the potential causal factor of interest – X – and the outcome, Y (Pearl 2009). The front-door condition is fulfilled if X becomes independent of Y again, once M is conditioned for. Such conditional independence implies that X causes M, which in turn causes Y.

The front- and back-door criteria – and thus all three strategies for causal effect estimation – are based on the logic of screening-off. Events that were dependent initially become independent, given the conditioning of some other events. This conditional independence indicates that the events must lie in the causal history of the event under consideration. Conditioning and instrumenting use the back-door criterion, since there is a movement backwards in the causal chain to establish causal relationships. Mediating through M (as shown in Figure 2.2c) uses the front-door criterion, since the factor M, which is a descendant of X, is used to establish the fact of X being causally relevant for Y. Durand and Vaara (2009) ultimately dropped conditioning and instrumenting, as the assumptions on which these strategies are based are often violated under real world conditions.

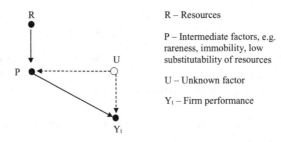

R – Resources

P – Intermediate factors, e.g.
rareness, immobility, low
substitutability of resources

U – Unknown factor

Y_t – Firm performance

Figure 2.3   Missing information on causally relevant events

Markov Condition

The fact that causal graph modeling is based on the logic of screening-off highlights one of the core assumptions on which this modeling rests – the Markov condition. This condition states that, once all of its parents are conditioned for, a variable will be probabilistically independent of all other variables except its descendants. It is important to recognize how fundamental this assumption is to Durand and Vaara's project and how quickly the arguments favoring causal graph theory break down once it is violated. More specifically, a major limitation of causal graph modeling is that the Markov condition frequently fails to hold under the kind of circumstances faced in management decision-making. We consider below two cases in which this is so: missing information and causal interdependence.

The Markov condition may fail to hold when there is insufficient information about potential causes and their effects. This includes cases in which not all relevant parents are specified and in which events have not been specified in a sufficiently fine-grained way (Arntzenius 1992). The problem of missing information can be illustrated using an adapted version of Durand and Vaara's prime example of the mediating strategy. Consider Figure 2.3, which is a simplified version of their Figure 2.4. In addition to excluding some variables, the main modification I have made is to place the unobservable event U in a slightly different position.

Suppose we want to establish whether certain resources R lead to high firm performance Y_t.[1] We assume that the individual and combined probabilities of these factors are known and that R is mediated by P (a set of intermediate factors such as rareness, immobility and low substitutability of resources). To be able to establish that Y_t is causally related to R in the way that Durand and Vaara propose, the following relationships would have to hold:

$$P(R) \times P(Y_t) \neq P(R \& Y_t)$$
$$P(R/P) \times P(Y_t/P) = P(R \& Y_t/P)$$

In this case R and Y_t would initially be probabilistically dependent but become independent once we condition for P. We would then establish that R influences firm performance Y_t through some mediating factor P.

However, given the relationships depicted in our example, the following probabilities actually hold:

$$P(R) \times P(Y_t) \neq P(R \& Y_t)$$
$$P(R/P) \times P(Y_t/P) \neq P(R \& Y_t/P)$$

P does not make R and Y_t independent because there is an unknown factor U, say, whether the technological environment of an industry is changing rapidly, that influences P directly. Durand and Vaara (2009), accordingly, have to assume that "the unobservable factors … do not influence P" (1259) for their approach to work. The presence of *any* such unknown factors that influence directly either the mediating factor P or the potential causal factor R and the phenomenon under consideration Y_t, will lead to the breakdown of the Markov condition, rendering causal graph modeling infeasible (Arntzenius 1992).

In order that the Markov condition would hold in Durand and Vaara's example, the relationship between R and P is deemed to be unaffected by any unknown factor U, which is highly unlikely to ever be the case in reality. Most readers, for instance, would probably have already found this example overly simplistic. In real world situations, firm performance is likely to depend on a complex web of causal relationships with "many back-door paths," as Durand and Vaara themselves argue.

The second reason for the Markov condition not being satisfied is causal interdependence. Unlike the previous reason, which is related to a lack of relevant information, here the Markov condition fails to hold even under conditions of perfect information. As mentioned, the Markov condition requires that once we condition for all its parents, a variable has to be probabilistically independent of all other variables except its descendants. To illustrate this requirement, take again the case represented by Figure 2.1a of a parent Z that causes X and Y. For the Markov condition to hold, X and Y must be statistically independent, given that Z has occurred. This would be equivalent to a situation in which, once Z has occurred, the likelihood of X and Y is determined by tossing two fair coins *independently* of each other. However, it seems to be much more likely intuitively that the effects of X and Y will depend on each other in some way, given that they share a common cause (Cartwright 1999).

Consider a more concrete example. Suppose a firm purchases a new machine (Z) that will, on average, reduce the defect rate of output (X) and the chance of machine breakdown (Y), as compared with the old machine. The Markov condition demands that, once the purchase of the new machine is taken into account, reductions in the defect rate and reductions in machine breakdown will occur independently of each other, as if the occurrence of each type of events were determined by tossing a coin. Yet, since both types of events result from a common cause, it is reasonable to expect that their occurrences are correlated. For instance, when the machine is close to a breakdown state, the defect rate is likely to be higher. In cases like this, it is highly unlikely that the Markov condition would hold.

An alternative example runs as follows. It has long been accepted that firms exist precisely because they are complex, interdependent structures (Coase 1937) in which the output of the combined work of employees is greater than the output of its constituent parts (Alchian and Demsetz 1972). Similar synergies are observed for firms' external relationships. Cohen and Levinthal (1990), for example, argue that firms that have prior knowledge in a particular area are better at acquiring new knowledge in the same area than firms without such prior knowledge. The newly acquired knowledge will contribute to the knowledge base, which enhances further the acquisition of knowledge in that area. Knowledge interactions of this kind create a virtuous loop that can help firms to get ahead of their competition.

Durand and Vaara acknowledge that "causal graphs are non-parametric and acyclic (i.e., they do not permit representation of circular causation . . .)" (1257). However, they do not mention that causal graph modeling also requires that causes lead to their effects independently, a particular form of atomism according to which causal factors exert their effects in isolation from each other. Such atomism is unlikely to hold in firms, which are composed of structured, interdependent relationships.

Vector Space Modeling

In contrast to causal graph modeling, vector space–based algorithms have a large number of successful scientific and business applications, such as search engines (Berry and Young 1995), literature-based discovery where previously unknown relationships between phenomena are inferred

(Swanson 1988), image recognition (Bulcão-Neto et al. 2011) and web-based translation (Bishop 2006). Vector space models such as latent semantic indexing or Dirichlet allocation were first developed to identify similarities in linguistic concepts (Blei et al. 2003). Although the models themselves can be highly sophisticated, the underlying logic is straightforward. States of affairs are represented as points in a multidimensional space, with each aspect of a state of affairs occupying a particular dimension. The points are modeled as vectors that have a length and a direction (hence the term vector space modeling).

The working of the algorithms can be illustrated using the analogy of linguistic text, the application for which they were originally developed. A text has two characteristics, namely (1) that it depicts a number of different entities, also called terms, and (2) that it contains information on how the entities are structurally related. In a piece of text, each word represents a basic unit of information. Words in turn are composed of letters. To infer the meaning of a word or string of words, vector space–based algorithms analyze how words and the letters they are composed of relate. By analyzing multiple texts, the meaning of words in their particular context can be identified. Texts do not have to be composed of the same words to have similar meanings. The algorithms are able to pick up similar structural arrangements, even if some of the words differ within the texts (Bishop 2006).

In management research, a firm's particular structural configuration might be regarded as analogous to text. This text comprises intra- and inter-organizational processes (the words) such as particular routines, how these routines are internally structured (the letters that comprise the words) and how the routines relate (as words form sentences in a text). Suppose that the way a firm is integrated with its suppliers is a key structural feature for achieving superior R&D performance and that it is difficult to imitate such integration because there is causal ambiguity as to whether and which elements of the relationship lead to the performance. Suppose further that whether a desired type of relationship can be achieved depends on the wider culture in which the firm operates. For instance, building relationships of mutual trust might require substantial investment and might be difficult to achieve in a society with a "transactional" culture. This example can be used to illustrate how vector space–based modeling differs from causal graph modeling in terms of (1) the nature of data used, (2) the mechanism that converts the data input into an output, (3) the nature of the output and (4) the assumptions made.

Nature of Data Used

A vector space–based modeling exercise might take information about meetings between a company and its suppliers from computer-based diaries as a source of data. Such diaries typically record the names of participants and their companies, their rank within these companies and the topic(s) of each meeting. Since we want to investigate R&D performance, this could involve collecting key R&D metrics such as which products were developed and how successful the products were in terms of indicators like speed of development, budget and sales. While researchers would still have to decide what data, such as the structure of meetings, they want to collect, the algorithm does not require the inputting of a classification of the structures that these meetings take. Establishing such structures will be, rather, an outcome of the analysis.

In contrast, causal graph modeling requires researchers to define a set of constructs and variables that measure the key factors they believe to be causally relevant. These constructs frequently describe whether firms possess particular characteristics or resources. Examples of the types of categories that the firms under investigation might have to be slotted into might include whether they have a matrix or a pyramid structure, how frequently they hold joint meetings with their suppliers, the level of trust established with the suppliers and whether they have joint development teams with their suppliers. Identifying in advance clearly defined entities or properties, rather than their structural relationship, therefore, becomes the main focus of data collection.

Conversion of Data Input into Output

In the vector space–based model, the composition of meetings is comparable to written text in the analysis of linguistic meaning. Each processual feature of a meeting, such as its participants and the departments they are affiliated with and the companies they belong to, is depicted in multi-dimensional vector space. The resulting vector represents the total structural description of each meeting. The similarity between structures can then be determined by calculating the angles between the vectors that represent them, with lower angles of deviation indicating higher structural similarity. If, for example, the same departments are present in a number of meetings, these meetings will be considered structurally more similar in this respect.

Causal graph modeling assumes perfect knowledge of probabilities. This implies that traditional statistical analysis is required to (1) identify the conditional probabilities between the entities in question and (2) assess whether the sample probabilities correspond to the population probabilities. For example, we might take 1,000 firms, determine whether they have an arm's length relationship with their suppliers or whether they form strategic alliances and then look at the conditional probabilities of arm's length relationships (or strategic alliances) in conjunction with R&D performance characteristics such as speed of product development.

Nature of Output

The way in which data are converted into an output influences the nature of that output. In the case of the vector space–based model, the output could be a characterization of the type and structure of interaction that is associated with the development of particularly successful products. Possible findings might include that:

- a particular structure of interaction (e.g., between different departments) is fruitful;
- a particular structural evolution of interactions over time is fruitful (e.g., initial interaction between certain departments of the focal firm and the supplier and then interaction between some of the firm's own departments);
- some structures of interaction are more common if strategic alliances are present; or
- particular compositions of teams may be effective.

Causal graph modeling, in contrast, would require population-based probabilities and that the Markov condition holds. The causal graph model structures the conditional probabilities in terms of causal relationships. We may then find, for example, that a long-term relationship with suppliers, such as a joint venture, lies in the causal history of successful product development.

Assumptions

The differences between vector space modeling and causal graph modeling boil down to the assumptions made. Vector space modeling combines the inference of structural relationship with the inference of causal directionality as two steps of an inseparable problem. Thus, it identifies *causal structures* where the relata have an internal structure and where interdependencies between relata drive the performance of firms. The aim is to explicate the causal mechanisms, the concept of which is discussed later in this chapter, underlying the phenomena of interest. Some of these structures may share similarities and, if so, it might then be possible to identify the types of structural relationship associated with performance. We can name and describe these structures, but no two will be exactly the same, as each varies in its elements and how the elements are arranged. As such, vector space modeling is particularly well suited to situations that involve a complex web of causation, where no single factor, but rather an interdependent web of causes, leads to performance outcomes. Uncovering the underlying causal mechanisms can be of considerable help in understanding these situations.

Causal graph modeling assumes perfect knowledge of the probabilistic relationship between events; the main task is to draw conclusions about causal relationships from these probabilities. Hence, this modeling represents a view of *event causation* (Lewis 1973) where clearly definable, identifiable and separable entities — which we call resources — exist. In particular, it is assumed that the influence of one entity is directed clearly at another so that there are no mutual interdependencies and that entities can be measured and their causal influence separated from each other. The effects of the entities are assumed to be conditionally independent and therefore it is assumed that the Markov condition holds. Further, while entities may causally relate to each other, they are denied any internal structure, which, according to vector space modeling, is crucial for generating causal mechanisms. Table 2.1 summarizes the comparison between vector space modeling and causal graph modeling.

Strengths

Perhaps the most important benefit of vector space modeling is that it can deal with causal complexity. As discussed above, vector space models do not depend on the Markov condition, which often breaks down in business phenomena. Furthermore, even if the Markov condition *were* to hold, causal graph modeling would not give us results that take sufficient account of causal complexity. Returning to the example of what causes superior R&D performance, a causal graph model may show that a pyramid structure is more effective than a matrix structure, or that cross functional meetings are more effective than single function meetings. These results are very limited, as they reduce causation to a few,

Table 2.1. *Comparison between causal graph modeling and vector space modeling*

	Causal graph modeling	Vector space modeling
Nature of data	• Clearly defined and separable constructs • Firms need to be classified in terms of the constructs of interest	• Main focus on structural elements and their relationships • Less pre-classification needed
Conversion of data input into output	• Inference of population statistics • Conditional independence	• Comparing deviation of angles between vectors • Identifying structural similarities (usually by calculating cosine between vectors)
Nature of output	• Causal relationships of various significance levels and strengths between constructs	• Structural similarities between objects or features of objects such as firms
Assumptions	• Perfect knowledge of probabilistic relationships between events • Separable, independently-acting resources drive performance (event causation) • Causal effects are conditionally independent (Markov condition)	• Structural characteristics of firms drive performance (structural causation) • Key to these structural characteristics are the relationships entities have with each other • Resources are mutually dependent entities that cannot be entirely isolated from their context

supposedly independent factors. In contrast, vector space models give us an understanding of the underlying mechanism and consequently provide insights into the complex web of causation that typically leads to superior performance. A vector space model may for example identify that joint product development teams between a company and its supplier, where a variety of ranks meet frequently inside and outside of work to create a high trust culture, lead to greater R&D success.

How does vector space modeling perform when applied to a complex web of causal interactions and missing data? Suppose researchers had access to the transcripts of R&D meetings but did not have access to other rich data sources, such as R&D expenditure by project and scientist locations. It turns out that vector space modeling outperforms methods that require traditional statistical analysis, such as causal graph modeling, in cases of causal complexity and missing data (Duch et al. 2007). Even if one had only the transcripts of R&D meetings, these documents would contain information on numerous potential causal factors. Thus an almost infinite number of potential combinations could explain the effect, leaving the internal structure of the relevant mechanism a black box. It is highly likely that methods such as multivariate regression or genetic algorithms would result in over fitting and the identification of spurious relationships. As causal graph modeling requires a similar type of data input, it suffers from the same problem. Vector space modeling, on the other hand, provides a sense of the internal structure of a mechanism, which is composed of a multiplicity of components, as *one* vector. It is thus much less likely to identify spurious correlations because (1) the number of potentially explanatory factors is substantially lower; and (2) we obtain a sense of the internal structure of the complex web of causation and can thus verify whether the causal mechanism, so identified, is plausible.

There is clear evidence for the advantages of vector space modeling in pharmaceutical research. This is an area in which significant advances have been made over the last several decades by focusing increasingly on the *mechanisms and pathways* through which drugs work, rather than on merely whether a drug is efficacious and safe (Rainsford 1995). Vector space modeling has been shown to be more effective than traditional statistical approaches in this context because it takes into account a variety of complex structures, such as the three-dimensional structure of molecules, as well as the interaction of a number of different genes (Nobel 2006).

Limitations

Vector space modeling often requires detailed data on underlying structures and processes. It may be difficult to acquire such data from firms and to transform the data into a format that can be used by the algorithms. Moreover, sometimes there may be only a few observations of key variables. For example, if a critical decision leading to R&D success is made in a single meeting and is not captured by the data, vector space modeling will not be able to identify this causal factor. Of course causal graph modeling will fail too in this instance, as no correlations can be identified.

A further limitation is that there is always some judgment involved; we need to select the structures to be studied, such as the meetings discussed in the example above. However, in contrast to causal graph modeling, it is not necessary to define in advance which particular properties of a meeting, such as their cross-functional nature, could be the cause of superior performance and to classify the meetings accordingly. Rather, such structural characteristics will emerge from the analysis.

Finally, while vector space modeling returns information that helps to uncover underlying causal mechanisms, it cannot guarantee that the mechanism identified was causally relevant in any particular case. Making causal attributions ultimately involves an unavoidable element of judgment, which will also depend on the background knowledge, experience and intuition of the researcher concerned. While causal modeling techniques offer little help in this respect, knowledge of judgment biases helps to avoid making mistakes (see Kahneman 2011). As an analytical technique, vector space modeling is also silent with respect to philosophical issues such as the debates between agent and event causalists discussed in the next section.

Agent versus Event Causation

Consider a scenario where Mary hit a red billiard ball with her cue, the red ball collided with a blue ball and the blue ball moved. Roughly speaking, the scenario consists of two events. First, Mary hit the red ball and the ball moved and second, the red ball collided with the blue ball and the blue ball moved. One key difference between the two events is that the first event involved Mary's action based on her intention to hit the red ball with her cue whereas the second event involved the movement of two inanimate objects without any human intention. Both events exhibit causation; the movement of Mary's cue caused the red ball's movement and the red ball's collision with the blue ball caused the latter's movement. Are the two incidents of causation of the same nature? There has been heated debate about the answer to this question. Those who answer "yes" are called event causalists while those who answer "no" are called agent causalists.

The answer depends on whether one thinks that an intentional action involves an irreducible causal relationship, whose subject is the agent carrying out the action, or involves an event or sequence of events (Bishop 1983). An agent refers to someone or something that makes things happen[2] and "to make something happen is to cause an event of some kind, that is, to exercise the power to cause an event of that kind to occur" (Alvarez and Hyman 1998: 221). Given the nature of management research, I focus on human agents and exclude the agency of animals, plants or inanimate things, although the latter can also make things happen – birds building nests or oxygen rusting iron, for example. When an agent acts intentionally, such as Mary hitting the red ball with her cue, an incident of agency occurs. Event causalists maintain that actions are movements of the agent's body parts that were caused in a particular way by mental events involving the agent's intentions, desires, emotions or beliefs. In this sense, they downplay the role played by agency in the process. In contrast, agent causalists argue that if an agent intentionally caused an event, we cannot "reduce it to the case of an event being a cause" (Davidson 1980: 128). Therefore, a correct account of agency has to preserve for the *agent* the role of an action's cause and the subject of the causal relationship in question is the agent, not the event in which the action occurred. The stress is on the causal power by virtue of which the agent has freedom of will to act (O'Connor 1996). To ascribe a power to an object is to say something about what it will or can do, under suitable conditions, in virtue of its intrinsic nature (Harré and Madden 1975). In brief, for the event causalist, "actions are events caused by intentions" whereas for the agent causalist, "they are events intentionally caused by agents" (Alvarez and Hyman 1998: 222). It is beyond the scope of this book to present the debate; suffice it to say, each side has some unique insights.

A related issue that is pertinent to management research is whether reasons can be considered causes. Davidson (1963), who subscribes to event causation, famously proposes that reasons are causes. Simply put, the reason for which an individual performs an action is the cause of the action. Actions are motivated by beliefs and desires. "We need beliefs and desires because our wanting this and believing that, besides being our reasons *for* doing what we do, are — sometimes at least — the reasons *why* we do" (Dretske 1989: 1). Suppose John's early retirement was due to his desire to spend more time on his hobbies. His desire constituted the reason that caused his decision to retire early. The role played by reasons in intentional explanation is discussed in Chapter 3.

Mechanisms

"To give a description of a mechanism for a phenomenon is to explain that phenomenon, i.e., to explain how it was produced" (Machamer et al. 2000: 3). Similarly, Bunge (1997: 410) highlights the central role played by mechanisms in formulating explanations in the natural and social sciences:

> If we wish to understand a real thing, be it natural, social, biosocial, or artificial, we must find out how it works. That is, real things and their

changes are explained by unveiling their mechanisms: in this respect, social science does not differ from natural science.

Social science *does* differ from natural science with respect to experiments. Scientists need to conduct experiments because of the open character of the world in which events are subject to diverse causal influences. Natural scientists design experiments with the objective of achieving the conditions of a closed system in which "a constant conjunction of events obtains; i.e. in which an event of type a is invariably accompanied by an event of type b" (Bhaskar 1978: 70). The ideal of experiments is to create closed systems so that extraneous causal factors are controlled for, regular sequences of events are observed and the causal relationships among the events can be analyzed. However, it is often very difficult, if ever possible, for social researchers to achieve conditions of closure, as shown by the artificiality of laboratory experiments performed by social psychologists (Harré and Second 1972). Sayer (1992) provides two main reasons for the openness of social systems. First, the configuration of social systems is continuously modified by human actions and, second, unlike inanimate objects or other animals, humans have the capacity for learning and self-change. Hence, social structures are less enduring than structures found in nature.

Given the impossibility of performing experiments under conditions of closure, a serious problem facing social researchers is to make reliable inferences about the causes of social phenomena. Some scholars maintain that a mechanism approach to research can ameliorate significantly this problem (e.g., Elster 1989; Little 1991; Hedström and Swedberg 1996). It should be noted that the notion of mechanism can be traced to the scientific worldview of the seventeenth century when natural science was dominated by mechanics, the exemplar of which was Newtonian mechanics. The idea then spread from physics and astronomy to other natural sciences such as chemistry and biology (Hedström and Swedberg 1996). The original concept of mechanism has been broadened over the centuries; while a few of the mechanisms studied by contemporary scientists are mechanical, most are not (Bunge 1997).

Whereas in economics the concept of market mechanism was evident as early as 1776, in Adam Smith's *The Wealth of Nations* published that year, the term "mechanism" came into use in social research much more recently. One of the earliest instances of its uses was in the prominent sociologist Robert Merton's (1968) paper "On Sociological Theories of the Middle Range," first published in 1949. In that paper, Merton advocates theories of the middle range that "lie between the minor but necessary working hypotheses that evolve in abundance during day-to-day research and the all-inclusive systematic efforts to develop a unified theory that will explain all the observed uniformities of social behavior, social organization, and social change" (39). Using the example of role-set theory, Merton shows how social mechanisms − "the social processes having designated consequences for designated parts of the social structure" (43) − serve as elementary building blocks of a middle-range theory. In management research, March and Simon's (1958) landmark work *Organizations* was an early attempt at explicating the mechanisms of differentiation and aggregation through which individuals are able to accomplish organizational objectives − individuals being grouped into hierarchically connected functional units and performing specialized yet coordinated tasks.

A mechanism-centered social science can also be seen as a reaction to Friedman's (1953: 14–15) famous challenge to the necessity of model or theory realism:

> Truly important and significant hypotheses will be found to have "assumptions" that are wildly inaccurate descriptive representations of reality, and, in general, the more significant the theory, the more unrealistic the assumptions . . . the relevant question to ask about the "assumptions" of a theory is not whether they are descriptively "realistic," for they never are, but whether they are sufficiently good approximations for the purpose in hand. And this question can be answered by seeing whether the theory works, which means whether it yields sufficiently accurate predictions.

Since core assumptions often constitute a significant element of a mechanism, incorporating false assumptions will render a mechanism unrealistic. For example, marginal theory in economics assumes that business executives arrive at their production decisions through consulting schedules or multivariate functions showing marginal cost and marginal revenue. However, Lester's (1946) empirical study of US business executives falsified the assumption, implying that the mechanism entailed by marginal theory was not realistic. Friedman's above view was a response to the heated debate aroused by Lester's study about whether core assumptions of a theory had to be realistic. Contrary to Friedman's instrumentalist stance, researchers who adopt a mechanism approach are not satisfied with a model that merely generates accurate predictions based on covariational analyses. Rather, they attempt to specify discrete causal paths that connect the variables together. This will enhance our knowledge of the phenomenon by allowing us to peer deeply into the box of causality (Gerring 2008).

From a policy perspective, it is surely important to know *what* effect a given policy has produced, but it is also useful to know *why* the policy has that effect. The latter knowledge, which is gained through studying the mechanism concerned, will help policymakers anticipate possible unintended side effects and improve the policy accordingly (Gerring 2010). In the management discipline, bridging the gap between theory and practice is no easy task. The key criticisms that managers make of theorists is that theorists "comment on practice but elide context, overlook constraints, take the wrong things for granted, overestimate control, presume unattainable ideals, underestimate dynamism, or translate comprehensible events into incomprehensible variables" (Weick 2003: 453). As discussed below, a mechanism approach commits to the locality of causal processes and thus situates mechanisms in context. The approach seems appropriate to address managers' concern. Hence, "a deeper understanding of mechanisms might be one way to better translate organizational theories into managerial action" (Anderson et al. 2006: 109).

Characteristics

In science, what constitutes a mechanism has evolved over time (Machamer et al. 2000). In social research, the concept of mechanism "contains a plethora of meanings" (Gerring 2010: 1500). Mayntz (2004: 238) laments that "a survey of the relevant empirical and methodological literature soon bogs down in a mire of loose talk and semantic confusion about what 'mechanisms' are." Mahoney (2001), for example, lists twenty-four definitions proposed by twenty-one authors. That various definitions of mechanism have been proposed is not surprising, given that the entities and processes studied by different disciplines are rather heterogeneous and that a mechanism is identified by the kind of effects or phenomena it generates. A mechanism is therefore always a mechanism for something (Darden 2006). For the sake of discussion, I adopt a general definition of mechanisms that is applicable to both natural and social phenomena and is modeled on the definition of Machamer et al. (2000): mechanisms consist of *entities* and *activities* organized so as to produce regular *changes* from a beginning state to an ending one. Entities can be understood as the actors, organizations, structures and so on that engage in activities, and the activities are the producers of change.[3] Let's illustrate this definition using Merton's (1948) well-known example of self-fulfilling prophecy in the context of a bank run. The *entities* here refer to the bank, its cash reserves, its depositors' belief that the bank is having financial difficulties, a banking system that lacks a deposit insurance scheme and so on. The *activities* are depositors' withdrawals of their deposits in large numbers within a short period of time and the bank paying the depositors from its cash reserves. The entities and activities are not random but are related and form an organized whole. Unless the government intervenes or other banks give a helping hand, the bank will eventually become insolvent (or even bankrupt) — the *change* from the beginning state of solvency. The mechanism is regular in that it always works in the same way from the beginning to end under the same conditions.

Since mechanisms involve change, "it makes no sense to talk about mechanisms in pure ideas or abstract objects, such as sets, functions, algorithms, or grammars, for nothing happens in them (when taken in and by themselves)" (Bunge 1997: 418). For example, 3+2=5 does not represent the mechanism of adding three and two to arrive at the answer of five. Similarly, a deductive inference is not a mechanism through which a conclusion is drawn. Therefore, the concept of mechanism is alien to logic, mathematics and linguistics, none of which are concerned with changes that take place in time. This point is also consistent with the nature of a mechanism being an irreducibly causal process that produces the effect of interest. Adding three and two, for instance, does not cause five to exist. Consider the following syllogism:

Premise 1. All human beings are mortal.
Premise 2. Mary is a human being.
Conclusion. Mary is mortal.

The two premises do not cause Mary to be mortal.

Including the terms "entities" and "activities" in the definition entails the philosophical intuitions of both substantivalists and process ontologists (Machamer et al. 2000). Substantivalists focus on entities and their properties, believing that talk of activities can be reduced to that of properties and their transitions. They speak of entities with capacities to act, such as aspirin's capacity to relieve a headache. Note here that entities refer to concrete things rather than pure ideas or abstract objects, such as functions, sets or algorithms (Bunge 1997). In contrast, process ontologists reify activities, believing that talk of entities can be reduced to that of processes that entities generate. Each side is biased and fails to capture fully the nature of mechanisms. In fact, entities and activities are interdependent in that "entities having certain kinds of properties are necessary for the possibility of acting in certain specific ways, and certain kinds of activities are only possible when there are entities having certain kinds of properties" (Machamer et al. 2000: 6). Mechanisms are active in generating phenomena and so need to be conceptualized as the activities of their entities. In the bank run example, the entities and their properties alone do not give rise to a bank run. Rather, a significant percentage of depositors have to, based on their belief, act within a short period of time in order to start a bank run. The definition is dualist in that both entities and activities constitute mechanisms. In short, "it is the activities that entities engage in that move the mechanism from an initial causal condition through different parts to an outcome" (Beach 2016: 465).

A mechanism is a causal chain producing the effect of interest. The effect of the bank run example is the insolvency of the bank that confirms depositors' initial belief. The mechanism perspective commits to the locality of causal processes in that whether X is a cause of Y depends on facts about the spatiotemporally-restricted causal process in question (Hedström and Ylikoski 2010). For example, if depositors withdraw their deposits over a longer period of time, the bank may be able to call back some of its loans and have sufficient cash to pay the depositors. Consequently, some depositors may change their initial belief that the bank is in financial trouble and so do not withdraw their deposits or even re-deposit their money. The bank run may stop; that is, the mechanism does not run its course. The notion of a causal *chain* implies that there should be some intermediate steps between cause and effect (Mayntz 2004). In the case of a bank run, there are a series of steps between the formation of depositors' belief and the eventual insolvency of the bank. On the other hand, when a cause directly leads to an effect, such as one billiard-ball colliding with another, the whole event does not constitute a causal chain.

Management research is concerned with social mechanisms. As a subset of mechanisms, social mechanisms are characterized by interactions among individuals that underly and account for social regularities (Little 1991). Such individuals are categorized into groups defined by salient features that members of a group share. In describing a mechanism, the relevant behavior of an individual depends on the group to which that individual belongs. In the bank run example, depositors form a group and an individual depositor's behavior is affected by the general concern of the group that if the bank fails, depositors will not be able to get back all of their money. Therefore, when the bank's financial situation is believed to be poor, it makes sense to withdraw one's deposit as soon as possible.

Another issue is whether a social mechanism refers to a recurrent or a unique causal process. Mayntz (2004: 241) opts for the former and proposes that mechanisms "'are' sequences of causally-linked events that occur repeatedly in reality if certain conditions are given." On the other hand, Boudon (1998: 172) deems a mechanism to be "the well-articulated set of causes responsible for a given social phenomenon" and that mechanisms "tend to be idiosyncratic and singular." Hedström and Swedberg (1996) are right regarding the point that the generality of mechanisms gives them explanatory power.[4] In reality, each bank run is unique. A mechanism can be formulated to tailor for the idiosyncratic features of a particular bank run. Yet, such a tailor-made description is only valid for that bank run and is better regarded as an account of a unique chain of events that led from one event to another than as a mechanism (Hedström and Swedberg 1996). An approach that is followed here and is more in line with scientific research is to work out a general bank run mechanism applicable to many bank run cases, although the mechanism may not describe accurately the details of any of the cases. The spirit of this approach is captured by Tilly's (2001: 25–26) definition of mechanisms in political science: "Mechanisms form a delimited class of events that change relations among specified sets of elements in identical or closely similar ways over a variety of situations." In other words, a mechanism is supposed to describe a variety of similar political situations, not one particular situation.

Temporality is an essential characteristic of social mechanisms, which take place in time (Mayntz 2004). That said, causal mechanisms, especially complex ones, do not always unfold in a linear manner; there may be branch causal chains, escalation processes and feedback loops. For example, during the early stage of a bank run, some depositors may not firmly hold to their belief that the bank is in financial difficulty and so hesitate to withdraw their money from the bank. However, when they see long queues of people outside the branches of the bank trying to get back their deposits, their belief is strengthened once more and motivates them to join the queue. This action in turn motivates more depositors to follow suit. This feedback loop escalates the process of deposit withdrawal.

Most of the mechanisms studied by natural or social scientists are unobservable or hidden and thus their description usually contains concepts that do not appear in empirical data (Bunge 2004). We do not see or observe the mechanism of self-fulfilling prophecy per se in an actual bank run. More likely, we read news about depositors scrambling to get back their money, their belief about the bank's financial situation and the bank trying to satisfy these depositors. We then link these entities and activities together and compare the information with our knowledge of self-fulfilling prophecy to determine whether our observation fits the mechanism. For new mechanisms, researchers have to use their skills of reasoning and imagination:

> To discuss mechanisms is to reason about possible and plausible states of the world as they bear on a particular causal relationship. In reasoning, writers build on their knowledge of a particular context and on general knowledge of the world. They may also play out elaborate reconstructions of the events as they actually occurred or might have occurred to test the relative plausibility of various hypotheses. (Gerring 2010: 1502)

Generally speaking, mechanisms cannot be inferred from empirical data and have to be conjectured (Bunge 1997). For instance, the mechanism of self-fulfilling prophecy cannot be inferred from the data about a bank run; it has to be conjectured by researchers "with imagination both stimulated and constrained by data, well-weathered hypotheses, and mathematical concepts such as those of number, function, and equation" (Bunge 2004: 200). As Harré (1970: 40) well stated about half a century ago, "making models for unknown mechanisms is the creative process in science, by which potential advances are initiated, while the making of models of known things and processes has, generally speaking, a more heuristic value." A certain degree of creativity on the part of the researcher is needed. Interestingly, Stinchcombe (1968:13) once noted, "a student [of sociology] who has difficulty thinking of at least three sensible explanations for any correlation that he is really interested in should probably choose another profession." As a staunch advocate of theorizing with mechanisms in the social sciences, his point concerns conjecturing at least three different mechanisms that can explain a correlation between variables.

It goes without saying that a conjectured mechanism has to be testable empirically in order that it is regarded as scientific. A conjectured mechanism must have survived empirical tests before it can be regarded as true to some degree and, according to Popper (1959), the mechanism should also be falsifiable (i.e., there is a chance of it being refuted by empirical tests). Pseudoscientific or superstitious practices, such as parapsychology, telepathy, astrology, horoscope, feng shui (風水) and faith healing, do not belong to the scientific domain unless they are based on falsifiable mechanisms; such practices, however, often do not work other than offering a placebo effect (Bunge 2004).

Causal Inference

Mechanisms assist researchers to make causal inference in two main ways:

> On the positive side, we can infer that X is a cause of Y if we know that there is a mechanism through which X influences Y. The negative flip side is that if no plausible mechanism running from X to Y can be conceived of, then it is safe to conclude that X does not cause Y, even if the two variables are probabilistically dependent. (Steel 2004: 56)

In particular, the second way implies that mechanisms can help to address the problem of confounders, which refer to common causes that explain observed but spurious correlations. We can exclude the possibility of a spurious correlation between two variables if we can formulate a plausible mechanism that links directly the variables in the circumstances (Little 1991). In the earlier example of peak hour traffic correlated positively with the sale of lipstick in Dallas, it is virtually impossible to come up with a plausible mechanism through which peak hour traffic would affect lipstick sales or vice versa. Hence the correlation is spurious. Here, the confounder was level of employment, which affected both peak hour traffic and lipstick sales. As discussed above, a plausible mechanism can be conjured to link level of employment with peak hour traffic or lipstick sales. Of course, a mechanism approach is not the only way to deal with the problem of confounders; vector space modeling, for instance, can also tackle the problem.

However, Steel (2004: 65) suggests that cases similar to the lipstick sales example are "too few and far between for the no-plausible-mechanism strategy to be of much use in distinguishing cause from mere correlation in social science."[5] A good example is the positive correlation between opportunity for advancement and level of frustration with the promotion system, found by Stouffer et al.'s (1949) study of American soldiers in World War II. Contrary to common sense, soldiers in the military police, which offered relatively few promotion opportunities, were on average more satisfied with the promotion system than those in the army air corps, which offered more opportunities. Gambetta (1998) summarizes five mechanisms that have been proposed by sociologists over the years to account for Stouffer et al.'s counterintuitive finding. For example, Merton (1957: 237) proposes that a "generally high rate of mobility induces *excessive hopes* among members of the group so that each is more likely to experience a sense of frustration in his present position and dissatisfaction with the chances of promotion." Here, the mechanism is one of excessive hopes that led more soldiers in the army air corps to frustration.

Gambetta (1998) fails, however, to consider the possibility that opportunity for advancement had little or no significant effect on the level of frustration with the promotion system. Steel (2004: 65) puts forward a possibility that Stouffer et al.'s finding was due to a confounder: "extremely ambitious people are much more likely to embark on career paths that promise greater opportunities for advancement and that their lofty aspirations are also more likely to make them dissatisfied with their current stations in life." Steel's self-selection bias argument implies that with sufficient imagination and luck, researchers can often conjure up mechanisms linking variables together. Given the complexity of human psychology, I believe that the five mechanisms reviewed by Gambetta and the confounder suggested by Steel were all possible in reality; that is, soldiers' levels of frustration could be accounted for by one or more of these mechanisms. If Stouffer and his colleagues had asked their subjects the reasons for their frustration over or satisfaction with the promotion system, they would have had a much better understanding of the mechanism(s) underlying their finding.

Amid the hype around the mechanismic turn in the social sciences – in particular, management (Anderson et al. 2006) – during the past three decades or so, Gerring (2010: 1504) issued a cautionary note by questioning the turn's novelty:

> It seems unlikely that anyone has ever published an article or book in any field that merely announces a covariational result as causal without *any* discussion of possible causal mechanisms. These are things that social scientists do, more or less self-consciously, when they argue about causes.

For instance, when Hempel – an arch-positivist who supposedly had serious reservations about the concept of causal mechanisms – attempted to substantiate the point that general laws serve similar functions in history as in the natural sciences, he offered the following description of what brings about a revolution:

> if a particular revolution is explained by reference to the growing discontent, on the part of a large part of the population, with certain prevailing conditions, it is clear that a general regularity is assumed in this explanation, but we are hardly in a position to state just what extent and what specific form the discontent has to assume, and what the environmental conditions have to be, to bring about a revolution. (Hempel 1942: 41)

Surely, he used mechanismic wording here. What distinguishes a mechanism-centered approach may be that researchers are more explicit in their theorizing with mechanisms and take more seriously the specification of discrete causal pathways compared to their peers following a different approach.

Process Tracing

As mentioned, if we know that there is a mechanism through which X affects Y, we can infer that X is a cause of Y. The question then becomes: How do we know that a mechanism exists? Little (1991: 30) proposes two ways that researchers may acquire knowledge of mechanisms:

> To credibly identify causal mechanisms we must employ one of two forms of inference. First, we may use a deductive approach, establishing causal connections between social factors based on a theory of the underlying process . . .. Second, we may use a broadly inductive approach, justifying the claim that a caused b on the ground that events of type A are commonly associated with event of type B . . .. But in either case the strength of the causal assertion depends on the discovery of a regular association between event types.

Little's suggestion implies that researchers possess some prior knowledge — theoretical knowledge in the case of deduction and empirical knowledge in the case of induction — of the connections between events. Since a mechanism often consists of a series of events, both kinds of knowledge may be needed to identify the mechanism.

Little's method may be categorized under a more general approach called "process tracing," which, in the case of social mechanisms, "consists in presenting evidence for the existence of several prevalent social practices that, when linked together, produce a chain of causation from one variable to another" (Steel 2004: 67). Simply put, process tracing is to trace a mechanism. A successful instance of process tracing provides empirical support for the existence of a mechanism linking the variables of interest. Process tracing is a fundamental tool of qualitative analysis, used usually by researchers who carry out within-case analysis (Collier 2011). Process tracing can be used in tandem with quantitative methods: "process tracing is used to establish qualitative claims about causal structure, and statistical analysis is called on to estimate the strengths of these relationships" (Steel 2004: 72).

To explicate process tracing, Bennett (2010) uses the analogy of a detective attempting to solve a crime by examining clues and potential suspects and collecting evidence that bears on suspects' motives, means and opportunity to have committed the crime. To uncover variables not previously considered in a mechanism, researchers may conduct process

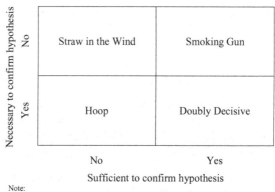

Note:
This figure is adapted from Table 10.1 of Bennett (2010)

Figure 2.4   Process tracing tests of evidential strength

tracing backward from observed outcomes to potential causes, or forward from hypothesized causes to eventual outcomes. Similarly, after a crime has occurred, a detective can work forward from potential suspects as well as backward from clues about the crime. In our bank run example, researchers may start their investigation by interviewing depositors who were among the first to withdraw their money or interviewing bank executives who were struggling to maintain the bank's solvency. Needless to say, the assumption here is that research access is readily available.

Since there exists detailed guidelines for process tracing (e.g., Collier 2011; Beach and Pedersen 2019), it is beyond the scope of this section to discuss these techniques. Yet, it is worth presenting in a simplified manner Van Evera's (1997) classification of four tests according to whether a piece of evidence is *necessary* and/or *sufficient* for accepting a hypothesis. The classification is useful for evaluating evidential strength in process tracing. As shown in Figure 2.4, the four tests are called "straw in the wind," "smoking gun," "hoop" and "doubly decisive." Let's illustrate the tests by returning to the example of self-fulfilling prophecy in the context of a bank run. Admittedly, this illustration may not be in line with the sophisticated banking and payment systems nowadays. Within this limitation, my aim is to demonstrate the nature of each of the four tests. Suppose a researcher wants to know whether a bank run has occurred after observing some events. The hypothesis here is that the mechanism of self-fulfilling prophecy has begun. The following events, corresponding to the four tests, provide different extents of support for the hypothesis.

- Straw in the wind: Outside the branches of a bank, there are long queues of depositors trying to withdraw their money. Is this a piece of evidence that a bank run of the self-fulfilling prophecy kind has started? No, the evidence is *neither necessary nor sufficient* for establishing the hypothesis. Depositors in large numbers may withdraw their money for various reasons, such as shopping during holidays. An essential element of the self-fulfilling prophecy is depositors' belief that the bank is experiencing financial trouble and so it is risky to keep their money with the bank. Without knowing the depositors' reasons, the observation of the long queues provides little information that favors or calls into question the researcher's hypothesis.

- Smoking gun: Here, there is additional information about the above event: these depositors believe that the bank is experiencing financial trouble. In this case, the event confirms the hypothesis. However, depositors may withdraw their money through other means, such as writing checks and transferring funds from their bank accounts to their mutual fund accounts. A bank run due to the same depositors' belief may occur without long queues outside its branches. In other words, the evidence is *sufficient but not necessary* for supporting the hypothesis. As Van Evera notes, when the suspect is holding a smoking gun right after a murder, this evidence implicates the suspect clearly. However, the absence of the gun does not exonerate the suspect.

- Hoop: The term "hoop" here means that a piece of evidence must "jump through the hoop" in order not to be eliminated; however, success in passing the hoop test does not support strongly the hypothesis in question. Suppose there is reliable evidence that a large number of a bank's depositors believe that the bank is having financial difficulties. Yet, most of these depositors have not acted on their belief and withdrawn money from the bank because of the expectation that the government will assists banks during a financial crisis. As mentioned above, the belief is a *necessary* element of the self-fulfilling prophecy, but the belief alone is *not sufficient* for the bank run to occur.

- Doubly decisive: Further to the above hoop test example, suppose the depositors do act on their belief and withdraw money from the bank through various channels. In this case, the evidence is both *necessary and sufficient* for confirming the hypothesis. Van Evera uses the example of a bank camera photographing the faces of all robbers, thereby implicating those caught by the camera and exonerating others.

While one piece of "doubly decisive" evidence may suffice to confirm a hypothesis and is better than many pieces of "straw in the wind" evidence, such high-quality data are hard to come by in reality. Instead, researchers may collect "hoop" and "smoking gun' data that together provide evidence of equivalent strength to "doubly decisive" evidence (Van Evera 1997).

Process tracing is not without limitations. Bennett (2010) mentions two key problems: degrees of freedom and infinite regress. The former is a usual problem of case studies in which there are too few cases included in a sample relative to the large number of variables studied. The latter is more specific to process tracing: when researchers pay attention to exceedingly fine-grained details of mechanisms, it can result in an infinite regress of studying "causal steps between any two links in the chain of causal mechanisms" (King et al. 1994: 86). Suppose researchers investigate a bank run and interview depositors who believe that the bank is experiencing financial trouble. After hearing that, say, a depositor's belief came from their friend, they may investigate further how the two individuals communicated for the belief to be transferred, what cognitive processes were involved and so on. Basically, this issue is concerned with the "stopping point" – that is, when an inquiry into a mechanism should stop. For example, in Checkel's (2006) study of the mechanism of socialization in the Council of Europe, he broke the mechanism into three sub-mechanisms, namely strategic calculation, role playing and persuasion, and focused on persuasion. The question then becomes: why should he stop at this point? It is plausible that persuasion could be broken down into further sub-mechanisms, such as more micro cognitive processes.

CHAPTER 3

Modes of Explanation

In spite of the various perspectives — such as positivism, realism, constructivism and pragmatism — being held by philosophers, there is consensus among them that "a fundamental aim of science is to provide explanations of natural phenomena" (Salmon 2006: 4).[1] It is not surprising that theories of explanation are a crucial topic in philosophy of science. There is much that management, as a relatively young social science discipline, can learn from the development of such theories.

At the beginning of the twentieth century, the dominant attitude of scientifically oriented philosophers and philosophically inclined scientists held mostly that "there is no such thing as scientific explanation — explanation lies beyond the scope of science, in such realms as metaphysics and theology" (Salmon 1999: 338). That is, explanation belongs to the domain of philosophy. This chapter introduces several major modes of explanation proposed by philosophers and ends with a brief discussion of "process organization studies" — an emerging genre of management studies — that is related to some of the modes of explanation.

Aristotle's Doctrine of the Four Causes

One can be easily misled by the word "causes" concerning Aristotle's doctrine if one thinks of "causes" in terms of the Humean notion of cause and effect. Only one of Aristotle's causes — the "efficient" cause — is remotely related to that notion. As discussed in Chapter 2, causation is objective in that it is a relationship between *events* out there. Thus, causes are events and so are their effects. On the other hand, Aristotle doesn't limit his causes to *events*; typically, it is *substances* that have causes. At this point, it is obvious that Aristotle does not intend to discuss the concept of cause. Rather, Aristotle attempts to develop a theory of *aitia*. The Greek word *aitia* (singular *aition*) has been translated in philosophy as "causes" and refers to whatever answers a why-question. Note that explanations are in fact answers to why-questions (see Chapter 1). One can explain something in terms of not only causal factors but also factors related to, say, function or purpose, as discussed in the sections below. Since *aitia* are whatever answers a why-question and whatever answers a why-question is an explanation, it follows that an *aition* is simply an explanatory factor rather than a cause. In short, Aristotle's doctrine of causes is actually a theory about the structure of explanations (Moravcsik 1974).

Physics (Ross 1936) and *Metaphysics* (Ross 1948) present Aristotle's account of the four causes that can be given in answer to a why-question:

- Material cause: the material out of which a thing comes to be, for example, the wood of a table.
- Formal cause: the form of what a thing is to be, for example, the shape of a table.
- Efficient cause: the thing that brings something about, for example, the carpenter who made a table is the efficient cause of the table.
- Final cause: the purpose for which a thing is done, for example, a table was made for the purpose it is supposed to serve.

One problem is that when Aristotle presents the four causes, he does so without providing the rationale for choosing these four (Hennig 2009). Ross (1936: 37) therefore claims that we "do not know how Aristotle arrived at the doctrine of the four causes." Various philosophers have attempted to figure out the connections among the four causes. For instance, Moravcsik (1974: 6) makes this concluding remark:

> In summary, the reason for selecting these four types as the main types is that they represent the main factors of what for Aristotle is the primary category of beings, namely substances. What gives unity to the list of four is that jointly they provide a complete explanation of the nature of a substance, and thus Aristotle supposes that they must contain the ingredients of a complete explanation of any other phenomena, since these must be in some way dependent on substances.

In addition to applying the four causes to the explanation of the nature of a substance, which can be an artefact or a natural substance such as an organism, Aristotle also attempts to use the four causes to explain natural changes. A change is natural when the thing that undergoes the change has "in itself" a principle that governs this change, which constitutes a development that is typical (i.e., natural) for the changing thing (Hennig 2009). Since natural changes are different from substances, they do not have the four causes in precisely the same way as substances do. In light of

Aristotle's claim that self-movements, including actions, are changes, Reece (2019) proposes a four-cause treatment of actions:

- Material cause: agents' bodies are material causes, constituting the underlying substrata of their actions.
- Formal cause: agents' psychological attitudes are formal causes, providing their actions the identity conditions.
- Efficient cause: agents themselves are efficient causes, bringing about actions.
- Final cause: actions are performed for the sake of achieving agents' goals, which are therefore final causes.

Reece (2019: 225) links nicely the four causes together to describe the nature of an action: "An action is a self-movement with the body as its substratum, performed by a self-moving agent who counts as the per se efficient cause of the self-movement because her active desire for a goal is what informs her activity, giving it the goal-oriented structure that it has." The description throws light on intentional explanation discussed below.

In spite of the significant position in philosophy of Aristotle's doctrine of the four causes, management researchers may not find it useful. However, since the field of entrepreneurship is concerned with bringing novel products and services into being, Aristotle's account for why things come into being may be relevant. Consider, for example, the case of bringing a new product to market (not the product itself). A *material* cause represents the resources, both tangible and intangible, that the entrepreneur works with. A *formal* cause pertains to the process that the entrepreneur goes through, such as generating product ideas, garnering financial support, researching the market, building a product prototype, testing the market, making adjustments to the product and manufacturing the product. An *efficient* cause refers to the entrepreneur, who engages in the abovementioned activities that create the product from scratch. A *final* cause represents the desired outcome — the successful launch of the product in the market.

Covering Law Model

An early and very important attempt at developing a theory of scientific explanation is the covering law model created by Carl Hempel (together with Paul Oppenheim). The model explains events by subsuming them under a law, which then, so to speak, "covers" the events to be explained. The model has two versions: the deductive-nomological (D-N) model and the inductive-statistical (I-S) model. This approach to explanation is consistent with the character of explanations given in natural sciences, which often proceed by deriving descriptions of particular events – or descriptions of empirical regularities – from sets of premises identified as laws. For quite a long period of time, the covering law model was regarded by philosophers of science as essentially correct, in part due to the fact that "its formalization has proved to be possible in a logical satisfactory way" (Janssen and Tan 1991: 255). The model has been criticized severely, however, since the 1980s as more and more counterexamples, some of which are discussed below, have emerged.

Before I present the two versions of the model, it is necessary to introduce the Vienna Circle, which provides some useful historical background. Hempel was not only a member of the Circle but was also influenced strongly by some Circle members such as Rudolf Carnap and Otto Neurath (Friedman 2000). The spirit of the Vienna Circle is reflected by the caution that enough restrictions are placed on the definition of explanation to rule out metaphysical explanations, but the definition should be sufficiently lax to allow those explanations that scientists traditionally accept as legitimate (Caldwell 1980).

Vienna Circle

The Vienna Circle refers to a group of eminent philosophers and scientists who met weekly or thereabouts from 1924 to 1936 at the University of Vienna. Physicist and philosopher Moritz Schlick is considered widely to have been the founder of the group. Fortuitously, it existed in the midst of the cultural, political and intellectual turmoil of the Weimar period. Members attempted to reexamine the philosophical foundation of science in view of the then-recent advances in the discipline, such as the dramatic replacement of Newtonian mechanics by Einstein's theory of relativity. The objective of the Circle was to establish a solid foundation for empirical sciences. The Circle was dissolved when the Nazi party came to power in Germany, partly because some of the key members were Jewish (Sigmund 2017). Many of its members, including Hempel, emigrated to the United States and taught at universities there. The Circle's influence on philosophy, in particular philosophy of science, has been immense, persisting even to the present day.

The manifesto of the Circle, as stated in 1929's *The Scientific World Conception: The Vienna Circle*, characterizes the scientific world-conception essentially on the basis of two features (in Sarkar, 1996: 331):

First it is *empiricist and positivist:* there is knowledge only from experience, which rests on what is immediately given. This sets the limits for the content of legitimate science. *Second,* the scientific world-conception is marked by application of a certain method, namely *logical analysis.* The aim of scientific effort is to reach the goal, unified science, by applying logical analysis to the empirical material.

Similar to its composition of members, the philosophical perspectives propounded by the Vienna Circle were constantly changing. Yet scholars usually associate the group with only one philosophical perspective — logical positivism, the label for which is derived from the view that philosophy is in the form of logical analysis and its subject matter is concerned with empirical or positive sciences (Caldwell 1980). The Circle, which believed that the task of philosophy was to analyze knowledge statements with the aim of making them clear and unambiguous, distinguished between analytic and synthetic statements. Statements in logic and mathematics were analytic. Without any empirical content, true statements of logic or true mathematical statements did not express factual truths. In contrast, synthetic statements were held to have meaning only to the extent that they were verifiable. This verifiability criterion implies testability because one must be able to test whether a synthetic assertion is true. Synthetic statements constitute justified knowledge claims based on successful empirical tests. The Circle only accepted synthetic statements a posteriori (i.e., scientific statements) and analytic statements a priori (i.e., logical and mathematical statements) as legitimate in scientific research. Metaphysical statements, such as "God lets people have the freedom to choose between good and evil," were, according to the Circle, neither analytic nor subject to empirical testing and thus were deemed meaningless, although not necessarily false. Such statements, according to the Circle, should be excluded from the domain of science. In brief, in the Circle's view, the basic percept of science could be encapsulated by Ernst Mach's ([1883] 1960: 587) dictum that "where neither confirmation nor refutation is possible, science is not concerned."

The philosophy of science proposed by the Circle was criticized severely over the years. For instance, its notion of meaningful statements (noted above) was disparaged as "too narrow — that it arbitrarily excludes other than empirical verifiability" (Blumberg and Feigl 1931: 294). Some philosophers even arrived at this somewhat damning conclusion: "there is no doubt about the truth of the statement that the philosophy of the Vienna Circle is dead" (Haller 1982: 25). In this connection, Popper (2002) famously claimed responsibility for killing logical positivism. In spite of its shortcomings, however, the Circle was a vibrant forum in which widely divergent ideas about how science at that time should advance were expressed and debated (Sigmund 2017). Since its demise, there have been no academic groups that could be considered to be similar to it.

Deductive-Nomological Model

The D-N model of scientific explanation was first proposed in Hempel's (1942) paper "The Function of General Laws in History" and then formalized by Hempel and Oppenheim's (1948) paper "Studies in the Logic of Explanation." Although Hempel (1965) admitted that the model was not totally novel because its core idea could be traced to definitions of explanation as subsumption under laws from Mill's (1973) landmark work *System of Logic* published more than a century ago, the historical significance of the model should by no means be underestimated. Niiniluoto (2000: 138) claims that these two seminal papers "opened a new research area in the philosophy of science." In Salmon's (2006) survey of four decades of scientific explanation from 1948 to 1987, he notes that "the 1948 Hempel-Oppenheim article marks the division between the prehistory and the history of modern discussions of scientific explanation" (10). In another place, this eminent scholar of scientific explanation remarks that the article "constitutes the fountainhead from which almost everything done subsequently on philosophical problems of scientific explanation flows" (Salmon 1990: 3). In short, the D-N model deserves management researchers' attention.

The D-N model consists of one or more general laws and statements declaring that certain events occurred. A general law is "a statement of universal conditional form which is capable of being confirmed or disconfirmed by suitable empirical findings" (Hempel 1942: 35) and is assumed to be deterministic in nature, depicting a regularity of the following type: whenever an event of a specified kind C occurs, an event of a specified kind E will occur. The claim that a set of events — say, C_1, $C_2, \ldots, C_n$ — have caused the occurrence of event E amounts to the following D-N explanation in the form of an *argument* that consists of three main steps:

(1) a set of general laws stating that if C_1, C_2, $\ldots$, C_n occur, then E will occur,

(2) a set of existential statements confirming the occurrence of C_1, $C_2, \ldots, C_n$,

(3) a deduced conclusion stating the occurrence of E.

Steps 1 and 2 are the premises and Step 3 is the conclusion derived from deductive reasoning. In other words, an explanation must be expressible in the form of a deductive argument in which a sentence describing the event to be explained (the explanandum E) is a logically valid consequence of the explanans (general laws and existential statements). It is the general laws (Step 1) that establish an explanatory connection between the antecedent conditions (Step 2) and the explanandum E (Step 3). The why-question concerned is construed as meaning "according to what general laws, and by virtue of what antecedent conditions does the phenomenon occur?" (Hempel and Oppenheim 1948: 136). The D-N model is intended to establish necessary and sufficient conditions for explaining why the explanandum took place (Fetzer 1974). Caldwell (1980: 58) lists four conditions of adequacy for the D-N model: "the explanandum must be a logical consequence of the explanans, the explanans must contain at least one general law, the explanans must have empirical content, and the sentences constituting the explanans must be true."

As discussed in Chapter 1, the chief function of explanation is to promote understanding. For the D-N model, "the link between explanation and understanding is secured by the notion of *expectability* – the reason that a sound deductive argument for the occurrence of some event explains that event is precisely that the argument justifies, to the extent that the premises are justified, the expectation that the event will (or did) occur" (Weslake 2010, 274–275). On the other hand, Friedman (1974: 7) laments that the D-N model does not tell us what it is about the explanation relation entailed by the model that gives us understanding of the explained phenomenon and thus makes the world more intelligible. Proponents of the D-N model seem to consider that concepts like "understanding" and "intelligibility" lie beyond the province of the philosopher of science. Hempel (1965: 413) wrote that "such expressions as 'realm of understanding' and 'comprehensible' do not belong to the vocabulary of logic, for they refer to psychological or pragmatic aspects of explanation," and these aspects vary from individual to individual. In the context of the Vienna Circle, pragmatics, though important, were empirical and hence did not belong to the rational construction of new scientific language on the positivistic basis, which was purely logical (Carnap 1936). Philosophers of science, in Hempel's opinion, should aim at "explicating the nonpragmatic aspects of explanation, the sense of 'explanation' on which *A* explains *B simpliciter* and not *for you or for me*" (Friedman 1974: 7).

The broad anti-metaphysical stance of the Vienna Circle made delving into explanation appear a dubious enterprise (Douglas 2009). In particular, the presence of general laws in the D-N model contradicts the Circle's verifiability criterion mentioned above. The criterion rules out as meaningless those statements of universal form (e.g., all ravens are black), which are often used in the specification of general laws. Such statements cannot be verified conclusively by any finite set of observations because no number of confirming instances can guarantee that an exception will never be found. Hempel (1950) observed that the verifiability criterion of the most conservative and dogmatic logical positivists was not justifiable. Though beyond the scope of this book, it is worth mentioning that he proposed a more sophisticated approach toward the logic and language of science, which has become known as logical empiricism.

The D-N model was originally designed to explain natural science phenomena. The Vienna Circle rejected the view that there is a radical distinction between natural and social sciences, a stance summarized clearly by Ayer (1959: 21): "The scale and diversity of the phenomena with which the social sciences dealt made them less successful in establishing scientific laws, but this was a difficulty of practice, not of principle: they too were concerned in the end with physical events." Hempel and Oppenheim (1948) themselves claim that the model is applicable to social sciences as well. To illustrate their point, they use the example of a severe drop in the price of cotton in the autumn of 1946 such that the cotton exchanges in New York, New Orleans and Chicago had to suspend their activities temporarily. To explain this incident, newspapers traced it back to a large speculator in New Orleans who had feared that his holdings were excessive and thus had begun to liquidate his position. Then, smaller speculators had followed in panic selling, resulting in the critical decline. In this incident, one general regularity in Step 1 refers to the law of supply and demand that accounts for the drop in cotton prices when the greatly increased supply was not matched by a corresponding change in demand. There are also certain regularities in the behavior of individuals who attempt to preserve or improve their economic position. Step 2 refers to the events that the first speculator had large stocks of cotton, that he liquidated his position due to fear, that there were smaller speculators with considerable holdings, that these speculators followed in panic selling, that there existed the cotton exchanges providing platforms for the transactions and so on. The severe drop in the price of cotton (Step 3) can be deduced from Steps 1 and 2.

Although the D-N model could be expected to be equally applicable to social sciences, it has been largely neglected or ignored by management researchers. Sayer (1992: 2) argues that "social science has been singularly unsuccessful in discovering law-like regularities." Compared to natural phenomena, invariant laws are far less common in management phenomena, partly because researchers' activities may change the beliefs and practices of managers, undermining the stability of the phenomena under investigation (Numagami 1998). Yet management researchers may benefit from the model's insights. For example, I discuss in a section below how the model could be used to explain the vertical integration between General Motors (GM) and Fisher Body in 1926. The integration is "the most commonly cited example of a holdup problem solved by vertical integration" (Klein 2008: 442) and is thus a classic example of market failure in the transaction cost economics (TCE) literature. In terms of explaining organizational actions, Susman and Evered (1978: 590) argue that the D-N mode of explanation takes the following form: "(a) Actions of type A always produce consequences of type C in a given class of situations, (b) Person X takes action A in a particular situation, thus (c) A consequence of type C occurs."

Inductive-statistical Model

Deterministic general laws that rule out exceptions are uncommon in some natural sciences such as medicine. Laws invoked in virtually all social sciences are of a probabilistic nature; that is, they state that a particular event will occur with such and such probability if certain specified conditions exist. As Hempel and Oppenheim (1948: 140) admit, "frequently, the regularities invoked cannot be stated with the same generality and precision as in physics or chemistry." Hempel (1965) consequently retreated on to the I-S model, which is a probabilistic version of the D-N model:

(1) a set of general laws stating that if C_1, C_2, . . ., C_n occur, then the probability is p that E will occur,
(2) a set of existential statements confirming the occurrence of C_1, C_2, . . ., C_n,
(3) a conclusion stating that E will occur with a probability of p.

Instead of deterministic laws, Step 1 consists of statistical laws. On the one hand, the I-S model does not seem to differ much in effect from its D-N counterpart in terms of explanation because in both cases, E did occur. On the other hand, when prediction is called for, the I-S model can only suggest the probable occurrence of E when the premises are true whereas the D-N model deduces E's occurrence with certainty.

Since it is impossible to *deduce* E's occurrence, Hempel (1965) deems the I-S model to be an *inductive* argument that would render E's occurrence predictable with a high inductive probability. That is, the statistical laws and existential statements together lend more or less strong inductive support to E's occurrence. His main example of I-S explanation is concerned with the curing effect of penicillin. Suppose we ask the question "Why did Peter recover quickly from a streptococcus infection?" We are told that he was treated with penicillin and that most (but not all) strep infections clear up quickly when penicillin is administered (the statistical law in this case). To explain organizational actions, Susman and Evered (1978: 591) propose this corresponding form of I-S explanation: "(a') The likelihood that a consequence of type *C* will follow action of type *A*, is some value *L*, (b') Person *X* takes action *A*, thus (c') A consequence of type *C* will occur with a particular likelihood."

Hempel (1965) requires that the probability value of *p* in Step 3 be close to 1 if an event is said to be explained. This requirement implies that low probability events cannot be explained by the I-S model. Suppose the answer to the question "Why did John develop lung cancer?" is that he had been smoking one pack of cigarettes a day. Given the research finding that the proportion of one-pack-a-day smokers who develop lung cancer is less than one in ten over a period of thirty years (Doll et al. 1994), we cannot apply the I-S model to explain John's lung cancer on the basis of his smoking habit. There is another problem associated with the high probability value of *p*. Suppose we have an experiment with only two outcomes, A and B, where the probability of A is close to 1 and thus the probability of B is close to 0. If the experiment is repeated frequently, in the long run, we will get some B events in spite of their far lower probability. If we have all the information relevant to the occurrence of A and B events, it seems arbitrary, as well as somewhat odd, to say that we can explain the A events (based on the I-S model) but not the B events (Gandjour and Lauterbach 2003).

Symmetry between Explanation and Prediction

Hempel (1965) requires that acceptable answers to the question "Why did E occur?" must offer information that shows that E *is* to be expected. Conversely, an adequate scientific prediction potentially provides an adequate scientific explanation for the occurrence of E it predicts. Hence, there is a symmetry between explanation and prediction — every adequate explanation is a potential prediction and every prediction is a potential explanation. Here, I expound on this issue using Hempel's (1942: 38) own lucid description:

> Quite generally, prediction in empirical science consists in deriving a statement about a certain future event (for example, the relative position of the planets to the sun, at a future date) from (1) statements describing certain known (past or present) conditions (for example, the positions and momenta of the planets at a past or present moment), and (2) suitable general laws (for example, the laws of celestial mechanics). Thus, the logical structure of a scientific prediction is the same as that of a scientific explanation .... While in the case of an explanation, the final event is known to have happened, and its determining conditions have to be sought, the situation is reversed in the case of a prediction: here, the initial conditions are given, and their "effect" — which, in the typical case, has not yet taken place — is to be determined.

The above quote indicates two asymmetries on which the symmetry thesis is built: "a temporal asymmetry (i.e., an explanation is offered for an event which has occurred, while a prediction is offered for an event which has not occurred)" and "an epistemological asymmetry (i.e., an explanation is offered for an event that is known to have occurred, while a prediction is offered for an event that is not known to have occurred)" (Fetzer 1974: 176). Hence, predictions are just explanations provided at a different epistemic-temporal location (Douglas 2009). Suppose one wanted to explain the trajectory of a cannonball using the D-N model. The trajectory could be derived from Newtonian mechanics and the initial conditions of firing the cannonball. This derivation explained the trajectory. Alternatively, if one wanted to know the trajectory before firing, one could use exactly the same derivation to predict the trajectory. Both processes take the same logical form. Likewise, the higher closing price of a commodity, such as oil, on a certain trading day could be explained by increased demand relative to supply of the commodity; when the demand of the commodity was observed to be increasing relative to supply, one might predict that the closing price on that day would rise.

Salmon (2006) distinguishes between a narrow symmetry thesis, which applies only to D-N explanations, and a broad symmetry thesis, which applies to both D-N and I-S explanations. According to the narrow thesis, every nonstatistical prediction is a D-N explanation; according to the broad thesis, every prediction is an explanation of either the D-N or I-S mode. Since Hempel and Oppenheim (1948) developed the D-N model only, the narrow symmetry thesis was asserted there. Later, Hempel (1965) advocated for the broad thesis, with certain limitations. The distinction between the narrow and the broad symmetry theses is useful for avoiding confusion. For example, Scriven (1959) criticized Hempel and Oppenheim's (1948) symmetry assertion by citing evolutionary biology, which provides explanations of what has evolved but not predictions of what will evolve. Since evolutionary biology abides by statistical laws instead of deterministic laws, Scriven's critique applies only to the broad symmetry thesis, whereas Hempel and Oppenheim's (1948) symmetry thesis is the narrow version. The critique therefore misses the point.

The part of the narrow thesis that posits that every explanation is a prediction given the right conditions seems to be defensible because it "amounts only to the assertion that the conclusion is a D-N argument follows from its premises" (Salmon 2006: 49). More dubious is the other part of the thesis, whether narrow or broad, that states that every prediction is an explanation given the right conditions. Many different criticisms were raised against the symmetry thesis in the late 1950s and early 1960s (Douglas 2009). For instance, Scheffler (1957) launched a critique challenging the logical parallel between explanation and prediction. No explanation is false because, as mentioned above, the sentences constituting the explanans must be true and an explanandum which, being a logical consequence of the explanans, cannot be false either. In contrast, there is a possibility of predictive failure (i.e., false predictions) and thus not all predictive statements are explanatory. In other words, "explanation and prediction have different logical characteristics: explanations are true, predictions need not be" (Scheffler 1957: 298). Moreover, predictions are made with or without rational grounds and some rational grounds that are adequate for *prediction* may fail to *explain* the predicted occurrences. A problem of Scheffler's critique is that an explanation is regarded by Hempel as one form of argument and, as such, it is inappropriate to label an explanation as true or false. An argument is valid or invalid, not true or false (Copi and Cohen 1998). What Scheffler talks about seems to be the fact that in the case of explanation, the occurrence of E must be true (i.e., explaining why E occurred) whereas in the case of prediction, the prediction of E's occurrence may turn out to be false (i.e., E does not occur as predicted).

Counterexamples

Scriven's (1959) above-mentioned example of evolutionary biology attempts to reveal the flaws of the D-N model (although the example is actually related more to the I-S model). Salmon (2006) provides nine further examples that challenge various aspects of the D-N or I-S model. Here, I discuss briefly three of his more straightforward counterexamples – the barometer, the birth-control pill and the flagpole.

Suppose there is a law saying that whenever the barometric pressure drops sharply, a storm will occur. If a sharp drop in the reading of a properly functioning barometer is observed, one may infer that there will be a storm. Although the inference fits the D-N model, it makes little sense to say that the drop in the barometric reading explains the occurrence of the storm. Rather, it is the change in atmospheric pressure that causes both the drop in the barometric reading and the occurrence of the storm. In other words, the D-N model fails to distinguish between spurious and real associations.

The second counterexample is concerned with irrelevant explanatory factors. Suppose John faithfully consumed his wife's birth control pills in order to avoid becoming pregnant during the past year and he succeeded in achieving his objective. Again this case conforms to the D-N model, with the law being that any male who regularly take birth control pills will not become pregnant. Obviously whether John took any such pills is irrelevant with respect to explaining why he was not pregnant. Hence, the D-N model fails to "capture the intuitive relation of *explanatory relevance* that holds between that which explains and that which is explained" (Hitchcock 1995: 304).

The final, and most interesting, counterexample, called the flagpole problem, concerns the issue of explanatory asymmetry. It was created by Bromberger (1966), who used the Empire State Building and a telephone post, instead of a flagpole, to illustrate his arguments. A flagpole of a certain height stands vertically on flat ground. The sun is shining at a certain elevation and a shadow of a certain length is formed. Given the height of the flagpole and the elevation of the sun, along with the law of rectilinear propagation of light, one may deduce the length of the shadow. According to the D-N model, this deduction is an explanation of the shadow's length. By the same token, given the elevation of the sun and the length of the shadow, one may apply the same law to deduce the height of the flagpole. Although this deduction is also in line with the D-N model, few people would accept that the height of the flagpole is explained in this way. That is, the derivation of the length of the shadow from the height of the flagpole promotes understanding whereas the other derivation does not. The reason for this explanatory asymmetry is that given the sun's elevation, the flagpole causes the shadow and so explains the shadow's length, whereas the shadow does not cause the flagpole. In other words, the direction of explanation should be parallel to the direction of causation (Strevens 2004). One may think of other similar examples, such as the length of a simple pendulum being part of an explanation of its period, but not the other way round. Examples of explanatory asymmetries are found throughout the natural sciences (Jansson 2015). Hempel (1965) proposed that there is no real difference between two derivations and that our feeling of the difference is a misconception from which we should liberate ourselves. His point, which contradicts layman's common sense, has not been well received by his peers.

These counterexamples indicate the failure of both the D-N and I-S models to take into account causal dependencies. This failure is understandable, given that Hempel's account of explanation follows an empiricist tradition where causal judgments are epistemologically problematic. As discussed in Chapter 2, the Humean conception of causality regards the constant conjunction of events as an indicator of a causal relationship and such a conception seems to "drain the concept of causality of all its content" (McBreen 2007: 421). Hedström and Swedberg (1996: 287) provide a trenchant criticism of Hempel's approach:

> Since this form of explanation simply entails applying a general law to a specific situation, the insights offered by the exercise are directly proportional to the depth and robustness of the "probabilistic law." If this law is only a statistical association, which is the norm in the social and historical sciences according to Hempel, the specific explanation will offer no more insights than the law itself and will usually only suggest that a relationship is likely to exist, but it will give no clue whatsoever as to *why* this is likely to be the case. Covering-law explanations in the social sciences therefore normally are "black-box" explanations and they do not attempt to reveal any mechanisms that might have generated the observed relationships.

By bringing in laws as an essential element of the definition of explanation, the covering law model relies on a very narrow definition and this is the main reason why the model fails (Faye 1999). Moreover, the model fails to capture the concept of explanation because it does not involve the notion of a mechanism (Bunge 2004). Hence, one way to rectify this deficiency is to place mechanisms at the center of a theory of explanation, as discussed in the next section.

Mechanismic Explanation

Chapter 2 presented the nature of mechanisms and their role in causation. Following the terminology of Bunge (1997), any explanation that refers to a mechanism is said to be *mechanismic*. This section discusses mechanismic explanation, which is also called mechanism-based explanation (Hedström and Ylikoski 2010) or mechanistic explanation (Baetu 2015). Since a mechanism is a causal chain producing the effect of interest and "to explain an event is to provide some information about its causal history" (Lewis 1986: 217), there is a natural connection between mechanisms and explanation. It may be too strong to maintain that the specification of mechanisms is essential for causal inference (Steel 2008). Yet "a fully satisfactory social scientific explanation requires that the causal mechanisms be specified" (Hedström and Ylikoski 2010: 54). As discussed in Chapter 1, the primary objective of explanation is to promote understanding and understanding is precisely what mechanisms aim to provide.

In Chapter 2, mechanisms are defined as consisting of entities and activities organized so as to produce regular changes from a beginning state to an ending one. A mechanismic explanation describes the cogs and wheels of a causal process through which the outcome to be explained was brought about:

> The focus on mechanisms breaks up the original explanation-seeking why question into a series of smaller questions about the causal process: What are the participating entities, and what are their relevant properties? How are the interactions of these entities organized (both spatially and temporally)? What factors could prevent or modify the outcome? And so on. (Hedström and Ylikoski 2010: 51–52).

Needless to say, a mechanismic explanation describes a causal process selectively in the sense that it only captures the essential elements of the process, removing irrelevant details.

The natural sciences abound in examples of mechanismic explanation. Glennan (1996) provides two such examples: a float valve to regulate the water level in a toilet tank and a voltage switch. Mechanismic explanation is especially prominent in contemporary biology. Francis Crick, who shared the Nobel Prize for his discovery of the molecular structure of DNA, deemed that twentieth century biologists preferred to reason in terms of "mechanisms" and not "laws." The notion of "laws," such as Newton's laws of motion or Boyle's law, is generally reserved for physics, which can provide explanations based on laws with few exceptions. The case of biology is very different. "What is found in biology is *mechanisms*, mechanisms built with chemical components and that are often modified by other, later, mechanisms added to the earlier ones" (Crick 1989: 138). An explanation for a natural phenomenon may not be well received by the scientific community until the underlying mechanism is established. For example, humans have suffered from allergies for centuries. The idea of allergic disease emerged only in the first half of the twentieth century after Clemens von Pirquet, an Austrian pediatrician, proposed in 1906 a concept of allergy founded upon antigen-antibody reactions. Nowadays, it is generally accepted that "mechanisms of allergic reactions are based on antigen-antibody reactions in cells or in tissues, and also that antigen and antibody for allergy are not harmful to their host by themselves and would cause allergic symptoms only after they have combined with each other" (Sindo 1973: 150).

In social science research, the self-fulfilling prophecy in the context of the bank run discussed in Chapter 2 is an excellent example of mechanismic explanation. In describing how events unfold, it explains why depositors' belief about a bank's financial difficulties may result in the bank's insolvency or even bankruptcy, which in turn confirms their original belief. Another example is TCE explanations. The basic structure of TCE consists of four main parts: (1) the behavioral assumptions of bounded rationality, opportunism, risk neutrality and transaction cost minimization; (2) the principal transaction attributes of asset specificity, uncertainty and frequency; (3) a variety of transaction costs; and (4) the various modes of governance. A core behavioral assumption of TCE is that business executives make contracting decisions in a transaction-cost-economizing manner (Williamson 1985). This assumption constitutes the foundation of the theory's mechanismic explanations.

A typical TCE explanation is concerned with a firm's make-or-buy decision; that is, why a firm manufactures a component of its product inhouse rather than purchasing it from the market, or vice versa. As the asset specificity of manufacturing the component increases, redeployability of the asset for alternative uses decreases. This in turn will increase bilateral dependency and contracting hazards between the firm and its potential supplier of the component. Owing to bounded rationality, contracts are necessarily incomplete and offer limited protection against opportunistic behavior. The high-powered incentives of the market form of governance impede adaptability between the firm and its potential supplier, resulting in high transaction costs associated with having to monitor exchange behavior and guard against opportunism. Thus the market is ill equipped to deal with situations of high bilateral dependency. Transaction-cost-economizing considerations of the firm will push transactions with high asset specificity, such as purchasing the component from the market, into more integrated forms of governance, such as manufacturing the component inhouse (i.e., hierarchical governance). How this mechanism actually generates observable events depends on a number of contingent factors, the most prominent of which concerns the institutional environment in which the firm is located. Changes in the institutional environment will shift the comparative costs of different forms of governance (Williamson 1997).

Peering into the Black Box of Causality

A defining characteristic of a mechanism is the role it performs in an explanatory account. This role is highlighted by Bunge's (1997) distinction between black-box explanations and mechanismic explanations that explicitly refer to generative mechanisms. Suppose we have observed a systematic relationship between two types of events or variables, I (input) and O (outcome). For mechanismic explanations, the way in which these two sets of events or variables are linked to one another is expressed using a certain mechanism M as I-M-O. The mechanism M plays the role of explicating an observed relationship between specific initial conditions I and a specific outcome O. The search for mechanisms means that we are not satisfied with merely establishing systematic correlation between variables or a constant conjunction of events. Rather, we aim at an explanation that allows us to specify the cogs and wheels that have brought the relationship into existence. In short, a mechanismic explanation "seeks to provide a fine-grained and tight coupling between explanans and explanandum" (Hedström and Swedberg 1996: 298).

For the same pair of I and O, there can be different Ms. That is, it is a one-to-many relationship. A simple analogy is the way of solving an arithmetic problem such as 6×47. The solution, 282, can be obtained by manual calculation with or without the use of pencil and paper, by using an electronic calculator, or by using a math software program. A black-box approach is only interested in the arithmetic problem and its solution, not *how* the calculation was done. For the TCE explanation of the make-or-buy decision discussed above, there can be alternative explanations, such as the natural-selection approach of evolutionary theory, which "adopts the population of organizations as the level of analysis, the environment as the primary selection mechanism that utilizes some selection criteria (e.g., transaction cost economizing), the long run as the appropriate time frame, and ex post objective view of costs" (Chiles and McMackin 1996: 76). Firms engage in a random series of configurational changes, some of which are, by luck, transaction cost reducing, while others are not. Other things being equal, firms that happen to arrive at a low transaction cost configuration will outperform those that do not (Buckley and Chapman 1997). In a free, competitive economy, governance structures that are more efficient for economic exchange will replace less efficient ones, with the result that observed structures are generally consistent with the TCE logic regardless of whether the choice of such structures was based on transaction-cost-economizing decisions proposed by TCE (Robins 1987). Obviously, the natural selection approach entails mechanisms very different from those of TCE. For instance, it does not need the assumption that managers make contracting decisions in a transaction-cost-economizing manner. In other words, for the same firm and transaction characteristics and the same decision outcome, the underlying mechanism that links the two together can be provided by TCE or the natural-selection approach. This example shows the importance of peering into the black box of M if one is interested in knowing how a decision outcome was arrived at.

Mechanismic explanation regards mechanisms as intervening between I (the explanans) and O (the explanandum). The approach takes correlational analysis as a point of departure and develops an alternative to it by adding the causal link M (Mayntz 2004). In contrast, what characterizes a black-box explanation is that the link between input and output, or between explanans and explanandum, is assumed to be devoid of any structure of interest, perhaps because such a structure cannot be observed (Hedström and Swedberg 1996). As discussed in Chapter 2, Friedman (1953) holds an instrumentalist view that the assumptions of a theory do not have to be realistic. Such a view represents a black-box approach to explanation; that is, as long as a theory can produce accurate predictions from a set of initial conditions, researchers should not be concerned about the structure that links these conditions with the predictions.

B. F. Skinner's behaviorism, which ignores the cognitive factors mediating between stimulus and response, is another famous example of a black-box approach to management research. Yet in the late 1970s when research methods had been improved, behaviorism was criticized: "Behaviorism, for its part, must accommodate itself to accepting the importance of what goes on inside the 'black box,' especially since we now have methods for investigating its contents" (Shevrin and Dickman 1980: 432). In responding to the challenge, Skinner (1985) described briefly these methods, namely introspection, brain science, simulation and linguistics. However, his vehement response failed to prevent the demise of behaviorism and the rise of cognitive psychology; the 1990s were designated by psychologists "the decade of the brain." Cognitive psychology deals with many of the classic topics of sensation, emotion, perception, decision making, learning and memory. The influence of cognitive points of view spread to the field of organizational behavior (Ilgen et al. 1994). For example, a key difference between Skinner's operant learning theory and Albert Bandura's social learning theory concerns the mediating effects of covert cognitive processes, which affect virtually all aspects of social learning (Davis and Luthans 1980). These cognitive processes constitute the mechanism through which social learning takes place. As Bandura (1977: 160) points out:

> If human behavior could be fully explained in terms of antecedent inducements and response consequences, there would be no need to postulate any additional regulatory mechanisms. However, most external influences affect behavior through intermediary cognitive processes. Cognitive factors partly determine which external events will be observed, how they will be perceived, whether they leave any lasting effects, what valence and efficacy they have, and how the information they convey will be organized for future use.

In contrast, Skinner (1953) adopts a positivist position and dismisses cognitive processes as being mostly metaphysical and having no rightful place in the scientific study of behavior.

Every mechanism has a structure that relates the entities and activities concerned together (Hedström and Ylikoski 2010). When a mechanistic explanation opens the black box of causality, it reveals this structure, making visible how the entities, activities and their relations produce the effect of interest. For instance, the above-discussed TCE and natural selection approaches to explaining a firm's make-or-buy decision involve mechanisms of different structures with different entities and activities.

Comparison with the Covering Law Model

The development of the mechanistic explanation has been motivated partly by the shortcomings of the once-hegemonic covering law account of explanation (Hedström and Ylikoski 2010). This section briefly compares these two important theories of explanation. The preceding section discusses three counterexamples – the barometer, the birth control pill and the flagpole – that challenge different aspects of the covering law model. It is imperative to see how mechanistic explanation addresses the problems highlighted by these counterexamples. Table 3.1 summarizes the comparison.

Table 3.1. *Comparison between the covering law model
and mechanismic explanation*

	Covering law model	Mechanismic explanation
Laws	Must include laws	May not include laws
Symmetry between explanation and prediction	Entails symmetry	Doesn't entail symmetry
Causality	Black box approach	Peering into the black box
Distinction between spurious and real associations	Unable to distinguish between spurious and real associations	Able to distinguish between spurious and real associations
Explanatory relevance	Unable to exclude explanatory irrelevant factors	Able to exclude explanatory irrelevant factors
Asymmetry of explanatory relations	Unable to make sense of the asymmetry	Able to make sense of the asymmetry

To start with, by definition, the covering law model includes at least one law statement, such as the law of supply and demand in the case of social science research, as well as a set of initial conditions, from which the explanandum phenomenon is deduced as a conclusion. In contrast, mechanismic explanation relies mostly on generalizations about the properties, activities and relations of underlying entities, but these generalizations do not have to satisfy the traditional criteria for laws (Hedström and Ylikoski 2010). They "are robust and non-accidental, but hold in virtue of the fact that they describe the behavior of the mechanism" (Glennan 2010: 257). For example, the self-fulfilling prophecy in the context of a bank run uses some generalizations, one of which is that people tend to protect their wealth. Therefore, when depositors of a bank believe that the bank is in financial trouble, they will withdraw their money in order to protect their wealth. That said, mechanismic explanations, especially in the natural sciences, may invoke law statements.

The logical structure of a prediction is the same as that of an explanation in the covering law model (Hempel 1942), resulting in a symmetry between explanation and prediction. Using the example of the course of an illness, Harré (1988) illustrates lucidly the main difference between explanation and prediction in terms of the information needed. Based on the symptoms reported by a patient with a known illness, such as flu, an experienced physician would be expected to be able to say what symptoms will occur as the disease progresses. That is, it is often possible for the physician to predict the course of the illness from its initial symptoms. However, to explain the succession of symptoms is a rather different matter:

> For prediction we need to know only facts of the same kind as those we wish to predict, in this case, observable symptoms. But to explain we need to know the causal mechanism that produces the symptoms. In general the entities that make up the causal mechanism are of a different kind from those we can ordinarily observe, and are known in some other way than that by which we know the kinds of things we can observe as regular antecedents of the disease states. (Harré 1988: 139)

Harré's illustration suggests that mechanismic explanation does not entail symmetry between explanation and prediction. As discussed in Chapter 2, a causal mechanism commits to the locality of causal processes in that whether X is a cause of Y relies on facts about the spatiotemporally restricted causal process in question (Hedström and Ylikoski 2010). The mechanism of self-fulfilling prophecy may explain satisfactorily a bank run that has occurred in a specific location and at a specific time. Yet the same mechanism is not in a position to predict whether a bank run will occur when long queues of customers trying to withdraw their deposits are seen outside the branches of a bank. Mechanismic explanation "emphasizes the difference between diagnostic and explanatory reasoning, and although explanatory understanding is constituted by an ability to make correct what-if inferences, this does not imply that it always provides a basis for empirical predictions" (Hedström and Ylikoski 2010: 55).

A satisfactory covering law explanation has to specify the law and the conditions that make the law applicable in the specific case concerned. The explanation offers no more insights than the law itself, whether it is a deterministic law in the case of the D-N model or a probabilistic law in the case of the I-S model. A law usually only suggests that a relationship exists but gives little clue as to why this is the case. As such, covering law explanations are "black-box" explanations and do not reveal any mechanisms that generate the observed relationships (Hedström and Swedberg 1996). It is more appropriate to say that the covering law model *justifies* certain expectations and predictions than to say that it *explains* what happens (von Wright 1971). By contrast, the discussion above describes how mechanismic explanation attempts to peer into the black box of causality. As shown below, mechanismic explanation is able to address the shortcomings of the covering law model that were revealed by the three counterexamples exactly because it takes causality seriously.

According to the covering law model, the drop in the barometric reading is a legitimate explanation of the occurrence of the storm whereas both are in fact caused by the change in atmospheric pressure. In other words, the model is unable to distinguish between spurious and real associations. Mechanismic explanation deals squarely with this problem. There is a mechanism connecting the change in atmospheric pressure with the drop in the barometric reading and another mechanism connecting it with the occurrence of the storm. However, there is no mechanism that links directly the drop in the barometric reading with the occurrence of the storm and thus there is no explanatory relationship between the two. In social science research, mechanismic explanation "is not built upon mere associations between variables, but always refers directly to causes and consequences of individual action oriented to the behavior of others" (Hedström and Swedberg 1996: 299).

Similarly, mechanismic explanation addresses the issue of explanatory relevance illustrated by the birth control pill counterexample. John's action of taking birth control pills cannot explain his not becoming pregnant because there is no mechanism that links the two events together. In fact, the mechanism that makes these pills effective in preventing women from becoming pregnant is not operative in men. As mentioned above, a mechanismic explanation describes a causal process selectively so that it only captures the essential elements of the process. Generally speaking, a mechanismic explanation excludes factors that are known to be irrelevant when a mechanism is conjectured. A caveat is that if a proposed mechanism is flawed, some of the entities and activities it entails may be irrelevant to the phenomenon in question.

The flagpole problem shows that the covering law model fails to make sense of the asymmetry of explanatory relations. Although effects do not explain their causes, the covering law model does not rule this out. According to the model, once the elevation of the sun is given, the height of the flagpole explains the length of its shadow and vice versa. Mechanismic explanation avoids this problem. There is a causal mechanism that accounts for the length of the flagpole's shadow given the elevation of the sun and the height of the flagpole. Since the flagpole's height is by no means caused by its shadow, there isn't any corresponding causal mechanism associated with the shadow that can account for the height. Simply put, the direction of causation determines the direction of the explanation (Salmon 1998).

Intentional Explanation

Intentional action is behavior rightly given an intentional explanation and reference to the agent's mental state plays a vital role in intentional explanation (Bishop 1983). Explanations of human behavior, whether individual or collective, make reference to a special kind of causation – intentional causation – defined as a "form of causation by which mental states are causally related to the very states of affairs that they represent" (Searle 1991 335). Recall that Chapter 2 discussed agent causation, the core idea of which is that an intentional action involves an irreducible causal relationship whose subject is the agent carrying out the action, not an event or sequence of events (Bishop 1983). Intentional causation is consistent with agent causation, as shown by Searle's (1991: 335) illustrative example: "a man whose thirst causes him to drink is engaging in behavior that can only be explained by intentional causation because his desire to drink causes the very behavior that is represented in the content of the desire, namely, his drinking." This example fits the meaning of agent causation in that the man is the agent and the intentional action is to drink water and the agent carries out the action with the belief that the action will quench his thirst. In an intentional explanation, which is also called intentionalistic explanation by Searle (1991), the explanans refer to the beliefs and desires of the agent and the explanandum is the agent's action.

Reason and Intention

An action is different from an accidental aggregate of movements, such as falling down on a slippery road, in that there should be a clear intention. Similarly, intentional action refers to behavior that is controlled by conscious decisions and choices, not behavior driven by nonconscious reasons. In the above example of drinking water, if the man nonconsciously picks up his cup and drinks water while talking to his friend, he does not have the intention to drink (although he does drink). Explaining this and the above example of falling down on a slippery road falls outside the domain of intentional explanation. Management research often studies collective intention in the sense that the intention is attributed to an organization. Consider the example discussed in Chapter 1 of Samsung's plan to shift much of its display production from China to Southern Vietnam in 2020.

The plan reflected the collective intention of Samsung, or at least the collective intention of those Samsung managers who made the decision.

As discussed in Chapter 2, reasons are causes, an argument proposed in Davidson's (1963) influential article "Actions, Reasons, and Causes." The article appeared at a time when there was substantial consensus that an agent's reasons for acting could not be causes of the agent's actions performed for those very reasons. It was widely believed that the article marked a turning point in analytic theory of action by offering a knock-down argument against the consensus (Wilson 1985). Putting Davidson's idea in a nutshell, an intentional action is one that is done for a reason and the reason for which an individual performs the action is the cause of the action. In other words, explaining an action by stating the intention with which it was done is a kind of causal explanation. Davidson (1963: 689) aptly describes the relationship between intention and reason:

> To know a primary reason why someone acted as he did is to know an intention with which the action was done. If I turn left at the fork because I want to get to Katmandu, my intention in turning left is to get to Katmandu.

A key problem of Davidson's argument is causal deviance: an agent has a reason R for doing X, R causes the agent to do X and yet it is not the case that she does X for reason R (or for any reason) precisely because she does X *unintentionally* (McGuire 2007). Davidson (1980: 79) himself provides a well-known illustrative example:

> a climber might want to rid himself of the weight and danger of holding another man on a rope, and he might know that by loosening his hold on the rope he could rid himself of the weight and danger. This belief and want might so unnerve him as to cause him to loosen his hold, and yet it might be the case that he never *chose* to loosen his hold, nor did he do it intentionally.

While the causal deviance problem, which is concerned with empirically rare situations that have little practical significance, may be a worthwhile topic for philosophers to chew on, it is more pedantic than impactful on empirical research. Davidson's core argument remains unscathed (Wilson 1985). In fact, regarding reasons as causes is in line with our commonsense view that individuals can reason, act for reasons, pursue intentions and implement plans. Searle (2007: 57) illuminates the role played by reasons in explanation:

> We have the first-person conscious experience of acting on reasons. We state these reasons for action in the form of explanations. The explanations are obviously quite adequate because we know in our own case that, in their

ideal form, nothing further is required. But they cannot be adequate if they are treated as ordinary causal explanations because they do not pass the causal sufficiency test . . . they are not of the form A caused B. They are of the form, a rational self S performed act A, and in performing A, S acted on reason R . . . I am claiming that the condition of possibility of the adequacy of rational explanations is the existence of an irreducible self, a rational agent capable of acting on reasons.

Davidson (1980: 11) poses a powerful challenge to his opponents: "If, as Melden claims, causal explanations are 'wholly irrelevant to the understanding we seek' of human action, then we are without an analysis of the 'because' in 'He did it because . . .' where we go on to name a reason." According to Davidson, it is necessary to have an analysis of the "because" in explanations that provide reasons and there is no way to conduct that analysis unless we suppose that the concept of causality plays some role in the analysis (McGuire 2007). An effective approach is to regard reasons as causes.

Hermeneutics

Searle (1991: 337) highlights a key feature of intentional explanation: "The propositional content given by the theorists in the explanation of the behavior must be identical with the propositional content in the actual mind of the agent or agents whose behavior is being explained; otherwise, the behavior is not properly explained." This apparently complicated statement can be illustrated by the example of drinking water. Suppose Tom drank water and Mary explained his behavior as him being thirsty. The propositional content of Mary's explanation is that Tom was thirsty, which caused him to drink water. Tom's behavior is properly explained only if the propositional content was indeed in Tom's mind; that is, Tom was in fact thirsty and so he drank water. If Tom drank because he wanted to take in some water before jogging so that he wouldn't feel thirsty during that exercise, the propositional content of Mary's explanation is different from the propositional content in Tom's mind and thus her explanation is false. Yet a third party has to interpret the propositional contents of both Tom and Mary in order to determine whether Mary's explanation is false.

Relatedly, criminal intent is an important concept in law. In the fraud trial of Elizabeth Holmes, the former CEO and founder of Theranos, mentioned in Chapter 1, the outcome of the trial would hinge on prosecutors' ability to prove beyond a reasonable doubt that Holmes acted with an "intent to deceive" (Oremus 2021). That is, when Holmes presented her venture to investors and customers (e.g., Safeway and Walgreens), did she intend to provide false statements? One explanation of her action is that she genuinely believed the content of these statements; the other explanation is that she knew the falsity of the statements and deliberately misled investors and customers. Holmes' fate depends on which explanation the jury accepts. While the jury will interpret her actions based on the evidence presented in court, she is the person who knows best which explanation is true, presuming that she is aware of her own intentions. This issue of interpreting one's action is concerned with hermeneutics, a leading genre of interpretive research.

The *Oxford English Dictionary* (1989) defines hermeneutics as "the art or science of interpretation, especially of Scripture," but over the past several centuries, hermeneutics has expanded beyond the theological domain. Friedrich Schleiermacher, a New Testament professor, created modern hermeneutics in the early nineteenth century by viewing it as a general theory of textual interpretation and understanding. The scope of contemporary hermeneutics is no longer confined to merely interpreting texts such as written documents and scripts. About half a century ago, Ricoeur (1971: 529) proposed the following insightful hypothesis:

> if there are specific problems which are raised by the interpretation of texts because they are texts and not spoken language, and if these problems are the ones which constitute hermeneutics as such, then the human sciences may be said to be hermeneutical (1) inasmuch as their *object* displays some of the features constitutive of a text as text, and (2) inasmuch as their *methodology* develops the same kind of procedures as those of *Auslegung* or text-interpretation.

Ricoeur attempted to establish an analogical link between interpreting text and interpreting human action and argued that action in general could be regarded as "text." Subsequent hermeneutic scholars have expanded substantially the meaning of *text* to include organizational and social practices, social structures, cultural artifacts and so on. These objects are texts in a metaphorical sense in that they may be "read," interpreted and understood in a manner similar to our reading, interpretation and understanding of written texts (Francis 1994). Hermeneutics treats social phenomena as a text to be interpreted through analyzing and reconstructing the significance of various elements of the action or event. Individual actions or beliefs can only be understood through an act of interpretation by which the researcher attempts to understand the meaning of those actions or beliefs (Little 1991). The emphasis is on interpretation and understanding.

Since the term "hermeneutics" does not have a clear and definitive meaning, management researchers have used the term in two broad senses, representing the two poles of a continuum. The weak sense refers to "research that may adopt (or that may be influenced by) any of a number of perspectives and approaches to inquiry, including interpretivism, qualitative or ideographic inquiry, existentialism, phenomenology, postmodernism, and so on" (Prasad 2002: 13). In this sense, hermeneutics is somewhat synonymous with "qualitative research." As such, the meaning of hermeneutics is not reflected properly in the usage. The strong sense is relatively more precise, referring to "research that engages in interpreting texts (and other organizational artifacts and activities)" (Prasad 2002: 13). This latter usage is the one that management researchers should adopt.

There are two fundamental elements of the hermeneutic process. First, an interpretation is dependent on the researcher's background, including earlier experiences, religion, education and familiarity with the object to be interpreted. These background factors together constitute what Gadamer (1975) calls "prejudice" (in a relatively neutral sense of the term), which may facilitate or hinder understanding of the text. For Holmes's trial, a juror's background will likely affect the interpretation of Holmes's action. If, say, a juror has the experience of creating a tech venture, she may know that technopreneurs tend to exaggerate the merits of their products in a way that could be seen as misleading and thus may be more charitable when judging whether Holmes had an intent to deceive than a juror who was previously fired by a new venture or who lost money investing in a failed venture. This is the reason why jury selection is a crucial element of the legal process. Hermeneutic researchers have to remind themselves of their own prejudice and take that into consideration when conducting their analysis.

The second element is concerned with the hermeneutic circle – there is a constant interplay between understanding the whole and understanding its parts. Prasad (2002: 18) illustrates the concept using an example of interpreting a written text:

> Consider, for instance, the task of understanding a paragraph in any piece of writing. The paragraph in question must, of course, be understood by means of understanding the individual sentences that make up that paragraph. On the other hand, it is often the case that the meaning of individual sentences in a paragraph becomes clear only when we already have an understanding of what the paragraph as a whole is trying to convey, or what the paragraph is "driving at," or what is the "direction" of the entire paragraph.

Since neither the paragraph nor any individual sentence can be understood without reference to one another, the process is like a circle. Alternatively, the idea of the hermeneutic circle may be seen as emphasizing the importance of understanding the context for the purpose of interpreting a text (Prasad 2002). Applying this view to Holmes's trial, her action has to be interpreted in the context of, say, Silicon Valley's hype-driven culture, in which technopreneurs often have incentives to tout products that are still in the development stage (Oremus 2021).

The hermeneutic perspective maintains that social science is fundamentally different from natural science because it depends on the interpretation of human behavior and social practices that have embedded meanings. Meanings developed by agents enter into the constitution of "social facts" whereas the object of natural science studies is not constituted as meaningful (Harbers and de Vries 1993). Natural science is concerned with describing and explaining objective causal processes and the researcher's relationship to the object of study involves a "simple hermeneutic" (Giddens 1976). In other words, the understanding of natural phenomena is a one-sided endeavor on the part of the researcher. By contrast, the study of objects in social science often involves a "double hermeneutic" – researchers have to interpret their subjects' interpretations because the latter's understanding and sensemaking are an integral part of the object of study (Danermark et al. 2002). The intersection of two frames of meaning is a logically necessary part of social science; the meaningful social world is constituted by lay actors and the theories invented by social scientists (Giddens 1984). Thus, the double hermeneutic is a distinctive characteristic of social science. Legal or management scholars who study Holmes's trial may want to understand how jurors arrived at their decision. In this case, they have a double-hermeneutic task of interpreting these jurors' interpretations of the evidence presented to them. Suppose a researcher manages to interview all the jurors after the trial is over. These jurors will reflect on how they digested the evidence, discussed it with fellow jurors and tried to reach a unanimous verdict. The researcher has to interpret not only each juror's interpretations but also all the jurors' collective interpretations that led to the verdict.

Teleological or Functional Explanation

Related closely to intentional explanation is teleological explanation. Starting from a young age, humans show a strong inclination to interpret observed behaviors of others as goal-directed actions (Csibra and Gergely

2007). Returning to Searle's (1991) example of a man drinking water, "to quench his thirst" can be an explanation of his action. In this case, the explanation is framed in terms of an attempt to achieve a goal or to attain an end. It is not the future state of quenching his thirst that explains his action; rather, it is his desire for quenching his thirst with the concurrent belief that drinking water will achieve that goal. In other words, his goal of quenching thirst causes his action. This teleological explanation would be correct even if he still felt thirsty after drinking the water. Another example is the question: "Why does the heart beat?" One plausible teleological explanation is: "To circulate the blood through the body." Again, the explanation here is framed in terms of what end the beating of the heart will lead to.

Some scholars use the terms "teleological explanation" and "functional explanation" somewhat interchangeably. For instance, Nagel (1979) lists "functional or teleological explanations" as one of his four types of explanation. Similarly, in Salmon's (2006) *Four Decades of Scientific Explanation*, there is a section titled "Teleology and Functional Explanation," in which he discusses the first decade (1948–1957) of scientific explanation. Both terms refer to what have been called "goal-directed activities," that is, activities being the means through which a goal is attained. A complication here is that there are two kinds of goals: those that are pursued consciously and those that are not. The example of drinking water and, in fact, all goals set by individuals and organizations, belong to the first kind. As to the second, the above example of the heart beating shows that the goal of circulating the blood through the body is not consciously pursued by the heart.

The Forward-looking Problem

A basic philosophical problem is that in both of the above examples, the explanation is forward-looking:

> Teleological explanations explain the means by the ends; a development or trait is explained by reference to goals, purposes or functions, and so the explanans refers to something that is an effect of the explanandum, something that is forward in time relative to the thing explained. Of course this is quite unlike ordinary causal explanations in which the explanans refer to prior causes of the explananda. Indeed, because teleological explanations seem to refer to effects, rather than prior causes, it looks at first sight as though backward causation is invoked. (Neander 1991: 455–456)

For simplicity of discussion, I call this problem the "forward-looking problem." Phrased another way, the problem is about whether the explanandum can be legitimately "explained as being causally related either to a particular goal in the future or to a biological end which is as much future as present or past" (Braithwaite 1946: ii).

In relation to the forward-looking problem, it is useful to distinguish between teleological and functional explanations. A teleological explanation involves a conscious intent to achieve a goal and thus is only applicable to human actions (Gruner 1966). Braithwaite (1946) argues that teleological explanations of intentional, goal-directed activities are always reducible to causal explanations with intentions as causes, with the goal-directed behavior being explained as goal-intended behavior. For the example of drinking water, the man's goal of quenching his thirst can be restated as his intention to quench his thirst. Using Aristotelian terms, the idea of the final cause is converted into that of the efficient cause. In brief, teleological explanations in this narrow sense are effectively the same as intentional explanations. Hence, teleological explanations do not have the forward-looking problem because an agent's action is explained by her concomitant intention, not by an expected future state (Neander 1991). Since intentional explanations have been covered in the preceding section, the following discussion focuses on functional explanations.

A functional explanation is defined "in terms of the contribution made by something, a thing or a process, to the future maintenance of a system of which it is a part, or to the future maintenance of the present state of such a system" (Gruner 1966: 517). This definition restricts the meaning of the word "function" to "function within a system" because this is the meaning that researchers usually adopt when speaking of a functional explanation. Following Gruner (1966), I place no restriction on the type of system and a function can occur in a biological, mechanical, social, organizational or any other system. The above example of a man drinking water falls within the domain of teleological explanation instead of functional explanation because there is no reference to any system. The man's action of drinking water is explained by his purpose of quenching thirst. His action can hardly be explained by claiming that the action serves a function within a system. In contrast, the explanation of a heart beating is functional because it is about the heart's biological function in the body, which is the system concerned.

Functional explanations belong to the group of backwards explanations, which are concerned with explaining an event that occurs at a certain time by another event that occurs at a later time (Jenkins and Nolan 2008). In other words, backwards explanations are related directly to the forward-looking problem. Backwards explanations are ubiquitous in our daily lives and include non-functional explanations. For example, Susan is upset because her mother, who is in the last stage of cancer, will die sometime next month, according to the doctor. This example, which is modeled on Jenkins and Nolan's (2008), is related to neither teleological nor functional explanation. Consider an example used by Jenkins and Nolan of a volcano that is smoking because it will erupt soon. This is not a functional explanation because the smoking is a symptom that the volcano is going to erupt; it does not serve any function that contributes to the eruption. Genuine functional explanations may have the forward-looking problem because they purport to explain something in terms of its beneficial consequences.

Some functional explanations, such as those concerned with a biological system, can escape the forward-looking problem. According to the theory of evolution, the biological system of an organism has a certain function when the function has a property that has contributed to the fitness of the organism's ancestors over a long period of competition and natural selection. The function is to do what it did during the organism's evolutionary history in order to contribute to that fitness. For example, the human heart circulates blood so that oxygen is brought to and carbon dioxide is carried away from the tissues. This function contributes to the survival of the human body. Since a biological function is itself a matter of how things developed in the evolutionary history of an organism, the related functional explanation is not forward-looking (Jenkins and Nolan 2008). In fact, functional explanation is critical to modern biology for two reasons. First, a large proportion of biological categories are defined functionally. Second, functional explanation plays a central role in "functional analysis," which is aimed at studying how an organism functions normally or, in the case of medicine, what happens when an organism functions abnormally (Neander 1991). However, interpreting functional explanation in terms of the covering law model, Hempel (1965) concludes that functional explanation is not a legitimate alternative form of scientific explanation at all because it is possible that several different entities could have brought about the beneficial consequence in question.

Functional Explanation in Social Science

In contrast with modern biology, in social science, functional explanations "are often objects of suspicion" (Steel 2005: 941). Yet their attraction stems from "the implicit assumption that all social and psychological phenomena must have a *meaning*, i.e. that there must be *some* sense, *some* perspective in which they are beneficial for someone or something; and that furthermore these beneficial effects are what explain the phenomena in question" (Elster 1994: 403). Merton (1957) was among the first to introduce functional analysis to social research. Put simply, in social research, "functional analysis examines social phenomena in terms of their consequences for the broader society" (Turner and Maryanski 1979: xi). After defining functions as "those observed consequences which make for the adaptation or adjustment of a given system," Merton defines manifest functions as "those objective consequences contributing to the adjustment or adaptation of the system which are intended and recognized by participants in the system" and latent functions as "those which are neither intended nor recognized" (51). In other words, the difference between manifest and latent functions is whether the adjustment or adaptation is intended and recognized by participants. The concept of latent function sensitizes sociologists to a range of significant social variables that would otherwise be easily overlooked. Merton maintains that it is in the pursuit of latent functions that the distinctive intellectual contributions of the sociologist lie.

The distinction between manifest and latent functions in empirical research can be illustrated by Merton's (1957) example of introducing a new system of wage payment in an organization. The sociologist is interested to know whether the new wage plan achieves its intended purpose of reducing labor turnover or increasing output. Armed with the concept of latent function, however, the sociologist may wish to extend his inquiry in those directions that are most promising for the theory development of the discipline. For example, he could consider the consequences of the new wage plan for the trade union in which the workers are organized. Merton seems to be arguing that the sociologist's interest should be extended beyond labor turnover or output levels to include such consequences of the new wage plan as certain changes in the organization of the trade union concerned. While the plan was designed to reduce labor turnover or increase output, its impact on the trade union is incidental. In this case, the former is the manifest consequence of the wage plan, and the latter its latent consequence. Here, the concept of manifest function is used mainly as a kind of stooge set-up such that the subsequent unveiling of the latent function can appear as a significant insight, resulting in the impression that sociology is an especially penetrating form of inquiry (Campbell 1982). In his trenchant critique, Helm (1971) shows that the terms "intended" and "recognized" used in Merton's definitions of manifest and latent functions are vague, resulting in ambiguity of the distinction between the two functions. As such, Merton's methodological guide of focusing on latent functions "can amount only to the vaguest maxim to sociologists to do their investigating with care" (Helm 1971: 60).

Elster (1994) agrees with Merton that when researchers develop functional explanations, their aim is to explain latent functions. However, he rejects functional explanations on the grounds that they rely on a dubious analogy between the biological and social worlds. As mentioned already, functional explanations in biology appeal to the mechanism of natural selection. On the other hand, "in societies there is no general mechanism — corresponding to natural selection — that could permit us to infer that the latent functions of a structure typically maintain the structure by feedback" (Elster 1984: 2). There are crucial differences in the details of animal and human adaptation. For instance, humans can let pass immediate opportunities that are perceived to be local maxima on the expectation that if they wait, some better opportunity will probably come along. They also do not mind incurring a loss in the short term in anticipation of a bigger gain in the future. Hence, humans are capable of surveying many alternatives in order to achieve global maximization. In contrast, natural selection operates through immediate advantages enjoyed by a species without consciously considering future possibilities. As a result, "what is maximized in natural selection is differential fitness not absolute fitness" (Elster 1984: 26). Natural selection thus leads to local maximization. Owing to this critical difference, the analogy between the biological and social worlds breaks down and "functional explanations are in principle unsuited to explaining social phenomena" (Wray 2002: 73).

Similar to Elster (1984), Little (1998) argues that in biology, natural selection provides the mechanism through which organisms adapt functionally to their environment but there is no comparable mechanism to which researchers may refer in justifying functional explanations in social science. Unlike Elster, however, Little does not take this as grounds for rejecting functional explanations in social research. Instead, he recommends developing an account of functional explanation that relies on mechanisms other than that of social selection:

> it is almost always possible to come up with some beneficial consequences of a given institution; so in order to justify the judgment that the institution exists because of its beneficial consequences we need to have an account of the mechanisms which created and reproduced the institution which shows how the needs of the system as a whole influenced the development of the institution. (Little 1998: 6)

Little considers that there are two mechanisms that can play this role. Both are based on intentional choices of individuals. The first is that "the benefits produced by a social feature are anticipated and pursued by the persons whose behavior gives rise to the feature" (Little 1991: 100). For example, a diversity practice is implemented in the R&D unit of a company because the unit head recognizes the generally positive relationship between innovation and employee diversity in terms of gender, age, ethnicity and education (Østergaard et al. 2011). However, it may be that the CEO, instead of the unit head, recognizes the relationship and the CEO instructs the unit head to implement the practice. Therefore, another mechanism underlying functional explanation is that "the practice may be encouraged by other powerful individuals who *do* understand the causal relationship between the practice and the benefit and who intend to produce the benefit" (Little 1991: 100).

Kincaid (1990) proposes a different solution based on a causal interpretation. To claim that a social practice A exists in order to do B or that the function of A is to do B, researchers have to satisfy two conditions: (1) A causes B; and (2) A persists because it causes B. While the first condition is a simple causal statement, the rationale of the second condition is as follows:

> A given social practice has a certain effect. When it has that effect, there is some causal mechanism that insures A continues to exist. When the practice stops having that effect, that mechanism stops operating. The second condition is thus an ordinary causal claim. (Kincaid 1990: 345)

As labor costs in China rose in recent years, some foreign companies moved their labor-intensive production processes from China to countries like Bangladesh, Vietnam and Indonesia. Kincaid's schema is able to provide a functional explanation of this phenomenon. For the first condition, relocating labor-intensive production from China to countries with lower labor costs causes a reduction in overall production costs. A complication here is that the anticipated cost-reduction function of relocating production causes the relocation practice to be adopted in the first place. This tricky point is illustrated aptly by Dore's (1961: 844) example of the balance spring of a mechanical watch:

> A small boy's examination of the interior of a watch may lead him to conclude that the function of the balance spring is to control the movement of the balance wheel. He would have little difficulty in using his functional insight to arrive at a causal explanation of the spring's presence – it is there because the man who made the watch realized a need for something to control the movement of the wheel, and the process of ratiocination which ensued led him to put in the spring.

Thus there is a mutual causal process: the anticipated cost-reduction function causes the relocation's existence and then the relocation causes cost reduction. As to Kincaid's second condition, the relocation persists because it causes cost reduction. An implication is that if, for whatever reason, the cost of labor in China becomes cheaper such that the labor cost differential between China and these countries is insignificant, the relocation will not persist because it has lost its cost-reduction function. Note that here it is about the *persistence* of the relocation whereas the first condition is about the relocation's *origin*.

In the field of management research, one of the most famous examples of functional explanation is organizational ecology, which borrows heavily from evolutionary biology and ecology (Hannan and Freeman 1989). Kincaid (1990) considers organizational ecology an empirically successful case of functional explanation. Treating an organization as if it were an organism, organizational ecology attempts to explain certain features of a particular type of organization – such as hotels, restaurants, churches, labor unions and newspapers – on the basis of differential mortality and founding rates. Organizations compete for resources, including financing, employees, raw materials and customers. Resources, however, are limited. As a result, some organizations survive and some fail. The availability of resources also affects founding rates because entrepreneurs are more likely to establish organizations when the needed resources are readily available.

According to Kincaid's schema, certain features of organizations are justified by their positive effects on survival. These features manage to persist because of the positive effects. Studies of organizational ecology identify selective mechanisms that underlie that connection. Therefore, when organizational ecology explains why organizations have certain properties, it actually provides a functional explanation. For example, Abbott et al. (2016) analyze the proliferation of private transnational regulatory organizations (PTROs) compared with the relative stasis of intergovernmental organizations (IGOs) like the World Trade Organization. Rare before 1990, PTROs refer to organizations established and governed by actors from sectors such as civil society and business. They adopt business standards of conduct on regulatory issues ranging from worker rights to climate change and promote, monitor and enforce these standards. According to Abbott et al. (2016), IGOs have limited organizational flexibility because of strong oversight and multiple veto points by member states and their growth is constrained by crowding in their dense institutional environment. By contrast, PTROs' mandates are more fluid and states generally exercise less formalized oversight of their activities. Hence,

PTROs benefit from organizational flexibility and low entry costs, which in turn allow them to enter niche areas with only limited resource competition, resulting in their high relative growth compared to IGOs.

Kincaid's optimism about functional explanation in general and organizational ecology in particular is not without challenges. The key challenge concerns the use of biological models of evolution. First of all, the typical analogy between organisms and organizations that is cited for supporting the use of biological models is naïve:

> There is some risk in adopting the biological metaphor, but there is reason to believe organizations have much in common with biological organisms. Both organizations and organisms are animate. Organizations and many advanced organisms are choiceful... Both are seen to adapt responsively to their environmental habitat, and both can bring about changes in their environments. (McKelvey 1978: 1429)

In spite of the caveat at the beginning of the above quote, McKelvey does not seem to recognize the risk. While organisms and organizations do share several so-called common characteristics, there are *numerous* differences between the two. As Reydon and Scholz (2009: 409–410) well point out: "But merely drawing analogies between different sorts of phenomena or between different kinds of entities is insufficient legitimization for applying a successful theory or model from one domain of investigation to the phenomena under study in another domain." Sometimes an analogy is drawn between life and the marathon. This does not imply that skills enabling one to win a marathon will be useful in planning one's life.

Echoing the above critique made by Elster (1984) and Little (1998) about applying the concept of natural selection to organizations, Reydon and Scholz argue that there is no concrete entity undergoing evolutionary processes in the case of organizational ecology. In addition to the huge differences between organisms and organizations, evolutionary processes in biology require populations to have at least minimal levels of closure and isolation from other populations, a requirement that is obviously not met in the case of populations of organizations. Since organizations are not real entities that can function in evolutionary processes, biological models of evolution are inapplicable to organizational populations. Hence, "organizational ecology lacks an explanatory mechanism that can be cited as the cause of the observed diversity of organizational forms" (Reydon and Scholz 2009: 430).

On another front, Turner and Maryanski (1979) raise the challenge that functional analysis is tautological. Adopting a definition of tautology that is consistent with but different from the one stated in Chapter 1, they regard tautology as "circular reasoning in which variables are defined in terms of each other, thus making causes and effects obscure and difficult to assess" (124). They apply the definition to the case of a structure being part of a system, with the structure serving a certain function. In this sense, there is some sort of circular reasoning:

> Because a structure is a part of a system, it must be involved in meeting the system's needs, while the structure exists because a system's needs are met and the system survives. In both of these statements, it is difficult to know what causes what and the explanations seem circular. (Turner and Maryanski 1979: 124–125)

Regarding a structure-system relation as an example of a more general part-whole relation, the above point can be illustrated by the following passage by noted anthropologist and early promoter of functional analysis A. R. Radcliffe-Brown (1935: 396):

> The continuity of structure is maintained by the process of social life, which consists of the activities and interactions of the individual human beings and of the organized groups into which they are united. The social life of the community is here defined as the *functioning* of the social structure. The *function* of any recurrent activity, such as the punishment of a crime, or a funeral ceremony, is the part it plays in the social life as a whole and therefore the contribution it makes to the maintenance of the structural continuity.

Although the writing is somewhat confusing, here the whole may refer to the social structure and the part the recurrent activity with the social life being in-between. While recurrent activities contribute to the continuity of a social structure, their own existence relies on the structural continuity because they are part of the social life, which in turn maintains the continuity of the social structure. Some kind of circular reasoning is evident in the passage.

Turner and Maryanski (1979) state that the most typical way of dealing with the tautological problem is to invoke the social selection argument: structures that contribute to the survival of a system have selective advantages and will remain as integral parts of the system. Yet, as shown by Reydon and Scholz's (2009) above critique of organizational ecology, the concept of social selection itself is problematic if the theory of biological evolution is applied indiscriminately to organizations.

Historical Explanation

About three decades ago, Kieser (1994) asked, "Why does organization theory need historical analyses?" and made a few suggestions for conducting historical analyses. At around the same time, Zald (1993: 519) called for "the development of a historically informed organizational theory." In more recent years, there have been repeated calls for a historical perspective in management studies. Some enthusiastic scholars even advocate the so-called historic turn initiated by Clark and Rowlinson (2004: 331), who link this turn to the "wider transformation that is alluded to in terms such as the 'discursive turn,' deconstruction and post-modernism." Given their positioning of the historic turn, it is unsurprising that the turn "would entail a move away from the view that organization studies are part of the social sciences" (Van Lent and Durepos 2019: 431). Such a move entails ideas "that knowledge is subjective, that historical writing should inspire rather than faithfully record, [and] that the past is a lost world" (Bowden 2021: 23). This is unfortunate and is not the position taken in this book, which considers management to be a social science discipline. No wonder Bowden (2021) dubs the historic turn the "historic wrong turn."

Following Glennan (2010: 251), I define historical explanation as something that "explains the occurrence of some *particular* event or state of affairs by describing how it came to be." John Gaddis (2002: 3), a noted historian, remarks that the past "is something we can never have. For by the time we've become aware of what has happened it's already inaccessible to us: we cannot relive, retrieve, or rerun it as we might some laboratory experiment, or computer simulation. We can only *represent* it." While debunking the misconception that historians do not use theory, Gaddis (2002: 62) briefly describes the way historians explain:

> In seeking to show how past processes have produced present structures, we draw upon whatever theories we can find that will help us accomplish that task. Because the past is infinitely divisible, we have to do this if we're to make sense of whatever portion of it we're attempting to explain. Explanation is, however, our chief priority: therefore we subordinate our generalizations to it.

In other words, historians tend to use theories, which are necessarily *general*, to explain *particular* historical events — Gaddis labels this task as "embedding generalizations within narratives." He laments that social scientists insist on developing analytical models that lead them to "*embed narratives within generalizations*" (62), with the principal objective of confirming or refuting a hypothesis. His insights would surely benefit social scientists who conduct historical studies, but his impression of how social scientists formulate historical explanations is somewhat simplistic, as indicated by the discussion below.

The Covering Law Model of Historical Explanation

Hempel (1942) is one of the first philosophers of science to comment on historical explanation. In fact, the title of his 1942 paper that develops the covering law model is "The Function of General Laws in History" and it has an explicit focus on history. He includes historical explanation under the general umbrella of scientific explanation by applying the covering law model to historical studies in that paper. Since the main objective of the covering law model is to explain natural phenomena, he first claims that there is no difference between natural science and history in terms of offering an explanation because "both can give an account of their subject-matter only in terms of general concepts, and history can 'grasp the unique individuality' of its objects of study no more and no less than can physics or chemistry" (37). That is, he upholds a naturalist position, deeming that the subject and methods of the natural and social sciences should be continuous. At the same time, he acknowledges that many historians "deny the possibility of resorting to any general laws in history" (39). Yet his concern is not with what historians actually do but with what they ought to do.

Hempel (1942) gives two reasons why most explanations offered in history or sociology do not include an explicit statement of general regularities. First, such statements — for example, people tend to improve their material being — frequently relate to individual or social psychology, which is somewhat familiar to people through their everyday experience; thus, these statements are tacitly taken for granted. Second, it could often be very difficult to formulate these taken-for-granted assumptions explicitly with sufficient precision and in such a way that they are consistent with all the relevant empirical evidence. He illustrates this second point using the Dust Bowl migration:

> Consider, for example, the statement that the Dust Bowl farmers migrate to California "because" continual drought and sandstorms render their existence increasingly precarious, and because California seems to them to offer so much better living conditions. This explanation rests on some such universal hypothesis as that populations will tend to migrate to regions which offer better living conditions. But it would obviously be difficult accurately to state this hypothesis in the form of a general law which is reasonably well confirmed by all the relevant evidence available. (40–41)

Hempel admits that the phenomena covered by historical explanation are of a statistical character and thus probabilistic statements of regularities rather than general deterministic laws (i.e., laws in the form of universal conditionals) are called for. In other words, the I-S model, rather than the D-N model, is more appropriate. Nevertheless, he treats historical events as replicable and expects to find enduring regularities that can be codified in generalizations or even laws (Sayer 2000).

Hempel also cautions that most historical explanations are of the form that he would label as an "explanation sketch." The sketch consists of a somewhat vague indication of the statements of regularities and initial conditions considered as relevant and needs "filling out" in order to offer a full-fledged explanation. This filling-out task requires further empirical research to add details and the sketch suggests a direction to guide the task. As the filling-out process progresses, the historical explanation becomes more precise and it is possible to indicate at least roughly what kind of evidence would be relevant in testing some of the arguments entailed in the explanation.

The D-N model of historical explanation can be illustrated by the vertical integration between GM and Fisher Body in 1926. The following brief description of the case is based on the TCE logic used by Klein et al. (1978) and Klein (1988) and a more detailed discussion provided by Tsang (2017: chapter 7). In 1919, to replace the open and largely wooden bodies used to build their automobiles, GM signed a ten-year contract with Fisher Body for the supply of closed, largely metal, auto bodies. Subsequently, GM acquired a 60 percent interest in Fisher by purchasing 300,000 shares of newly issued Fisher common stock. The contract included an exclusive dealing clause whereby GM would buy substantially all its closed bodies from Fisher. The clause served as an incentive for Fisher to make the required specific investments and reduced significantly the likelihood of GM acting opportunistically by demanding a lower purchase price after Fisher had made those investments. However, the clause allowed Fisher to take advantage of GM by setting a monopoly price for the bodies. Over the next few years following the signing of the ten-year contract, the market experienced a significant rise in demand for automobiles and a shift from open bodied to closed bodied models. Fisher held up GM by using a relatively inefficient, highly labor-intensive technology and by refusing to locate the body-producing plants next to the GM assembly plant. Having Fisher's plants close to GM's was necessary for GM to achieve production efficiency but would have required a large specific investment on the part of Fisher, which was possibly appropriable by GM. By 1924, GM found the contractual relationship with Fisher to have become intolerable and began negotiations for purchasing the remaining stock in Fisher. This culminated in a final merger agreement in 1926.

Based on the format of the D-N model presented above, the explanans of a historical explanation must contain not only a set of instantial conditions but also general statements of some kind; the explanandum must be deducible from the explanans. The model can be applied to frame Klein et al.'s (1978) historical explanation for the acquisition of Fisher Body by GM as follows:

(1) If a firm finds itself trapped in a holdup situation by an opportunistic supplier and if its financial condition permits, the firm will attempt to acquire the supplier;

(2) In the early 1920s, GM found itself trapped in a holdup situation by the opportunistic Fisher Body and GM was in good financial shape;

(3) GM attempted to acquire Fisher Body and did so successfully in 1926.

The explanation is in the form of an explanation sketch, lacking many details that have to be filled out. Nevertheless, it presents the gist of the TCE logic in explaining the merger.

I discussed above the shortcomings of the covering law model but the model also has problems specific to its application to historical explanation. First of all, as admitted by Hempel (1942), the model does not reflect what historians actually do when they explain. Rarely do they seek to explain the occurrence of a complex historical event by subsuming it under one or more general laws. Roberts (1996: 9) summarizes the prevailing sentiment thus: "ordinary historians find his [Hempel's] model strange and irrelevant." Moreover, it is difficult to identify any general laws or statements of general regularities required by the model for explaining historical events. Human behavior is rule- rather than law-governed. Unlike natural laws, rules are made and followed by human agents but can be violated for various reasons (Murphey 1986). The covering law model cannot explain "collective events that are appreciably complex" (Nagel 1979: 574). Yet these events are precisely the ones that historians are interested in. As a matter of fact, historians do explain successfully many important events in history using methods different from Hempel's (Weingartner 1961).

Comparison with Functional Explanation

In his monumental work *The Visible Hand: The Managerial Revolution in American Business*, Chandler (1977: 11) explains the rise of the modern business corporation:

> This institution [modern business corporation] appeared when managerial
> hierarchies were able to monitor and coordinate the activities of a number
> of business units more efficiently than did market mechanisms. It continued
> to grow so that these hierarchies of increasingly professional managers
> might remain fully employed. It emerged and spread, however, only in
> those industries and sectors whose technology and markets permitted
> administrative coordination to be more profitable than market coordina-
> tion. Because these areas were at the center of the American economy and
> because professional managers replaced families, financiers, or their repre-
> sentatives as decision makers in these areas, modern American capitalism
> became managerial capitalism.

Chandler's explanation is functional in nature. The modern corporation
came into existence in nineteenth-century America because it monitored
and coordinated the activities of business units more efficiently than the
market could. Technological changes created economies of scale, under-
mined the effectiveness of traditional organizational forms and challenged
the market's ability to coordinate efficiently the flow of goods and services
through the economy. Managers played the role of innovating agents who
monitored the environment and adapted rationally to changes. They saw
needs and did what was necessary to solve problems. If they perceived that
new organizational forms were needed for adaptation, they would create
and adopt such organizational forms. If these forms succeeded in competing with existing ones, they would survive and persist. In short, the
corporation replaced the coordinating function of Adam Smith's "invisible
hand" with the "visible hand" of professional management, which would
ensure that the corporation fulfilled the functions it was supposed
to perform.

In response to Chandler's functional explanation for the rise of the
modern corporation, Roy (1990) proposes an alternative, historical explanation. In contrast to Chandler's approach that takes technology as the
exogenous transformative force in promoting corporate ascendence, Roy
identifies "the state as a major transformative agent, institutionalizing the
original corporate form, allowing it to privatize, legalizing the socialization
of property, mobilizing large scale capital, stimulating institutional structures of finance capital and stifling resistance to corporate ascendance"
(38). The state laid the legal and institutional foundation for the corporate
revolution. Industrial capital was split into two segments: a corporate
segment affiliated with financial capital and institutionalized through the
large corporation and an entrepreneurial segment tied to commercial and
local banking capital that preserved the dominance of personal ownership.
The latter segment declined with the marginalization of individually

owned firms whereas the former rose to hegemony with the rapid development of the modern corporation. In brief, while Chandler pays scant attention to the role of the state, Roy treats the state as an actor that defines its own interests, develops structures and capacities for action and responds to mobilization by other actors.

In the process of providing his historical explanation, Roy (1990) also compares briefly the functional and historical logics of explanation. As discussed in the preceding section, in a functional explanation, a social structure or relationship emerges because it serves the needs of some larger system. That is, the structure or relationship's existence is explained in terms of its consequences and so incurs the forward-looking problem. A new structure or relationship is subject to the process of social selection. Chandler explains the timing of the modern corporation's emergence in terms of its consequences of being more efficient than the market. Its persistence indicates that it outperformed some other organizational forms. A historical explanation focuses on the sequence and conjuncture of events. A new social structure or relationship is explained by tracing its unfolding steps and potential turning points. Each turning point is regarded as a conjuncture of preexisting structures and relationships in which actors, whether individual or collective, interact within a given historical context to alter the structures or relationships or to create new ones. Social selection may or may not play any role in the explanation, depending on the actual historical development. Roy describes the key events in the historical context of nineteenth-century America that facilitated the emergence of the modern corporation. For example, there were fundamental legal changes that enabled collective ownership and privatized the corporation.

Although functional explanation and historical explanation are both capable of conducting counterfactual analysis, they differ with respect to how counterfactual possibilities are identified and how actual outcomes are explained. Functional explanation considers the function of a particular structure and proposes alternative structures that could have the same function. It then examines actual events and shows how the structure in question fulfilled the function better than alterative structures. In the case of the rise of the modern corporation, a functional approach could conjure up an organizational form other than the corporation that monitored and coordinated the activities of business units more efficiently than the market. Based on actual events in nineteenth-century America, the approach shows how the corporation would fulfill that function better than the alternative organizational form. Yet Roy laments that Chandler's functional approach limits consideration of counterfactuals. For example, Chandler "does not seriously consider whether entrepreneurial organization could have managed technologically sophisticated production" (27). In contrast, by means of counterfactuals, historians "would revisit the past, varying conditions as they did so to try to see which would produce different results" (Gaddis 2002: 100). To explain the rise of the corporation, Roy identifies a number of counterfactual possibilities, such as the entrepreneurial form (including partnerships and limited partnerships); organizations borrowed from or linked to other sectors, like the producers' cooperative used in agriculture; and bureaucratic hierarchical structures pioneered by the military. It is then necessary to identify the critical junctures in history that account for why particular alternatives were realized; Roy traces some key historical events that favored some alternatives to the corporation but not others.

A final issue is the role of contingencies in the path that leads to the outcome. A functional explanation tends to not take such contingencies seriously so that the outcome appears to be inevitable. In Roy's words, Chandler's argument gives an impression of inevitability:

> the modern business enterprise seems inevitable, developing *when* managerial hierarchies were able to monitor and coordinate better than market mechanisms. There was a function to be performed: monitoring and coordinating different business activities. To explain why one social structure fulfilling that function replaced another, Chandler argues that modern business enterprise did it better. The consequence, superior monitoring and coordination is also the cause. (28)

Historical explanations, by contrast, fully acknowledge contingent events that changed abruptly the course of history. One well-known example is the assassination of Archduke Franz Ferdinand, the heir presumptive to the throne of Austria-Hungary, on June 28, 1914. The assassination led to the idea among some historians that the outbreak of World War I was an accident. Roy's explanation of the rise of the modern corporation is more contingent in tone. He argues, for example, that the merger movement among corporations between 1898 and 1903 was due to a number of contingent factors occurring at more or less the same time:

> The merger movement can best be explained in terms of the conjuncture of political, economic and social factors at the end of the century. The legal and institutional structures of finance capital, the collapse of that structure in the depression, the judicial decisions abolishing antitrust common law, a procorporate administration in Washington and the widespread belief that entrepreneurial capitalism was inevitably waning, all contributed to this movement. (36)

Table 3.2. *Comparison between functional explanation*
and historical explanation

	Functional explanation	Historical explanation
Forward-looking problem	Needs to be addressed	Avoided by focusing on past and current situations
Explanatory logic	In terms of serving the functions of some larger system	As the outcome of a sequence of unfolding events in which actors interact
Social selection	Plays a key role in eliminating changes or creations that fail to function efficiently	May or may not play a role
Counterfactual analysis	Show how a counterfactual entity serves a function less efficiently than the entity in question	Show why some counterfactual entities were realized rather than others in a historical context
Contingencies	Not seriously taken into account	Fully acknowledged

Table 3.2 summarizes the comparison between functional and historical explanations.

Process Organization Studies

In recent years, a genre of management studies called "process organization studies" has emerged. This stream of research addresses "questions about how and why things emerge, develop, grow, or terminate over time, as distinct from variance questions dealing with covariation among dependent and independent variables," and "draws on theorizing that explicitly incorporates temporal progressions of activities as elements of explanation and understanding" (Langley et al. 2013: 1). This temporal focus represents a distinct mode of explaining management phenomena, although the content of the explanation may involve human intention or be in a historical context. Process organization studies can be considered a reaction to the dominant form of scholarship in social science in general and in management in particular that neglects or ignores the relevance of time, sequence, movement or flux in research (Langley and Tsoukas 2010).

The initiation of the process organization research stream was also inspired by process metaphysics, which prioritizes activity over product and change over persistence. Substance metaphysics, in contrast, recognizes the occurrence of processes but considers them transient and incidental, explaining processes in terms of substances — "processes contingently *happen* to substances, but the latter are essentially unchanging in character" (Langley and Tsoukas 2010: 2). Again, consider Samsung's plan to relocate much of its display production from China to Southern Vietnam. Let us assume that the relocation of production did occur. Substance metaphysics would consider the relocation as something that happened to Samsung. That is, Samsung changed from a state where all of its display production was in China to another state where much of it was in Southern Vietnam. However, Samsung remained basically the same, except for the relocation, which was a one-off change. This substance metaphysical orientation is adopted by most management researchers. On the other hand, process metaphysics would deem that Samsung is not an unchanging entity but is constituted by its own experiences. In short, process metaphysics considers substances to be subordinated to and constituted by processes.

Variance versus Process Theorizing

The distinction between process organization studies and the approach to addressing variance questions mentioned above indicates that the former originates from Mohr's (1982) famous distinction between "variance" and "process" theorizing. Variance theorizing refers to explaining phenomena in terms of the relationships between independent and dependent variables. Borrowing the term "efficient cause" from Aristotle, Mohr (1982: 41) refers to it as "a force that is conceived as *acting on* a unit of analysis (person, organization, and so on) to make it what it is in terms of the outcome variable (morale, effectiveness, and so on) or change it from what is was. It may be thought of as a *push-type* causality." For instance, a firm's rewarding of innovative behavior encourages its employees to create new products or services, marketing techniques, organizational practices and so on. Variance theorizing emphasizes necessary and sufficient causality. According to Mohr, an ideal variance explanation identifies conditions necessary and sufficient for the outcome. Returning to the above example of rewarding innovative behavior, researchers may attempt to identify a set of variables necessary and sufficient for such rewards to lead to the firm's desired outcome of more innovation.

Mohr's concept of necessary and sufficient causality is nothing but nebulous, lacking the precision one usually finds in philosophical discourses. This is not surprising; his book belongs to the management literature, after all. Consider this passage:

Each contributory necessary and sufficient condition in a variance model is an efficient cause. Furthermore, each such cause, whether standing alone as an additive contributor or combined multiplicatively with other causes, has a separable impact on the outcome; the extent of its impact is not lost in the intertwining of causes and conditions. (Mohr 1982: 41)

The first sentence seems to suggest that there is more than one efficient cause in a variance model, as indicated by the word "each." Suppose a variance model has two efficient causes, A and B. If A is necessary and sufficient for bringing about the outcome, B will be a redundant cause in the model and vice versa, contradicting the second sentence. This example shows a key function of this book, which is to bridge the philosophy and management literatures by presenting the topic of explanation to management researchers using largely philosophy-based language.

Researchers usually use a set of well-developed variables and test their hypotheses with statistical techniques. Most of the quantitative empirical studies published in management journals are based on variance theorizing. Variance theorizing is suitable for predicting specific outcomes that are unaffected by the temporal ordering of the independent variables. When researchers include several independent variables in a statistical model, the temporal order in which the variables come into operation makes no difference to the outcome, as long as the theory employs a time frame in which all of these variables are operative. The level of the dependent variable Y is the same whether independent variable M occurs before independent variable N or vice versa, on the condition that the influence of M and N is brought to bear fully on Y. This temporal treatment is consistent with the usual statistical modeling methods, such as ordinary least squares regression, that uses a linear combination of independent variables to predict a dependent variable. Such methods generate identical results no matter which independent variable affects the dependent variable first in reality.

In contrast to variance theorizing, process theorizing deals with events rather than variables and final causes rather than efficient causes. A final cause is concerned with an end state whose existence presupposes the occurrences of a series of prior states. Using Mohr's (1982: 59) terminology, "a process model involves *pull-type causality*: X (the precursor) does not imply Y (the outcome), but rather Y implies X." The emphasis on the outcome reflects the operation of the final cause. For example, the desire of a firm to be seen as a responsible employer may "pull" the firm toward implementing over time a series of policies that improve its employees' welfare, such as constructing a nursery to take care of employees' children, increasing the number of vacation days and allowing flexible working hours. Unlike variance theorizing, process theorizing emphasizes necessary causality rather than necessary and sufficient causality:

> Each causal event imparts a particular direction and moves the developing subject toward a certain outcome. This influence is necessary for development and change to proceed down a particular path. However, subsequent events, conjunctions, and confluences also influence the subject, and may alter the direction imparted by earlier events. Because causal influences come to bear "event wise" — through one or more events — rather than continuously, no cause can be sufficient in narrative explanation. (Van de Ven and Engleman 2004: 352)

For the above example of corporate social responsibility, suppose that as part of the firm's plan to set up a nursery for its employees, it first asks a consultancy firm to conduct a feasibility study. The consultancy report indicates that there will probably not be a sufficient number of enrollments to make the project sustainable in the long term. The firm therefore abandons the idea and instead decides to pay an allowance to employees who need to enroll their children in day nurseries. That is to say, an initial policy initiative was replaced by another one in view of the new information (the consultancy report in this example).

The discussion so far suggests that process theorizing takes time sequencing and ordering to be critical. It tells a story about how and why a phenomenon evolved as a result of the temporal ordering and probabilistic interaction of a sequence of events over time. In other words, it explains an outcome in terms of "diachronic patterns — who does what when and what happens next — rather than in terms of the synchronic presence of higher or lower levels of specific attributes" (Langley and Tsoukas 2010: 6). Since process models often address multiple levels and units of analysis and utilize both qualitative and quantitative analysis techniques to make sense of time-ordered data, they tend to be more contextual, complex and dynamic than variance models, which rely mostly on quantitative analysis (Langley 1999).

Connection with Other Modes of Explanation

Over the years, process studies have developed far beyond Mohr's (1982) idea of process theorizing. Researchers delve into the conceptual terrain of events, activities, episodes, temporal ordering and change and use different conceptualizations of process, different contexts in which processes unfold, different measurements of change, different data collection methods, different units or levels of analysis and so on. What remains common among these studies is that they provide understandings of causality as constituted through sequences of events rather than through correlations among variables (Langley et al. 2013).

While this research stream represents a distinct mode of explaining management phenomena, there are linkages between its explanatory approach and other modes of explanation discussed in this chapter. For instance, mechanismic explanation breaks up the original explanation-seeking why-question into a series of smaller questions about the causal process and is therefore connected naturally with process organization studies. In fact, Van de Ven and Poole (1995) identify a typology of four basic process theories, each associated with a generative mechanism, that explain how and why an organizational entity changes and develops. Their four mechanisms that govern the process of change are:

- Life-cycle: the process of change in an entity progresses through a sequence of stages.
- Teleological: change is a cycle of goal formulation, implementation, evaluation and modification based on the entity's learning.
- Dialectical: modelled on Hegel's dialectics, conflicts emerge between entities displaying thesis and antithesis that collide to produce a synthesis, which then becomes the thesis for the next cycle of a dialectical progression.
- Evolutionary: change consists of a Darwinian sequence of variation, selection and retention events among entities in a population.

Although the four mechanisms are not exhaustive and observed change and development processes in organizations are often more complex than any one of the mechanisms, Van de Ven and Poole's (1995) typology serves as a useful guide for researchers to analyze the processes they observe.

Another connection with other modes of explanation is the issue of meanings and interpretations. Buchanan and Dawson (2007) argue that research narratives shape the meaning and understanding given to a sequence of events. Narratives seeking to develop understanding of change processes are necessarily selective and sieved through particular discourses. Multiple interpretations of events and conflicting explanations can make an organizational change process a battlefield of competing narratives. Each of these narratives provides a certain lens through which to view lived experiences of change. Langley and Tsoukas (2010: 17) also maintain that many process studies consider the meanings or interpretations of individuals to be their raw material or primary object of investigation, suggesting a double-hermeneutic task of the type discussed earlier in this chapter.

Finally, a significant number of process studies excavate the past, with the data collection effort focusing precisely on materials linked directly to the outcome in question. This task connects process studies with historical explanation in that case researchers are required to explain or interpret some past events in their projects. These researchers would also benefit from historians' expertise of discovering, collecting, preserving and interpreting historical data.

Here I illustrate the connections between process studies and historical explanation using Bingham and Kahl's (2013) process study of how groups in the life insurance industry developed a new schema for the business computer during the period 1945–1975. After World War II, the process for the industry to adopt the new technology of business computers involved "developing interpretations of what computers were – that is, a collective schema that captured an understanding about computers" (19). Bingham and Kahl define schemas as "knowledge structures that contain categories of information and relationships among them" (14). Schemas simplify information processing by acting as cognitive frameworks and so help managers interpret their environment to make decisions. The objective of Bingham and Kahl's study was to provide a more complete account of how a new schema emerges, becomes distinct and persists as an independent cognitive structure. Their archival efforts focused on the proceedings of three occupational groups and trade associations – the Society of Actuaries, Life Office Management Association, and Insurance Accountant and Statistical Association – during the period 1945–1975. These organizations set up committees to investigate computers and held related conferences. The proceedings also included detailed discussions concerning the use or planned use of computers.

Through analyzing the proceedings, Bingham and Kahl identify and measure changes in the collective schema of the computer. The life insurance industry gradually developed a new schema to *interpret* what became known as business computers. Bingham and Kahl provide an example of the interpretation in the 1952 Society of Actuaries report:

> These new machines have been called computers because they were developed primarily for mathematical work. It is a mistake, however, to think of them today as purely computing machines capable only of a large amount of arithmetic. In recent years, some very important improvements have

converted them into machines capable of a wide variety of operations. Nowadays we must think of them as information processing machines with computing representing just a part of their total capabilities. (Davis et al. 1952: 5)

Bingham and Kahl *interpret* the above passage as the adoption of the machine analogy for developing "the *interpretation* of a computer as a machine that processes transactions through the use of such relations as 'merge,' 'punch' and 'match.'" (20). In other words, their research involves double-hermeneutics.

Bingham and Kahl identify three key processes — assimilation, deconstruction and unitization — that explain collectively schema emergence. Each process can also be regarded as a mechanism, which consists of entities and activities organized so as to produce regular changes from a beginning state to an end state. For example, assimilation is the starting point of schema emergence and is concerned with the cognitive recognition of a new object, in this case, the computer. Assimilation is essentially a mechanism that connects the state where the computer is not recognized to the one where it is. Entities include computers, managers who have to deal with computers, analogies between the computer and existing machines and so on. Activities include managers' perceptions of the computer's functions, comparison between the computer and other machines, recognition of the uniqueness of the computer, and so on.

Since Bingham and Kahl's data covers the period 1945–1975, they supplement their analysis of association proceedings with historical analysis of the life insurance industry's use of computers. They even label their study as an "in-depth historical analysis" (14), commencing their analysis by picking up the clue from Yates's (2005) historical analysis that reveals insurance companies' beginning to examine seriously and discuss publicly what became known as business computers in the mid-1940s. Bingham and Kahl's analysis surfaced the processes of assimilation, deconstruction and unitization, which constitute their core contributions to the literature. In sum, Bingham and Kahl's process study is in effect also a historical explanation involving double-hermeneutics and mechanismic reasoning.

CHAPTER 4

Microfoundations

Recently, there has arisen in management studies a so-called microfoundations movement, following in the footsteps of economics and sociology. The central impetus of the movement is "to unpack collective concepts to understand how individual-level factors impact organizations, how the interaction of individuals leads to emergent, collective, and organization-level outcomes and performance, and how relations between macro variables are mediated by micro actions and interactions" (Felin et al. 2015: 576). The movement's aim is to link macro management phenomena, such as corporate governance, corporate social responsibility and strategic alliances, with more micro disciplines, such as organizational behavior and psychology.

The notion of "microfoundations" can be traced to the heated debate in social science between methodological individualists and methodological holists (or methodological collectivists) that has been going on for over a century. The debate touches upon our deep-seated beliefs about the nature of the individual and of society (Udehn 2002). The gist of the debate can be summarized as:

> When the individualist contends that only individuals are responsible actors on the social and historical stage, the holist retorts that society is more than merely a collection of individuals. To this retort the individualist answers that there is no mysterious additional entity which turns a collection of individuals into a society; a collection of individuals is a society if there is strong interaction between them; this interaction is due to the fact that when any one individual acts (rationally) on the basis of his own aims and interests, he takes into account the existence of other individuals with aims and interests. To this the holist retorts that the individualist misses the point; that people's aims do not constitute a society but rather depend on society; so that members of different societies have different aims and interests. (Agassi 1960: 244)

That the issues involved in the debate seem so difficult to resolve is probably because they are mostly philosophical in nature and thus not amenable to direct empirical testing that would yield clear-cut answers (Udehn 2002). This chapter offers a far more in-depth philosophical analysis of the topic than what has been presented in management literature, such as Felin et al.'s (2015) review article of the microfoundations movement. The analysis provides new insights to management researchers.

Unlike sociologists or economists, management researchers seldom investigate the relationship between individuals and society or between individuals and the economy. Rather, their concern is more about the relationship between individuals and organizations. For example, in the domain of organizational learning research, there is a nagging issue of how learning at the individual level is related to learning at the organizational level:

> All learning takes place inside individual human heads; an organization learns in only two ways: (a) by the learning of its members; or (b) by ingesting new members who have knowledge the organization didn't previously have. But what is stored in any one head in an organization may not be unrelated to what is stored in other heads; and the relation between those two (and other) stores may have a great bearing on how the organization operates. (Simon 1991: 125)

The above quote suggests that when management researchers study organizational learning, they should also examine individual learning in the organization, which constitutes the microfoundation of organizational learning.

Methodological Individualism

The core ideas of microfoundations are based on or at least closely related to methodological individualism (Lindenberg and Foss 2011). Although the term "methodological individualism" has different meanings (Hodgson 2007), it generally refers to the epistemological stance that stresses the explanatory primacy of individuals and their purposeful behavior, that is, "social explanations and descriptions must be grounded in facts about individuals" (Little 1991: 183). Udehn (2002: 479) distinguishes between "strong versions of methodological individualism, which suggest that all social phenomena should be explained only in terms of individuals and their interaction, and weak versions of methodological individualism, which also assign an important role to social institutions and/or social structure in social science explanations." Joseph Schumpeter (1909) was the scholar who first brought the term "methodological individualism" to the English-speaking academia in his article "On the Concept of Social Value." For him, the term "describes a mode of scientific procedure which naturally leads to no misconception of economic phenomena" (231). Schumpeter (1909: 231) stresses the individual as the starting point for studying economic relationships:

> Every one has his marginal utility for each commodity; and for every one, if equilibrium is to be attained, it must be true that for the commodities to which they relate prices must express ratios between his marginal utilities, and that prices must have the same proportions to each other as every one's marginal utilities for the same commodities. But this is brought about only by the joint action of marginal and intra-marginal sellers and buyers; and the result would be different if the marginal utilities of any of them were not what they are. All of them contribute towards fixing prices. It appears, therefore, that the theory of prices is not to be dispensed with in a full explanation of social distribution; and this theory of prices is based on individual values.

This passage refers not just to methodological individualism but also ontological individualism. It is necessary to distinguish between the two because statements about the nature of reality (such as those about marginal utilities in the passage) are very different in character from statements concerning how one should explain observed phenomena in reality (such as the last statement about "full explanation"). The former kind of statement is ontological, while the latter is methodological.

Ontological individualism and methodological individualism are surely related, not least because researchers' ontological beliefs influence their methodological approach. Yet, believing that society is made up of individuals and nothing else does not imply necessarily that social phenomena must be explained in terms of individuals and their interactions (Udehn 2002). That is, ontological individualism does not necessarily imply methodological individualism. Conflating the two kinds of individualism may lead to muddled discussions. Consider, for example, Watkins's (1957: 105–106) principle of methodological individualism, which means that

> the ultimate constituents of the world are individual people who act more or less appropriately in the light of their dispositions and understanding of their situation ... we shall not have arrived at rock-bottom explanations of such large-scale [social] phenomena until we have deduced an account of them from statements about the dispositions, beliefs, resources and interrelations of individuals.

Hodgson (2007: 214) criticizes that Watkins "conflates both ontological and methodological individualism in a single passage" because the statement concerning "the ultimate constituents of the world" is ontological in character, while the statement concerning "rock-bottom explanations" is methodological. Like Watkins (1957), Demeulenaere (2011: 4) summarizes the two core ideas of methodological individualism as follows:

(1) Social life exists only by virtue of actors who live it.
(2) Consequently a social fact of any kind must be explained by direct reference to the actions of its constituents.

Demeulenaere argues that since social entities are *composed* of individual actions alone, social outcomes must be *explained* on the basis of facts about these actions. The first idea is concerned with the existence of entities and so is ontological, while the second idea is about the method of explanation and so is methodological. The distinction between methodological individualism and ontological individualism is necessary because many of the arguments for the former seem in fact to be arguments for the latter (Sawyer 2002). Udehn (2002) laments that many methodological individualists fail to make the distinction and this failure has been the source of much confusion in the methodological individualist-holist debate.

It should be noted that the literature is not uniform with regard to terminology. For instance, Epstein (2009) maintains that the thesis of methodological individualism is divided commonly into two different claims – explanatory individualism and ontological individualism. He defines explanatory individualism as the assertion that "explanations in the social sciences can or ought to be provided in terms of individuals or their properties" (188). His definition is in line with the usual meaning of methodological individualism. One problem with Epstein's approach is that a researcher's stances on the two kinds of individualism may not be highly correlated. For instance, a high ontological individualist position may be coupled with a rather low explanatory individualist position; to believe that society or an organization is made up of individuals alone does not imply that all social or organizational phenomena must be explained in terms of individuals and their interaction. Lumping explanatory individualism and ontological individualism together serves little purpose because each has to be discussed separately anyway.

Another terminology issue is Felin et al.'s (2015) claim that the microfoundations movement can be seen as promoting and pursuing Elster's (1989) version of reductionism, which refers to the process of explaining a particular phenomenon in terms of lower-level phenomena, rather than methodological individualism. Felin et al. justify their choice of terminology by giving two examples: "the actions of a cartel may be explained in terms of the actions of the participating firms" and "the functioning of a routine may be explained in terms of the coordinated actions of individuals." Hence, "microfoundations may or may not directly involve individuals" (619). In this sense, methodological individualism has a narrower scope than reductionism but follows a reductionist approach. While Felin et al.'s choice makes sense, methodological individualism is more established in the social science literature than is reductionism, probably because social entities and individuals are the focus of social research. In fact, they mention the term "reductionism" only twice in their text, while "methodological individualism" is mentioned eleven times. Little (1991: 191) also claims that "methodological individualism may be considered as the application of reductionism to social science." The discussion below focuses on methodological individualism first and then ontological individualism.

Max Weber, Schumpeter's teacher, is commonly credited for introducing the doctrine of methodological individualism to social science in his classic work *Economy and Society*. Weber, after taking the chair in sociology at the University of Munich, wrote in a letter dated March 9, 1920, to the economist Robert Liefmann, who had attacked sociology:

> I do understand your battle against sociology. But let me tell you: If I now happen to be a sociologist according to my appointment papers, then I became one in order to put an end to the mischievous enterprise which still operates with collectivist notions (*Kollektiabegriffe*). In other words, sociology, too, can only be practised by proceeding from the action of one or more, few or many, individuals, that means, by employing a strictly "individualist" method. (Roth 1976: 306)

According to Weber, social phenomena should be explained by explicating how they result from individual actions, which in turn should be explained through reference to the intentional states that motivate the actors. His version of methodological individualism is based on the idea of an interpretive sociology that treats individuals and their actions as the basic unit of analysis and is concerned with the understanding and causal explanation of social action. Here, understanding involves double hermeneutics in that the researcher needs to know the subjective meaning individuals attach to their own actions as well as the motives individuals have for behaving in a certain way. Weber's interpretive sociology adopts an individualist method because only individuals can attach subjective meanings to their behavior and there is no such thing as a collective personality or actor. Udehn (2002: 485) argues that "Weber was not really interested in the nature of social reality as such. Subjectivism was a feature of his methodology, nothing more." In other words, Weber was not interested in ontological individualism, which proposes a kind of dependence of the social on the individual.

Ontological Individualism

Methodological individualism follows from the ontological thesis that all social phenomena are created, or caused, by individuals, who are also "the ultimate constituents of the social world" (Watkins 1957: 106). Ontological individualism "is the thesis that facts about individuals exhaustively determine social facts" (Epstein 2009: 187). Contrast this thesis with that of methodological individualism − "facts about society and social phenomena are to be explained solely in terms of facts about individuals" (Lukes 1968: 120). The former is concerned with the nature of reality; the latter, the method of explaining reality. Ontological individualism is often seen as a response to the view that there is an autonomous sphere of social properties or facts and social groups are prioritized conceptually over individuals.

The earlier-noted ontological individualist quote of Simon (1991) describes his perception of the facts about organizational learning, individual learning and their relations. Similarly, von Mises (1949: 41–43) notes regarding ontological individualism:

> The hangman, not the state, executes a criminal . . . . For a social collective has no existence and reality outside of the individual members' actions. The life of a collective is lived in the actions of individuals constituting its body . . . . There is no substratum of society other than the actions of individuals.

According to this view, "social entities are *nothing but* ensembles of individuals in various relations to one another" (Little 1991: 183). Examples of social entity include classes, castes, schools, churches, charities, government and companies. Only individuals exist; social objects and properties are just combinations of the individual participants and their properties (Sawyer 2002). This ontological thesis is a truism. A school is nothing but a group of teachers and students engaging in teaching, learning and other related activities. When a school loses its students and teachers, it will no longer be a school. However, the claim of methodological individualism extends beyond this straightforward ontological thesis to a more ambitious thesis that "whatever complex and reciprocal relations there are between social entities and individuals, it is the totality of individual facts which determines the totality of social facts" (Currie 1984). That is, methodological individualism is basically about the determination of social facts or properties and it is here that we run into problems.

As Pettit (2003: 191) puts it, "individualism insists on the supervenience claim that if we replicate how things are with and between individuals, then we will replicate all the social realities that obtain in their midst: there are no social properties or powers that will be left out." The challenge faced by ontological individualists can be illustrated using the idea of supervenience. Using non-technical language, Lewis (1983: 358) encapsulates pithily the nature of supervenience with an illustrative example:

> To say that so-and-so supervenes on such-and-such is to say that there can be no difference in respect of so-and-so without difference in respect of such-and-such. Beauty of statues supervenes on their shape, size, and colour, for instance, if no two statures,[1] in the same or different worlds, ever differ in beauty without also differing in shape or size or colour . . . . One might wish to say that in some sense the beauty of statues is nothing over and above the shape and size and colour that beholders appreciate, but without denying that there is such a thing as beauty, without claiming that beauty exists only in some less-than-fundamental way, and without under taking to paraphrase ascriptions of beauty in terms of shape etc.

Lewis's example can be interpreted thus: if two statues have different degrees of beauty, they cannot have the same shape, size and color. However, the relation is asymmetric in that the inverse is not true because two statues having the same degree of beauty may have different shapes, sizes or colors. That is to say, a certain degree of beauty can be realized by different combinations of shape, size and color. Supervenience is about the relation between a class of facts, events or characteristics in a pair of domains (Currie 1984), which in this example refers to the domain of appreciating the beauty of a statue and the domain of the physical attributes of a statue. In short, the essence of supervenience is that "higher-level properties can be multiply realized by lower-level properties, but once the lower-level properties are fixed, the higher-level properties are fixed as well" (Ylikoski 2014: 119).

Kincaid (1986: 499) applies the doctrine of supervenience to the context of methodological individualism:

> Individuals determine the social world in the intuitive sense that once all the relevant facts (expressed in the preferred individualist vocabulary) about individuals are set, then so too are all the facts about social entities, events, etc. Or, to put this idea in terms of supervenient properties, the social

supervenes on the individual in the sense that any two social domains exactly alike in terms of the individuals and individual relations composing them would share the same social properties.

In the case of organizational learning, if two organizations are exactly alike in terms of their members and the members' relations, both organizations should have the same learning outcome. Yet Hodgson (2007: 215) raises a crucial issue of whether "the social world simply consists of individuals, or of individuals and *interactive relations between them.*" Rephrasing Hodgson's issue in terms of supervenience, we have the following scenarios:

(1) The social world supervenes on individuals *alone*, and
(2) The social world supervenes on individuals *plus* interactive relations between them.

The first scenario does not seem plausible. If individuals are considered isolated entities, as depicted by the scenario, we lack the complete building blocks for the *social* world, which by virtue of the fact that it is social, should include individuals' interactive relations. A situation that is close to the first scenario is Searle's (1990) example illustrating non-collective behavior displayed by a group. A group of people sat on the grass in various areas of a park. Suddenly it started to rain heavily and the people all got up and ran to the only shelter, located at the center of the park. In this case, the behavior of the group as a whole can be said to be the sum of each person's behavior. There was no collective behavior in the sense that there was virtually no organization involved. Rather, there was simply a sequence of individual acts that happened to converge on a common goal – avoiding getting wet. Social science researchers are not typically interested in this kind of situation.

The individual interaction aspect of social ontology is explicated by Hayek (1967: 70–71), who is often considered an advocate of methodological individualism:

> The overall order of actions in a group is in two respects more than the totality of regularities observable in the actions of the individuals and cannot be wholly reduced to them. It is so not only in the trivial sense in which the whole is more than the mere *sum* of its parts but presupposes also that these elements are related to each other in a particular manner. It is more also because the existence of those relations which are essential for the existence of the whole cannot be accounted for wholly by the interaction of the parts but only by their interaction with an outside world both of the individual parts and the whole.

For Hayek, society consists of not only individuals, but also interactions between individuals, as well as interactions between individuals and their environment including, presumably, both the social and natural worlds. Applying Hayek's insight to organizational learning, when we say that two organizations being alike in terms of their members and the members' interactive relations will have the same learning outcome, we refer to members' relations not only within but also outside the organization. For example, if a member is an engineer, we also take into account the member's interactive relations with the engineering profession outside the organization.

Generally speaking, the interactive relations of the second scenario above are concerned with social positions filled by individuals (such as engineer, sales representative, production supervisor and marketing director). An individual occupying a social position not only possesses his or her own qualities or powers but also acquires additional qualities or powers associated with that position, by virtue of relations with others (Hodgson 2007). Social structures are essentially groups of interacting individuals who occupy social positions, with emergent properties resulting from this interaction (Weissman 2000). Such properties are not the properties possessed by individuals taken in isolation. Like water that has properties not possessed by either hydrogen or oxygen, a listed company has properties not possessed by any individual employee of the company. Cautioning against reifying social structure as something more than an interacting pattern of individuals, Hodgson (2007) considers that social structures are equivalent to relations between individuals. Substituting "interactive relations between them" with "social structures" in the second scenario, we arrive at:

(3) The social world supervenes on individuals *plus* social structures.

Given the social character of interactive relations in the second scenario and of social structures in the third scenario, it does not make much sense to regard either scenario as representing ontological *individualism*. In sum, ontological individualists face a formidable conceptual challenge. The argument presented here is just one version of the challenge. Interested readers may refer to Epstein (2009), who presents an elaborate version of the challenge in terms of local and global supervenience.

Coleman's Macro-Micro Relations

As already mentioned, methodological individualism emphasizes the explanatory primacy of individuals and their purposeful behavior. Some

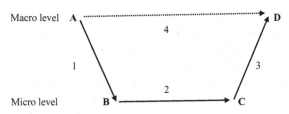

Figure 4.1   Coleman's macro-micro relations

scholars have brought the concept of causal mechanisms discussed in Chapter 2 into the picture. For example, Demeulenaere (2011: 15–16) holds that social causal mechanisms occur solely at the level of the actors and not at the macro level:

> Therefore the focus has to be on the causal "process" occurring at the action level. The idea that there are laws directly implemented at a macro level can be easily rebutted, since the effectiveness of the outcome necessarily leads to the "active" level, the level of action. One general implication of the notion of "mechanism" is to move analysis away from an "inactive" level to an "active" level, where effective actions occur. A strong correlation between variables should not therefore be interpreted in causal terms unless a mechanism linking the two dimensions is identified.

Demeulenaere's argument is in line with the approach of mechanismic explanation discussed in Chapter 3 that regards mechanisms as intervening between the explanans and the explanandum.

The version of methodological individualism held by scholars like Demeulenaere is often illustrated by reference to the famous "Coleman's boat" or "Coleman's bathtub," which is pictorially shown in Figure 4.1 and is a rare example of a visual representation in sociological theory. I shall simply call it "the diagram" here. The diagram was developed for sociologists, who want to understand both how large-scale entities (the macro) influence smaller-scale entities (the micro) and how a macro phenomenon is composed of microscale events and activities. The diagram distinguishes between the explanandum and the explanans, as suggested by the direction of an arrow. It offers a systematic way to think about such micro-macro relations and serves as a cognitive tool for theorizing. It is therefore not surprising that the diagram has also been used by political scientists (e.g., Dunlop and Radaelli 2017), economists (e.g., Hartley 1997), and management researchers (e.g., Felin et al. 2015). Based on the diagram, Hedström and Swedberg (1996) develop a typology of mechanisms: macro-micro mechanisms, micro-micro mechanisms and micro-macro mechanisms.

Coleman (1990) maintains that there are two types of explanation for the behavior of social systems. The first type "depends on either a sample of cases of system behavior or observation of the system as a whole over a period of time" (2) and sticks to the "macro" or "system" level. In contrast, the second mode of explanation "entails examining processes internal to the system, involving its component parts, or units at a level below that of the system" (2). He argues that the first type, as represented by Arrow 4 in Figure 4.1, cannot discriminate between potential alternative explanations of macro-level behavior derived from different combinations of unobserved, lower-level factors and mechanisms. An explanation of the second type based on analyzing actions and orientations of lower-level units, as represented by Arrows 1, 2 and 3, is likely to be more stable, general and fundamental than a macro-level explanation. Arrow 1 represents the constraining, shaping or forming of individual behavior that occurs when a macro-level entity, such as laws and regulations, social norms, or schools and companies, affects the individual. Arrow 2 represents connections within the individual's psychology and cognition and Arrow 3 the composition of the macro-level phenomenon through the activities of individuals at the micro-level (Little 2012). Since macro-level behavior is resultant of the actions of its component parts, knowledge of the mechanism through which such actions produce the behavior gives greater predictability than would statistical relations of macro-level variables. In sum, using the terminology of causal mechanism, the diagram implies that "there exist no macro-level mechanisms; macro-level entities or events are linked to one another via combinations of situational, individual action, and transformation mechanisms, i.e., all macro-level change should be conceptualized in terms of three separate transitions (macro-micro, micro-micro, and micro-macro)" (Hedström and Swedberg 1996: 299). The diagram is, admittedly, simplistic because many mechanisms cannot be represented by the nodes and arrows of the diagram. The nodes, especially Nodes B and C, are chosen to denote only key variables of a mechanism, with other variables included in the description of the mechanism.

As depicted in Figure 4.2, Coleman (1990) uses his model to illustrate the relationship between the macro variables – improved social conditions and occurrence of revolution (Arrow 4) – as conceived of by the so-called frustration theorists of revolution. Improved social conditions in a country followed by relative setbacks at the macro level generate frustration among the public at the micro level (Arrow 1), which in turn leads to expressions of aggression (Arrow 2). As a result of cumulative aggression, a revolution

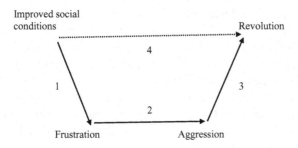

Improved social
conditions

Revolution

4

1   3

2

Frustration   Aggression

Note:
This figure is adapted from Figure 1.3 of Coleman (1990)

Figure 4.2   Coleman's macro-micro relations illustrated by revolutions

breaks out at the macro level (Arrow 3). Here, the micro-level nodes "frustration" and "aggression" correspond to Coleman's plea for explaining macro-level behavior based on actions and orientations of individuals. Although this explanation bottoms out at the level of individual action, Coleman (1990: 4) allows for the micro level being at a higher level: "a natural stopping point for the social sciences (although not psychology) is the level of the individual – and that, although an explanation which explains the behavior of a social system by the actions and orientations of some entities between the system level and the individual level may be adequate for the purpose at hand, a more fundamental explanation based on the actions and orientations of individuals is more generally satisfactory." For example, entities "between the system level and the individual level" can be households, companies, schools, churches, charities and so on, while the system level refers to society. Therefore, Coleman accepts quite readily non-individual agents and his micro-macro distinction is relative, not attached to any fixed "levels."

Management researchers usually study phenomena that are less macro than sociologists or political scientists. Thus, Arrow 4 of the diagram often points at actions or outcomes at the organizational level (Node D of Figure 4.1) while the cause may be at the social, economic, political, institutional, industrial or organizational level (Node A); Arrows 1–3 involve micro-level actions and cognition at the individual level (Nodes B and C). The diagram can be illustrated by the case of organizational learning. Based on what Hong et al. (2006) call the "routine-oriented" approach, organizational learning is the process of "encoding inferences from history into routines that guide behavior" (Levitt and March 1988:

320). Following Feldman and Pentland's (2003) reconceptualization, organizational routines refer to repetitive patterns of interdependent actions carried out by multiple organizational members involved in performing organizational tasks. They emphasize the critical role of human agency and distinguish between the ostensive and performative aspects of a routine. The former refers to the schematic form of a routine, or the routine in principle, while the latter is the routine in use, denoting the specific actions performed by specific individuals in specific places and at specific times when a routine is enacted. One of Feldman and Pentland's (2003) key contributions is their argument that both the ostensive and the performative aspects are necessary to constitute a routine, whereas previous conceptualizations emphasized the ostensive aspect only. When a routine is changed intentionally in both aspects, organizational learning is said to have occurred (Tsang and Zahra 2008). Yet this does not imply that learning necessarily leads to improved performance, partly because the acquired knowledge may be inaccurate and partly because putting the lessons learned into practice can be complex (Tsang 1997).

The change of a routine may be caused by incidents at the macro level. Consider, for instance, the hiring of new faculty members by business schools. Within the hiring routine, a common practice at many business schools in North America is to invite shortlisted job applicants for a campus visit so that they can experience the environment and meet the faculty in person. However, Covid-19 prevented schools from continuing this practice and forced them to use online job interviews instead. In other words, when the hiring routine was enacted by members of the search committee, the performative aspect was changed. Some search committee members might have gradually come to recognize the unique benefits of online interviews, such as convenience, low cost and flexibility. Accordingly, they informed the dean of their school, who subsequently changed the ostensive aspect of the hiring routine such that even after the pandemic, the school would arrange online job interviews for, say, applicants who had already visited their campus in the past, who were located overseas, or who had difficulties in traveling during the specific hiring window. This example can be used to illustrate Coleman's boat (Figure 4.3). What is observed at the macro level is the pandemic causing the change in the hiring routine (Arrow 4) and organizational learning having occurred. That is, the pandemic is the macro-level cause of the learning. A microfoundational explanation is that the pandemic made campus visits infeasible. Search committee members therefore replaced campus visits with online job interviews (Arrow 1). While using online

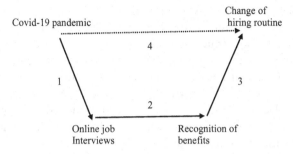

Figure 4.3   Coleman's macro-micro relations illustrated by hiring new faculty members

interviews, search committee members gradually came to appreciate the unique benefits of this new way of recruitment (Arrow 2). They informed their dean of these benefits and recommended that online interviews be a legitimate alternative to campus visits. If the dean accepted the recommendation, the hiring routine would then be officially changed (Arrow 3). This explanation of organizational learning describes the micro-level mechanism that links the two macro-level nodes "Covid-19 pandemic" and "Change of hiring routine."

Felin et al. (2015) distinguish between three types of microfoundational explanation that can be generated from the diagram: A (Arrow 3), B (Arrows 2 and 3) and C (Arrows 1 to 3). Type A explanation focuses purely on aggregating micro actions and does not inquire into the specific causes of these actions. For example, a simple aggregation of individual votes indicates the political preference of a population. However, the above example of faculty hiring does not involve any aggregation; it is the Dean's decision – not the search committee's or the result of the faculty's vote – to revise the hiring routine that leads to organizational learning. Unlike political elections, routines do not reflect a simple aggregation of individual behavior. In fact, Coleman (1990: 10) cautions against simple aggregation: "the micro-to-macro transition is made simply by aggregation of individual orientations, attitudes, or beliefs. If, however, the theoretical problem is one of involving the functioning of a social *system* ... then it should be obvious that the appropriate transition cannot involve the simple aggregation of individual behavior." In his example of revolution mentioned above, Coleman argues that Arrow 3 does not represent a simple aggregation of individual aggression to produce a revolution because "a revolution involves organization and the interplay of actions on the part of a number of actors" (10). In addition to simple aggregation, which Felin et al. (2015)

call "linear aggregation," they also mention non-linear aggregation, which "deals with the social interactional complexities where individuals influence each other, learn from each other, or where structures may impose certain non-linearities in aggregation" (591). Non-linear aggregation corresponds to Coleman's point about the organization and interplay of actions on the part of the actors. However, the change of a routine may not even involve non-linear aggregation. For instance, the change may be imposed from the top of the organization, such as from the foreign parent of an international joint venture (Tsang 2008). Type B explanation includes the proximate causes of micro actions. In the hiring example, the proximate cause is the use of online job interviews, resulting in unique benefits. Nevertheless, the explanation is odd in that it does not mention why online interviews replace traditional campus visits. Finally, Type C explanation includes the more distant, macro-level causes, which in the hiring example refer to the pandemic. Although the pandemic is considered a distant cause according to Felin et al.'s (2015) terminology, it is an essential element of a satisfactory explanation of the change in the hiring routine. Hence, Types A and B explanation do not seem to work well for the hiring example.

De Massis and Foss (2018: 387) label Type C explanation as "the *full* microfoundational explanation." An alternative is to consider microfoundations playing a justificatory rather than an explanatory role; a macro-level explanation is satisfactory as long as an account of the lower part of Coleman's boat can be provided, without having to include it in the explanation. Little (2012: 143) explicates this position:

> The requirement of microfoundations is not a requirement on explanation; it does not require that our explanations proceed through the microfoundational level. Rather, it is a condition that must be satisfied on *prima facie* grounds, prior to offering the explanation . . . . In short, we are not obliged to trace out the struts of Coleman's boat in order to provide a satisfactory macro- or meso-level explanation or mechanism.

Accordingly, the pandemic is a satisfactory explanation of the change in the hiring routine (Arrow 4) as long as the underlying factors at the individual level are available for clarification, if needed. When a situation calls for a succinct explanation of an event, a macro-level explanation serves the purpose well.

These contrasting attitudes toward whether microfoundations should play an explanatory or a justificatory role in research correspond somewhat to the attitudes regarding methodological individualism as a universal principle or a heuristic device guiding researchers:

There are some who see methodological individualism as an *a priori* and universal principle of social scientific research: an obligatory rule or categorical imperative, unconditionally binding for all social scientists, because it is based on certain self-evident truths about society and our knowledge about it. There are others who see methodological individualism as a heuristic device or research program, the fertility of which can only be ascertained *a posteriori*. (Udehn 2002: 501)

These two attitudes reflect the ongoing debate between methodological individualists and methodological holists. This should not be a surprising development because despite the fact that methodological individualism is intuitively appealing, it has some significant limitations, a major one of which is concerned with emergent properties, discussed next.

Emergent Entities and Properties

The term "emergence" denotes the possibility that "when certain elements or parts stand in particular relations to one another, the whole that is formed has properties – known as 'emergent properties' – that are not possessed by those elements or parts taken in isolation" (Lewis 2012: 368). In simple terms, the principle of emergence claims that "things have causal powers that their parts would not have if they were not organised into this kind of whole" (Elder-Vass 2014: 41). As elaborated below, certain explanations at the level of a whole cannot be reduced to a lower level based on its parts. The notion of emergence suggests that reality is stratified such that there is a hierarchy of levels of emergent entities, each of which has its own distinctive and irreducible properties. The distinct levels range from "the physical (including both the sub-atomic and atomic), the chemical, the biological (embracing both molecular and cellular phenomena), the mental (psychological), the individual, and the social" (Lewis 2012: 374). Emergent properties are structural or relational in the sense that their existence depends not only on the presence of the lower-level parts but also those parts being organized into a particular structure that positions them in specific relation to one another (Stephan 1992).

In an influential early account of emergence, Alexander (1920) argues that life is a new quality that emerges from a constellation of physical and chemical processes but is not merely physical and chemical. Although the higher quality of life emerges from the lower level of existence, it does not belong to that level and has its own order of existence with special laws of behavior. He claims further that the existence of emergent qualities is a brute empirical fact and admits no explanation. Another, more lucid, illustration of emergence is the case of water. A water molecule is composed of hydrogen and oxygen atoms. Elder-Vass (2007) distinguishes between resultant and emergent properties. The resultant properties of a whole are those properties that its parts also possess in isolation. The property of mass possessed by a water molecule is a resultant property because this property is also possessed by its oxygen and hydrogen atoms in isolation, or in an unstructured aggregation. In contrast, the emergent properties of a whole are those properties that its parts do not have in isolation. Many properties of water, such as being liquid at room temperature, are not possessed by its parts — hydrogen and oxygen atoms — in isolation. If these atoms exist simply as atoms or are combined into molecules of types other than water, the resulting substance will not have the properties of water. It is the fact of being combined into the specific structure of water molecules that gives the collection of hydrogen and oxygen atoms the particular properties of water. Water, then, is an emergent entity, while its many properties are emergent properties that enable water to exercise causal powers, such as being able to extinguish a fire or to quench a person's thirst.

Lewis (2012) distinguishes between explanatory reduction and eliminative reduction. It may be possible to achieve an explanatory reduction of emergent properties in the sense that one can explain how the properties of an emergent entity result from the properties of its parts and the interaction of these parts when they are arranged in a specific way. That is to say, one can identify the causal mechanism responsible for the existence of emergent properties. On the other hand, it is impossible to have eliminative reduction, in which the properties of an emergent entity itself can be explained away and thus eliminated entirely from explanations involving the exercise of the entity's causal powers. Simply put, the emergent entity itself cannot be eliminated from the explanation. Lewis (2012: 369) illustrates lucidly the contrast between explanatory reduction and eliminative reduction, using the case of water:

> For example, while we can explain the liquidity of water in terms of its atomic constituents and the relations (chemical bonds) obtaining between them when they assume the form of water molecules, the property of liquidity obtains only when the emergent entity, water, is present. The causal power to extinguish fires and to slake one's thirst is a property of water, not of the individual atoms of which it is composed. It follows, therefore, that causal explanations of how fires can be extinguished or thirst quenched have to make reference, if only implicitly, to that emergent entity, because it only when hydrogen and oxygen atoms are arranged into the form of water that the relevant causal power is present.

The explanation of water's liquidity is concerned with explanatory reduction while the explanation of its causal power is concerned with eliminative reduction. For the latter, water, as an emergent entity, cannot be eliminated from the explanation of its causal power.

Emergent entities and properties are common in management research. As a legal entity separate from the natural persons that are its members, an organization possesses special powers. For example, an organization can hire employees, sign and enforce contracts, file lawsuits, submit patent applications, own property, borrow money, be listed on a stock exchange and so on. These powers are conferred legally on the organization — not on any of its members — and are not legally ascribable to its members and their relations (Tsilipakos 2015). People refer to organizations as entities independent of their members, such as: "Apple on Tuesday sued NSO Group and its parent company, accusing the Israeli firm of violating a federal anti-hacking law by selling potent software that clients have used to spy on Apple customers" (Lyngaas 2021). This situation is in line with a basic ontological principle of emergence:

> entities have emergent causal powers when they are capable of exerting an influence on the world that their parts would not be able to exert were they not organised into such a whole. Such powers are produced by mechanisms, processes in which the parts of the entity interact to generate the influence concerned, and we may be able to explain such mechanisms scientifically. This, however, does not alter the fact that these powers would not exist if the whole did not exist, and therefore we may conclude that these are causal powers of the whole and not of the parts. (Elder-Vass 2014: 46)

This is not to deny the fact that an organization acts through its members; in order for an organization to take an action, one or more of its members need to take that action on its behalf (Tsilipakos 2015). Regarding the above news about Apple's lawsuit, the legal action was taken by the company's corporate lawyers based on senior management's decision.

In a similar vein, an organization learns through its members. Yet, according to the routine-oriented approach, researchers have to examine whether the routine related to the learning activities, such as a hiring routine, has been revised before organizational learning can be said to have occurred. The organizational members who perform a routine usually do not all have access to the same information about the routine. They act in a context created by the actions of other participants who include non-organizational members, such as the job applicants in the hiring example. Since such actions can create or close off alternatives, participants have to coordinate their actions and cannot just do as they please. Each performance of a routine is a collective performance in the sense that participants' actions are interdependent (Feldman and Pentland 2003). This is similar to the case of collective behavior of, say, a football team or an orchestra, which is somehow not analyzable in terms of members' separate individual behavior (Searle 1990). In sum, while a routine is composed of participants' actions, it has emergent properties not shared by any of these actions. Returning to the example of hiring new faculty, Figure 4.3 shows that the organization-level explanation can be reduced to an individual-level one. However, individual actions are constrained as well as enabled by the structure of the hiring routine. A proper individual-level explanation has to incorporate − not eliminate − the organization-level concept of routine, defeating methodological individualists' stress on the explanatory primacy of individuals.

Crossan et al.'s (1999) 4I framework presents organizational learning as four processes − intuiting, interpreting, integrating and institutionalizing − linking the individual, group and organizational levels. Intuiting and interpreting take place at the individual level, interpreting and integrating at the group level and integrating and institutionalizing at the organizational level. With a focus broader than that of the routine-oriented approach of organizational learning, the last process of institutionalizing refers to changes in not only routines but also structures or systems. Like the routine-oriented approach, the 4I framework also subscribes to the principle of emergence, with its underlying assumption being that "organizations are more than simply a collection of individuals; organizational learning is different from the simple sum of the learning of its members" (Crossan et al. 1999: 529). In short, organizational learning is in sharp contrast to the earlier example of people running to the park shelter when it rained.

While the microfoundations movement in management studies is a laudable attempt to generate better quality explanations, the principle of emergence shows one of the movement's serious limitations: emergent entities and properties cannot be eliminated by the process of explaining a particular phenomenon in terms of lower-level phenomena. As Steel (2005: 950–951) well says using the language of mechanism:

> Everyone will agree that social mechanisms inevitably do involve individual interactions. But the fact that societies are composed of interacting agents, and hence that whatever happens ultimately depends on these interactions, does not entail that every adequate *description* of a social mechanism must be phrased in individualist terms. Whether a description of a mechanism is adequate depends on the purpose for which it is intended.

For instance, in network analysis, a node of a network may be occupied by an individual, an organization, a city or even a country. Many network-related phenomena can be explained by analyzing the structure of a network — such as an open versus a closed structure — without the need to move one level down and study the characteristics of the nodes themselves (Borgatti et al. 2009). To conclude, when commenting on methodological individualism versus holism, Bunge (1997: 440) notes pithily, "I shall argue that neither is sufficient, though each contains a nugget." His advice is worth management researchers' attention when they consider whether to join the microfoundations movement.

CHAPTER 5

Theory versus Non-theory–Based Explanation

Most explanations we give in our daily lives do not involve any theory. When someone asks me why I had lunch at McDonald's yesterday, I might answer, "To save time, because I could only squeeze out thirty minutes for lunch." This is an acceptable explanation that is related only remotely to theory. Such atheoretical explanations are also common in business. Chapter 1 mentioned Toyota's recall of millions of vehicles in the United States in early 2010; the reason was a problem with the gas pedal. The recall was to satisfy federal requirements for motor vehicle safety. Unless one invokes some legal theory about why such federal requirements were created, the explanation is, again, non-theory based.

Researchers create theories to explain phenomena of interest by imposing order on unordered human experiences (Dubin 1978). Admittedly, the word "theory" is used loosely and with little consensus in scientific research:

> Like so many words that are bandied about, the word *theory* threatens to become meaningless. Because its referents are so diverse – including everything from minor working hypotheses, through comprehensive but vague and unordered speculations, to axiomatic systems of thought – use of the word often obscures rather than creates understanding. (Merton 1967: 39)

Yet this confusion is not a reason for abandoning the word. In fact, Merton (1968) himself promotes sociological theories of the middle range. Over past decades, there have been discussions in the management literature that aim to clarify the meaning of theory. For example, Sutton and Staw (1995) caution that references, data, variables, diagrams and hypotheses are not theory. Although management studies are often guided by theory, there are exceptions, especially during the initial investigation of a phenomenon. In the next section, I share my own experience of studying superstitious decision making.

Atheoretical Explanation

The story began when I was working as a corporate banker in HSBC, Hong Kong, prior to switching to my current career. During the lunar new year, some of my clients admitted frankly that they sought advice from fortunetellers or prayed in temples in order to plan ahead for the upcoming year. They also divulged that they would sometimes engage in superstitious activities when making strategic decisions, such as investing overseas, creating new products or services, investing in new technologies, selling existing business operations, forming business partnerships or hiring senior executives. Such practice is a common phenomenon among Chinese business executives and entrepreneurs. It is also an important business phenomenon; almost three decades ago, Kao (1993) argued that privately owned Chinese firms, most of which were located outside mainland China itself, constituted the world's fourth economic power after Japan, North America and Europe. Since the implementation of economic reforms in mainland China at the end of the 1970s, the number of large, privately owned companies, such as Alibaba, Huawei and Tencent, has been growing, implying that the phenomenon is even more important now.

When I embarked on my study of the phenomenon during the late 1990s, I was surprised to find that there was not even a single piece of academic research on the topic of superstition *and* decision making.[1] My literature review indicated that existing decision-making theories failed to explain the phenomenon (see Tsang 2004a). Although Popper (1994: 86) claims that "we always operate with theories, even though more often than not we are unaware of them," I attempted to start my research without any theoretical preconceptions. I intended to answer a single question: "Why do Chinese managers engage in superstitious activities when making strategic decisions?" My fieldwork included a questionnaire survey in Singapore and dozens of interviews with fortune-tellers and Chinese businessmen in Singapore and Hong Kong. The data I collected provided rich information about the phenomenon. I systematically coded and analyzed the data, publishing my study in *Organization Studies* (Tsang 2004a) and a practitioner version of it in the *Academy of Management Executive* (Tsang 2004b), both journals being the first outlets I attempted to publish in. During data analysis, I realized that the phenomenon could be linked to two important concepts in the decision-making literature – rationality and uncertainty. I developed my description of the phenomenon around these two concepts:

> Superstition helps Chinese businessmen cope with uncertainty by provid-
> ing a sense of certainty and alleviating the anxiety associated with uncer-
> tainty. Although superstition is often regarded as irrational and unfounded,
> practitioners try to justify it on the grounds of superstition's substantive
> validity or instrumental value. (Tsang 2004a: 923)

Another significant finding was that fortune-tellers played simultaneously
the roles of expert, provocateur, legitimizer and comforter when providing
advice to their business clients.

Although my study presented a golden opportunity to create a theory
that explained how superstition affected strategic decision making in
Chinese business communities, I thought my research was exploratory in
nature and, at that stage of the research, my priority was to present my
findings carefully and faithfully, establishing an empirical foundation on
which future research could be built. Moreover, I was pleased that I had
achieved the objective of answering the abovementioned why-question.
There were also encouraging developments during and after the publication of my study. Despite the study's meagre contribution to theory, one
of the three anonymous *Organization Studies* reviewers of my manuscript
commented that it "could become a classic *Organization Studies* piece in
the spirit of its founder, David Hickson, who believed that rigor and
boredom did not need to go together. It is pieces like [this] that often
make a single *Organization Studies* issue more interesting to me than the
entire year's crop of *AMJs*."[2] Not long after my study was published,
I received messages from researchers in Brazil and Mexico, saying that they
also encountered a similar phenomenon in their own country. My conversations with colleagues indicated that Indian, Japanese, Korean and
Thai managers were also rather superstitious. In my email exchange with
the late James March in 2006, he stated appreciatively that my "observation that 'superstition' is used to resolve choices among apparently equivalent (by rational standards) alternatives is insightful."

Some of the subsequent studies on superstition are more theory-based.
For example, drawing heavily on my study, Andrews et al. (2022) argue
that superstition is a pervasive informal institution affecting the decision
making of organizational members. The qualitative study of Andrews et al.
investigates how Western multinational corporations (MNCs) affect – and
are affected by – the use of superstition among local subsidiary managers in
Myanmar. The results indicate a complex, changing and surreptitious
relationship between MNC practice and the informal institution of
superstition. Although this informal institution is practiced widely by
locals, it remains forbidden according to its formal institutional

counterpart (i.e., Buddhism) and is illegal according to Myanmar state law. Andrews et al. propose a typology that theorizes Western MNC response to the primary informal institution of superstition in an emerging economy context where the informal institution plays a relatively significant role in relation to its formal counterpart. Their study also contributes to theories concerning institutional legitimacy and liability of foreignness.

Although my exploratory study provides a largely atheoretical explanation of why Chinese managers engage in superstitious decision making, it has attracted citations from researchers in various non-management disciplines such as economics (Fortin et al. 2014), finance (Gurd and Or 2011), marketing (Block and Kramer 2009), psychology (Huang and Teng 2009), hospitality (Pratt and Kirillova 2019), gambling studies (Tang and Wu 2012), architecture (Chang and Lii 2010), sustainability studies (Adomako and Amankwah-Amoah 2021), urban studies (Madeddu and Zhang 2017) and even studies of death and dying (Wong 2012). This citation pattern, which is rare among management studies, suggests that superstition significantly affects a wide variety of human activities and deserves more research attention. As I intended, my study has contributed to the empirical foundation that paves the way for future research.

Luck as an Explanation

Some of my respondents who engaged in superstitious decision making cited as one of their reasons that they wanted to pursue good fortune and avoid disaster (趨吉避兇). They considered luck an important factor affecting their career or business. It is not difficult to find cases in business where luck alone accounts almost completely for a company's change of performance during a certain period of time. An excellent example is Zoom, a company whose services many of us started using following the onset of the Covid-19 pandemic. In the words of its founder and CEO, Eric Yuan, when looking at the company's performance in the first quarter of 2020:

> We were humbled by the accelerated adoption of the Zoom platform around the globe in Q1. The COVID-19 crisis has driven higher demand for distributed, face-to-face interactions and collaboration using Zoom. Use cases have grown rapidly as people integrated Zoom into their work, learning, and personal lives. (Hayes 2020)

Few would dispute that luck provides a better explanation than any management theory for Zoom's sudden jump in performance in the first quarter of 2020. To be fair, the pandemic also brought bad luck to some companies, such as those in the airline or hotel industry.

Probably because luck is not only an atheoretical but also a naive explanation, people tend to provide more sophisticated and high-sounding explanations publicly. I once taught a part-time MBA course in strategic management. Virtually all of my students were either managers or professionals. Every time I taught the course, in the first lesson, I asked students to cite factors affecting a company's performance. Very rarely was luck mentioned as a causal factor. Pundits, who are supposedly more knowledgeable than my students, do not seem to fare any better. For example, Dell Computer was ranked first among the World's Most Admired Companies by *Fortune* magazine in February 2005. The company's performance plummeted just two years later. At that time, observers offered all sorts of "profound" explanations:

> According to *Business Week*, "Dell succumbed to complacency in the belief that its business model would always keep it far ahead of the pack." It had been "lulled into a false sense of security." An unsuccessful acquisition was said to be evidence of "hubris." In *Leadership Excellence*, a management consultant explained that Dell "got stuck in a rut" and became "reluctant to change." When rivals had matched Dell's strategy of customization, managers "fell back on an old practice: they cut costs to maintain market share." The *Financial Times* quoted a business school professor at the University of Maryland who opined: "[Dell has] forgotten how to make customers happy. I have to believe the problems with the company are cultural and they begin at the top." (Rosenzweig 2007: 6)

Each of the above explanations can be traced to a certain management theory. For instance, the comments that Dell became "reluctant to change" is rooted in the theory that a company's core capabilities (e.g., Dell's customization ability) may become its core rigidities (Leonard-Barton 1992). Rosenzweig (2007: 7) refutes these explanations forcefully and attributes the error to the halo effect, which refers to "the basic human tendency to make specific inferences on the basis of a general impression." In other words, a company's performance creates an overall impression that shapes how people perceive its strategy, leaders, employees, corporate culture and so on.

As Rosenzweig (2007: 15) well says, "in business, performance is inherently relative, not absolute." A highly plausible reason that explains at least partially Dell's drastic change in performance is that the company's superior performance in 2005 was due to extreme luck and its demise two years later was a result of regression to the mean. The phenomenon of a regression of data towards mean values was first discovered by Francis Galton, a half cousin of Charles Darwin. In a study of relationships between the heights of parents and their children, Galton observed that parents with an above-average height tended to have children who were shorter than themselves, whereas those who were short tended to have children who were taller than they were (Galton 1886). Regression to the mean suggests that good performance is likely to be followed by decline whereas poor performance is likely to be followed by improvement. Even if some of the above pundits who commented on Dell's performance believed that regression to the mean should be the explanation, they would probably refrain from mentioning it for a simple reason: "A business commentator who correctly announces that 'the business did better this year because it had done poorly last year' is likely to have a short tenure on the air" (Kahneman 2011: 182). What is true for a business commentator is also true for a management researcher when submitting manuscripts to journals. Few journal reviewers, including myself to be honest, would evaluate positively, say, an argument that the difference in performance between Companies A and B in Year X was smaller because Company A was having extraordinary luck in the preceding year, even if the authors managed to provide empirical evidence that indicated Company A's luck.

Although luck could provide a valid explanation for performance differences between individuals and organizations and for performance changes within an individual and organization, luck has rarely been a key construct in management research, especially empirical studies. Liu and de Rond (2016) surveyed the use of luck in six leading management journals (*Academy of Management Journal, Academy of Management Review, Administrative Science Quarterly, Management Science, Organization Science* and *Strategic Management Journal*) up to 2014 and found that only 2 percent of articles included the word "luck" (and related words like "lucky," "unlucky" and so on) in the main text, abstract or title. In addition to the perception that luck is not a typical theoretical construct, Kahneman (2011: 182) provides a psychological reason for the neglect of luck — and thus neglect of regression to the mean — by researchers:

> our mind is strongly biased toward causal explanations and does not deal well with "mere statistics." When our attention is called to an event, associative memory will look for its cause — more precisely, activation will automatically spread to any cause that is already stored in memory. Causal explanation will be evoked when regression is detected, but they will be wrong because the truth is that regression to the mean has an explanation but does not have a cause.

Luck (in the usual meaning of randomness) or regression to the mean fits neither Hume's conception of cause nor Suppes's (1970) definition of cause as a probability-raising event (see Chapter 2). Yet, an explanation need not involve a cause (based on a certain definition of cause), not to mention involve a theory. This does not imply that an explanation invoking luck must not contain any cause. For example, the immediate cause of Zoom's sharply improved financial performance in the first quarter of 2020 was that there was a much higher demand for its service. But it was luck that accounted for this higher demand.

Theory-Ladenness of Observation

My experience of studying superstitious decision making suggests that not aiming at a theory-based explanation of the phenomenon in question helps to free the researcher from the theory straitjacket that might compromise the accuracy of observation. My view is in line with Hempel's (1965) distinction between observational and theoretical terms. According to Hempel, data are accessible to direct observation by researchers and may be represented in the form of "observational reports," which are constructed by "observational sentences." Such sentences assert or deny that the objects under study have certain observable properties or stand in certain observable relations to each other. In contrast to Hempel's thesis of theory-neutral observation, Hanson (1969) argues that we usually "see" through spectacles made of our past experience and our knowledge and tinted by the logical forms of our languages and notations. Hence, there is a limit to how far we can make theory-free observations:

> There is no such thing as a "pure" observation, that is to say, an observation without a theoretical component. All observation – and especially all experimental observation – is an interpretation of facts in the light of some theory or other. (Popper 1994: 86)

One of the recurrent topics in the philosophy of science has been the debate about whether scientific theory influences scientific observation. Theory-ladenness of observation can be demonstrated by Gunstone and White's (1981) gravity experiment with first-year college physics students. They showed the students an iron sphere and a plastic sphere of the same diameter (10 centimeters) that were held next to each other two meters above a bench. They asked the students to predict the time it would take for the metal sphere versus the plastic sphere to fall to the bench. They then dropped the spheres three times. The students recorded their observations and explained any discrepancy with their prediction. They found that students whose initial hypothesis was that the heavier metal ball would fall faster than the lighter plastic ball were more likely to report observations supporting their theory — regardless of whether the theory is true or false — than were students whose initial hypothesis was that the two balls would fall at equal speeds. Gunstone and White's result seems to support the theory-laden view, which challenges the traditional empiricist account of scientific observation as the passive reception of sense-data (Greenwood 1990).

Modern scientific research often involves not direct perceptual observations but "more abstracted and reduced observations that we will call data" (Brewer and Lambert 2001: S181). In fact, with the exception of organizational behavior, management researchers often analyze archival data or data collected from questionnaire surveys, rather than engaging in observation. Modeling a typical situation in the process of scientific research, Brewer and Chinn (1994) conducted an experiment to test whether prior beliefs influence the evaluation of empirical data. One group of participants read passages supporting a theory that dinosaurs were cold-blooded, while the second group read passages supporting another theory that dinosaurs were warm-blooded. The participants reported a strong belief in whichever theory they had read about. Then they were presented with a piece of data that confirmed one theory and refuted the other theory. The same piece of data was rated as more believable when it was consistent with the participant's theory than when it was inconsistent. Brewer and Chinn's experimental results provide clear evidence supporting the view that evaluation of scientific data is theory-laden.

In addition to influencing data interpretation, theory may also affect how data are collected. An illustrative example is related to the three major ontological views about the nature of entrepreneurial opportunities, namely discovery, creation and actualization discussed in Chapter 1. It is somewhat natural that researchers adopting one of the views design a data collection method based on that view. For instance, subscribing to the discovery view, Corbett's (2007) study examines the relationship between opportunity identification and learning. As summarized in his figure 1, he develops hypotheses about how general human capital, specific human capital, information acquisition and information transformation affect the number of opportunities identified. To test his hypotheses, he conducted a questionnaire survey on a random sample of 1,592 founders, owners, top management team members, engineers and researchers of technology firms based in Colorado in the United States and received 380 usable returns.

His questionnaire asked the respondent to list as many new business or product opportunities as he or she could, based on a description of the Bluetooth wireless protocol. The Bluetooth technology was relatively new at the time of Corbett's study. Although his respondents were technology professionals, the level of familiarity and knowledge of Bluetooth varied to a great extent among them. Following is a passage from that Bluetooth wireless protocol:

> In this section we would like to examine your ability to find new potential business opportunities. After reading the passage below on a new emerging technical protocol, take a few minutes to list any potential business opportunities based on this protocol that come to mind. The ideas you list may or may not be related to your current business. (Corbett 2007: 107)

As explained in Chapter 1, since a business opportunity has to be profitable, a fatal flaw of the discovery view is that this profitability attribute of the outcome is known with certainty at the moment of "discovery" even before the opportunity is exploited. Corbett's asking his respondents to "find new potential business opportunities" suffers exactly the same problem: unless these so-called opportunities are proven profitable subsequently, they are probably not opportunities at all. According to the actualization view, what Corbett in fact asked his respondents was to *imagine* business opportunities that may turn out to be real opportunities.

As to the creation view of entrepreneurial opportunities, Harima and Freudenberg (2020) studied a social entrepreneurial acceleration program called Refugee Innovation Challenge in Hamburg, Germany. The program brought together social entrepreneurs and members of the refugee community to develop innovative solutions for refugees and asylum seekers who had just arrived in Germany. Harima and Freudenberg conducted interviews with both local and refugee participants in the program, as well as organizers of the program. It is obvious that their subscription to the creation view influenced their fieldwork significantly. For example, they regarded the acceleration program as "an initiative that provided a unique platform for local people and refugees to *co-create opportunities* in the context of innovative solutions to new challenges emerging in European countries due to the recent influx of refugees" (44–45, emphasis added). After several iterations of data coding, Harima and Freudenberg developed categories based on logical similarities and ontological levels of each element, which was then used to create a model of co-creation of social entrepreneurial opportunities, as visually presented in their figure 1. What they called "creating opportunities" is in fact "generating ideas."

Consider, for example, this quote from a refugee respondent in their section "Social opportunity evaluation":

> Because they never had the experience to be refugees. So, they have these great ideas, but they need someone. For example, when they say an idea "let's do this," and then I have the perspective of the refugee. So, I say "Okay but people maybe would think about it." (48)

Harima and Freudenberg actually used the term "idea evaluation" in that section. An entrepreneurial idea is different conceptually from an entrepreneurial opportunity in that the latter has to result in a positive outcome, which is known only after the so-called opportunity is exploited. Since their study focused on the generation and evaluation of entrepreneurial ideas, whether such ideas could lead to positive outcomes – that is, whether these ideas (or, imagined opportunities, according to the actualization view) really represented opportunities – was unknown. Hence, it makes little sense to talk about opportunities, not to mention creating opportunities.

If observations are theory-laden, this will endanger the objectivity of empirical testing as the foundation for the claim that science is objective: "Science strives for objectivity in the sense that its statements are to be capable of public tests with results that do not vary essentially with the tester" (Hempel 1970: 695). The objectivity of empirical tests is premised on, among other things, the presumed existence of a theory-free or theory-neutral observation language (Hunt 1994). Since the 1960s, the theory-laden view has been so popular that it was once regarded as one of the two dogmas concerning the observational evaluation of scientific theories; the other dogma was the Quine-Duhem thesis. They were called dogmas because "many contemporary philosophers of science appear to accept them uncritically and concede (however grudgingly) that they pose some threat to the objectivity of science" (Greenwood 1990: 553). The theory-laden view has also spread from the natural sciences to the social sciences:

> A person does not have to read very widely in the contemporary methodological or theoretical literature pertaining to research in the social sciences and related applied areas, such as education, in order to discover that objectivity is dead. When the term happens to be used, it is likely to be set in scare-marks – "objectivity" – to bring out the point that a dodolike entity is being discussed. (Phillips 1990: 19)

However, the theory-laden view is not without challenges. Hunt (1994: 141) distinguishes between two types of theory: "Explanatory theories are the theories being tested by a process involving (among other things) observation reports, whereas measurement theories are the ontological and other theories that are assumed (explicitly or implicitly) in the process of testing the explanatory theories under investigation." For example, the cause of lung-tissue scars and how the scars affect the functioning of the lung are concerned with explanatory theories, while measurement theories are about how lung-tissue scars are captured on X-ray plates. Hunt argues that, in addition to other problems, the theory-laden view blurs the distinction between explanatory and measurement theories. By making the distinction and tackling other problems, he develops a realist theory of empirical testing that debunks the theory-laden view. Space limitations do not permit a description of his theory here. Yet his distinction between explanatory and measurement theories may not be applicable to management research. As shown by the studies of Corbett (2007) and Harima and Freudenberg (2020), research design and measurement, as well as data interpretation and analysis, are often guided by the explanatory theory that a study aims to test.

Franklin (2015) distinguishes between the philosophical and practical components of the theory-laden view. The former is the view that "observation cannot function in an unbiased way in the testing of theories because observational judgments are affected by the theoretical beliefs of the observer" (156), while the latter is concerned with "experimental design, failure to interpret observations correctly, possible experimenter bias, and difficulties in data acquisition" (155). Similar to Hunt's (1994) suggestion, a usual approach to dealing with the philosophical component is to distinguish between explanatory and measurement theories; Franklin (2015) deems that the philosophical component has been tackled adequately and that the theory-laden view no longer poses a threat to unbiased observation. In contrast, the practical component is more complicated. For example, subscribing to a particular theory may lead to an experimental design that precludes observation of phenomena not predicted by that theory. This is as true in experimental designs in physics, on which Franklin bases his argument, as in management research. When Corbett (2007) and Harima and Freudenberg (2020) design their research methods through the discovery and creation views respectively, this narrow focus prevents them from recognizing in their fieldwork that entrepreneurial opportunities do in fact exist as propensities, as the actualization view advocates.

Incommensurability of Paradigms or Theories

When different researchers subscribe to different theories, the theory-laden view predicts that their observations will likely be different too, as indicated by Gunstone and White's (1981) experiment. Since explanation is affected by empirical observation, this implies that, for the same phenomenon, different theories may generate different explanations, which may not be comparable. The issue is part of a broader problem – incommensurability of theories or paradigms. The concept of incommensurability originates from Thomas Kuhn's (1970) highly influential book, *The Structure of Scientific Revolutions*, which represented a watershed in how people viewed the progress of science. The book also popularized terms like "scientific revolution," "paradigm" and "paradigm shift." Kuhn's concept of incommensurability has undergone substantial transformation since the publication of the first edition of that book in 1962 (Sankey 1993). The following description of the concept is based on his original position, which is also the version most discussed in the literature.

According to Kuhn (1970), one can divide scientific activities into periods of "normal science" punctuated at intervals by episodes of "revolution." Normal science is "research firmly based upon one or more past scientific achievements, achievements that some particular scientific community acknowledges for a time as supplying the foundation for its further practice" (10) and a scientific revolution occurs when "an older paradigm is replaced in whole or in part by an incompatible new one" (92). Kuhn considers paradigms to be "universally recognized scientific achievements that for a time provide model problems and solutions to a community of practitioners" (viii) and, as such, paradigms "provide models from which spring particular coherent traditions of scientific research" (10). Yet it has been noted widely in philosophy of science that Kuhn fails to use "paradigm" in a self-consistent manner; Masterman (1970) identifies at least twenty-one different uses of the term by Kuhn himself.

In spite of the confusion in philosophy of science caused by the term "paradigm," it has been used indiscriminately (or, abused, to be more precise) in a wide variety of ways by management researchers. The inappropriate use of "paradigm" in the management literature was probably made popular by Burrell and Morgan's (1979) seminal work, *Sociological Paradigms and Organizational Analysis*. Burrell and Morgan (1979: 23) used the term "paradigm" to "emphasise the commonality of perspective which binds the work of a group of theorists together in such a way that they can be regarded as approaching social theory within the bounds of the same problematic." Subsequently, management researchers used the term in a more problematic manner. For example, Donaldson (1995) distinguished between structural contingency, population ecology, institutional, resource dependence, agency and transaction cost theories. He considered each theory a paradigm and used the terms "theory" and "paradigm" interchangeably. Perrow (1994) also used the two terms interchangeably, as indicated by the terms "rational choice paradigm" and "rational choice theory" in his critique of Pfeffer's (1993) essay "Barriers to the Advance of Organizational Science: Paradigm Development as a Dependent Variable." The term "paradigm" is not needed for Pfeffer's argument; in fact, what he cautions against is the proliferation of management theories. As Hassard (1988: 248) well says, the term is "being substituted freely for terms such as perspective, theory, discipline, school or method." This is unfortunate because clarity of concepts is a pre-condition for healthy theory development.

At the heart of Kuhn's (1970) thesis of scientific revolution is revolutionary transition between competing paradigms, the point at which incommensurability enters:

> the proponents of competing paradigms practice their trades in different worlds . . .. Practicing in different worlds, the two groups of scientists see different things when they look from the same point in the same direction . . .. That is why a law that cannot even be demonstrated to one group of scientists may occasionally seem intuitively obvious to another. Equally, it is why, before they can hope to communicate fully, one group or the other must experience the conversion that we have been calling a paradigm shift. Just because it is a transition between incommensurables, the transition between competing paradigms cannot be made a step at a time, forced by logic and neutral experience. Like the gestalt switch, it must occur all at once (though not necessarily in an instant) or not at all. (150)

In addition to proponents of competing paradigms practicing their trades in different worlds, another major reason for incommensurability is that within the new paradigm, old terms, concepts and experiments fall into new relationships with each other, resulting in miscommunication and misunderstanding between the two groups of scientists. One of the most cited illustrative examples is the contrast between Newtonian mechanics and the theory of relativity. Kuhn argues that the analogues of Newton's laws that follow from the theory of relativity as a special case are not identical with those laws because Einstein's version of the laws employs relativistic concepts that represent Einsteinian space, time and mass.

Although Kuhn's intended audience consists of natural scientists and his peers in philosophy of science, management researchers prima facie jump on the bandwagon and apply his concept of incommensurability — arguably the most contentious aspect of Kuhn's thesis — to management theories. Similar to the case of "paradigm," there are signs that the term "incommensurability" has also been abused by management researchers. For example, Scherer (1998) argues that situations of incommensurability may emerge in both science and management practice. For the latter, he imagines a situation in which "managers do not agree about the interpretation of an organizational problem or strategic issue, e.g. a new product introduction in an unrelated industry" (150). It is strange to call this a situation of incommensurability. Rather, it is a usual case of differences in managerial judgement. No wonder Weaver and Gioia (1994: 584) lament that the notion of incommensurability has been used by management researchers in a "loose and imprecise fashion."

As mentioned, Burrell and Morgan (1979) popularized the term "paradigm" in management. They also sowed the seeds of incommensurability in the minds of some management researchers. Burrell and Morgan proposed a two-by-two matrix along two dimensions – assumptions about the nature of society (sociology of regulation vs. sociology of radical change) and assumptions about the nature of social sciences (objective vs. subjective), resulting in four sociological paradigms, namely interpretivism, functionalism, radical humanism and radical structuralism. They argued that a synthesis between paradigms cannot be achieved and that these four paradigms will develop independently and remain discrete. That is to say, the paradigms are incommensurable. The incommensurability stems from the commitment to opposing beliefs in either or both sets of assumptions mentioned above, with each paradigm having a language of its own (Jackson and Carter 1991). As researchers identify themselves with their own paradigm and establish research programs, journals and divisions at academic conferences accordingly, this will give rise to pluralism and fragmentation in the management discipline (Scherer et al. 2016). Although inter-paradigm debate is possible, Burrell and Morgan (1979: 25) stressed that "one cannot operate in more than one paradigm at any one given point in time, since in accepting the assumptions of one, we defy the assumptions of the other."

An excellent illustration of incommensurability in management research is the debate between finance researchers Amihud and Lev (1999) and Denis et al. (1999), on the one hand, and strategy researchers Lane et al. (1999), on the other, concerning the influence of equity ownership structure on corporate diversification strategies. The former group of researchers adopts agency theory. Diversified firms trade at a discount relative to their undiversified peers, hurting shareholders' interests. Yet diversification benefits managers by reducing the risk of the managers' undiversified personal portfolio and increasing their power and prestige derived from managing a larger firm. Diversification strategies thus represent decisions in which a fundamental conflict of interest between managers and shareholders emerges. Accordingly, agency theory predicts that manager-controlled firms have a greater propensity to implement diversification strategies, such as undertaking conglomerate mergers. In contrast, Lane et al. (1999) argue from a strategic management perspective that agency theory is unlikely to be applicable to corporate diversification because "the costs related to diversification are not as extensive or as far-reaching as suggested by Amihud and Lev (1981)" (1084). Lane et al. invoke Kuhn (1970) and raise the issue to the level of the two disciplines:

> In summary, we argue that strategic management and financial economics hold different world views, and that these differences in turn influence the disciplines' views on the ownership structure of corporations. Strategic management holds a more complex, less reductionist view, and therefore leads to the conclusion that neither owner-control nor management-control is a panacea. As such, the difference between the two disciplines is largely theoretical in nature. Contrary to the assertions by Amihud and Lev (1999) and Denis et al. (1999), therefore, we believe that the differences in theory cannot be rectified solely by appeal to empirical evidence. (1080)

The above comment hints that the two world views are incommensurable. Lane et al. go on to discuss the differences in measuring the key constructs between the two disciplines. For example, strategy researchers tend to have a more refined measure of merger relatedness. Lane et al. also highlight several other methodological differences. Contrary to their claim that the two disciplines hold different world views and that the differences cannot be rectified by appeal to empirical evidence alone, their discussion shows precisely that as long as the two groups of researchers make an effort to understand the other party's view, it is possible to settle those methodological differences and for both parties to design a test of agency theory together concerning the influence of ownership structure on corporate diversification strategies.

Lane et al. elevate the debate unnecessarily from the theory to the discipline level — "important differences exist between financial economics and strategic management, leading to differing beliefs, norms, methods, and interpretations of empirical results" (1077); doing so only serves to shut down dialogue. After all, the crux of the debate concerns "the theoretical importance of agency theory in explaining managerial attitudes towards corporate diversification" (Dennis et al. 1999: 1071). Amihud and Lev (1999: 1068) claim that "extant evidence strongly supports the proposition that corporate risk strategy and corporate acquisitions are affected by agency problems, proxied by ownership structure," whereas Lane et al. (1999: 1077) claim that their findings indicate otherwise: "agency theory's cornerstone assumptions about the principal/agent problem have little relevance in explaining the strategic behaviors of public corporations when their managers are neither under siege nor confronted with a situation in which their interests clearly conflict with those of shareholders." In fact, the methodological differences mentioned by Lane et al. can be spelled out without referring to any differences between strategic management and financial economics. For example, even within strategic management, some researchers may measure merger relatedness in a more refined manner than others.

Lane et al. (1999: 1079) highlight a conceptual difference between the two disciplines: "whereas finance scholars and agency theorists view managerial discretion as an opportunity for self-serving behavior, strategy scholars believe that it is also an opportunity for value-enhancing entrepreneurship." They fail to note that such a difference in managerial attitude proposed by the two groups of scholars, which is concerned with the underlying mechanism of the phenomenon, cannot be sorted out by analyzing quantitative archival data using a reduced model, the details of which are presented in Chapter 7. Other research methods, such as questionnaire survey and case study, are needed. However, all the empirical studies cited in the debate are of the reduced model format and, as such, it is unlikely that the debate can be "rectified solely by appeal to empirical evidence" (Lane et al. 1999: 1080). The problem here is due to research methods and has nothing to do with the alleged incommensurability between financial economics and strategic management.

The above debate is about two conceptual frameworks – not paradigms – explaining the influence of equity ownership structure on corporate diversification strategies. Unlike "paradigm," the meaning of "theory" is less ambiguous. Hintikka (1988: 25) defines the commensurability of two theories "(relative to a given set of questions) as the ratio of the total information of their shared answers to the total information of the answers yielded by the two theories combined." In other words, if there is little overlap in terms of the explanations given by two theories for a certain phenomenon, the theories are said to be highly incommensurable with respect to explaining that phenomenon. Incommensurability may refer to the unintelligibility of theories to outsiders due to alien assumptions (e.g., ontologies and epistemologies) and vocabularies (i.e., the absence of a neutral observation language). Similar to the case of incommensurable paradigms, a frequently *perceived* consequence of having incommensurable theories is that without common ground, meaningful communication between researchers operating within distinct theories is virtually impossible. The above debate clearly shows that such a perception is a myth rather than the reality.

To conclude, even Kuhn (1990), who originated the concept of incommensurable paradigms in the 1960s, admitted subsequently that incommensurability does not necessarily rule out meaningful communication and mutual understanding between researchers working within distinct paradigms. Similarly, Feyerabend (1987: 81), who contributed to the development of the concept after Kuhn, later conceded that incommensurability is a "rare event" and "is a difficulty for philosophers, not scientists." Likewise, Laudan (1996: 9) maintains that "incommensurability has been a philosophical conundrum in search of instantiation." In a stronger tone, Hintikka (1988: 38) laments that "the frequent arguments that strive to use the absolute or relative incommensurability of scientific theories as a reason for thinking that they are inaccessible to be purely scientific (rational) comparisons are simply fallacious." That is to say, paradigms and theories are commensurable and can be fairly compared and appraised based on common standards (Losee 2005). In light of these critiques of incommensurability, it is unfortunate that incommensurability has been used by some management researchers as "an excuse for not trying to understand or reconcile different theories" (Donaldson 1998: 269).

Substantive Theory and Metatheory

As mentioned in the Preface, I met in the summer of 2018 an ethnic Chinese scholar who was an enthusiast of yin–yang (陰陽) theory. He attempted to persuade me that the theory could explain virtually all natural and social phenomena. Obviously, he mixed up substantive theory with metatheory. In this section, I discuss these concepts' distinction with respect to explanation, using yin–yang theory as the example. Yin–yang theory, which is rooted in Chinese philosophy, is in essence one form of dialectical thinking that describes how opposite forces may actually be complementary, interdependent and interconnected in the natural or social world and how the two forces may give rise to each other as they interrelate to one another.

In recent years, some scholars have recommended using yin–yang theory in management research. Peter Ping Li is this theory's staunchest advocate and has published the largest number of academic papers promoting the theory. Therefore, my discussion is based on his arguments. To start with, Li makes this bold claim about the explanatory power of the theory: "In general, the lower-order value of Yin–Yang balancing is its ability to explain holistic, dynamic, and duality issues, while the higher-order value is its ability to absorb the 'either/or' logic, and allow it (other systems) to primarily manage fragmented, static, and consistent issues" (Li 2016: 70). Li (2014) illustrates his claim by the example of organizational ambidexterity, which refers to "an organization's ability to be aligned and efficient in its management of today's business demands while simultaneously being adaptive to changes in the environment" (Raisch and Birkinshaw 2008: 375). Li (2014: 329) argues that "the extant views of ambidexterity fail to account for the original insights concerning both trade-off and synergy, thus failing to adequately explain the dual nature of the exploration-exploitation link" whereas yin–yang theory can explain adequately this link.

Research interest in organizational ambidexterity was aroused by March's (1991) seminal article, proposing that exploitation and exploration are the two fundamentally different learning activities between which firms allocate their attention and resources. Exploitation is associated with activities such as "refinement, efficiency, selection, and implementation," while exploration refers to activities such as "search, variation, experimentation, and discovery" (March 1991: 102). Hence, exploitation and exploration may require different organizational strategies and structures. Levinthal and March (1993: 105) argue that an organization's long-term survival and success depend on its ability to "engage in enough exploitation to ensure the organization's current viability and to engage in enough exploration to ensure future viability." In other words, successful firms have to be ambidextrous in balancing between exploitation and exploration activities. Note that this can serve as a prescriptive statement, which is supposedly supported by empirical evidence that successful firms are often ambidextrous.

Li (2014) divides the extant views of ambidexterity into two camps, with the first camp recognizing "the trade-off between exploration and exploitation" (328) and the second one seeking "to balance exploration with exploitation by integrating the opposites into a unified system without explicitly taking their inherent trade-off into consideration" (329). For either camp, Li (2014: 328–329) laments that it is "insufficient to explain why and how concerning the coexistence of trade-off and synergy as the duality required for the balance between exploration and exploitation (March, 1991)." There is a grammatical error in the quote. I would interpret the quote as something like "insufficient to explain why and how the duality (i.e., the coexistence of trade-off and synergy) is required for the balance between exploration and exploitation (March, 1991)." First of all, March (1991) discusses neither synergy nor duality; the two terms are not even in his article. Based on the above interpretation of Li's quote, Li's criticism of the two camps makes little sense. Putting aside the complications associated with measuring constructs like trade-off, synergy, balance, exploitation and exploration, whether trade-off and synergy coexist and whether the so-called duality is required for achieving the balance are empirical questions that cannot be answered through theorizing alone. For instance, it is possible empirically that there is significant synergy between exploitation and exploration in one firm but virtually none in another, or that the synergy is present in one period of time but not in another period for the same firm. There are basically endless empirical possibilities. All Li (2014: 329) can provide is this piece of empirical evidence:

> In support of the Yin-Yang frame, the empirical evidence in a large-sample study (Li et al., 2012) shows that both exploration and exploitation are necessary for both radical and incremental innovations (in support of the holistic and duality tenets), but distinctively asymmetrical balances between exploration and exploitation are required (with exploration as the dominant for radical innovation in contrast to exploitation as the dominant for incremental innovation), and the interaction between exploration and exploitation follows an inverted U-shaped pattern as a curvilinear balance for both radical and incremental innovations.

The study of Li et al. (2012) was based on a sample of 508 Chinese firms. In addition to the issue of generalizability of results, this kind of quantitative study is not likely to test the three so-called operating mechanisms of yin–yang balancing described by Li (2014).

Another, and more serious, problem with Li's arguments is concerned with the nature of yin–yang theory. Li (1998: 837) regards the theory as "Chinese cognitive logic." Yin–yang theory "can be integrated not only with dialectical logic, but also with Aristotle's formal logic" (Li 2016: 61). If yin–yang is a logical system akin to Aristotle's formal logic, its main function is to help people make valid inferences and avoid errors in reasoning. Logic cannot be used to explain empirical phenomena such as organizational ambidexterity. Confusingly, in a more recent article, Li (2021: 55) also calls "the frame of yin–yang balancing a meta-perspective, similar to the approach to frame paradox as the meta-perspective or meta-theory." He does not seem to be aware that a logical system and a metatheory are two different things, serving different functions. Since Li (2021) does not define metatheory, I search for the definition in the paradox management literature because he claims that yin–yang theory makes a superior contribution to that domain of research – "It is obvious, among all five cognitive systems, the 'either/and' system (i.e., the meta-perspective of yin-yang balancing) is the only one that fully embraces paradox by truly accommodating and appreciating both tradeoff and synergy between true opposites in both spatial and temporal terms (at the same place at the same time)" (68). Two central figures of paradox management research, Lewis and Smith (2014: 129), adopt the following definition:

> Described as an overarching perspective (Ritzer, 1990) or paradigm (Qui et al., 2012), metatheory is unconstrained by particular contexts, variables or methods, rather delineating core elements, such as underlying assumptions and central concepts, for a scholarly community. Such a lens informs research practice, guiding advocates as they select specific variables and explicate their interrelationships within a theorized and testable model.

Further details related to the above definition can be found in Ritzer (1990), who proposes three ways of metatheorizing. The one picked up by Lewis and Smith (2014) is "the production of overarching theoretical perspectives" (Ritzer 1990: 9). These overarching perspectives (or metatheories) include philosophical perspectives such as "positivism, antipositivism, and postpositivism" (Ritzer 1990: 8).

Contrary to Li's (2014) framing of yin–yang balancing as a metatheory, his attempt to use it to explain organizational ambidexterity suggests that he actually regards yin–yang as a substantive theory, or what people refer to as "theory" in scientific research. One key difference between substantive theory and metatheory is that the former serves the function of explaining empirical phenomena but the latter does not. For example, Ritzer (1990: 8) argues that "theories like structural functionalism and exchange theory have clear roots in positivism." While structural functionalism and exchange theory are used to explain social phenomena, positivism serves as the philosophical foundation for the two theories. When scholars of the Vienna Circle created logical positivism, they did not intend to use it for explaining, say, why gas expands when heated. Ritzer (1990: 10) highlights this feature of metatheory:

> Overarching orientations have also been criticized for being framed at such an abstract level that they are of little use to practicing theorists and empiricists. Overarching perspectives must, almost by definition, be remote from the interests of practitioners.

Unfortunately, Li's discussion of yin–yang theory is nothing but confusing: it is not even clear whether yin–yang is a logical system, a metatheory or a substantive theory.[3] If he intends to use yin–yang as a substantive theory for explaining empirical phenomena, as what the scholar I met in 2018 did, he has to derive falsifiable hypotheses from yin–yang theory; otherwise, according to Popper (1959), it is not a scientific theory. If Li regards yin–yang as a metatheory, he should first stop the temptation to explain empirical phenomena. Then he may show how substantive theories may be developed based on the yin–yang perspective. If he considers yin–yang a logic system, he has to at least show how it helps improve our argumentation and inference processes over and above Aristotelian logic in scientific research.

Being ethnically Chinese, I appreciate the zeal of scholars like Li to bring Chinese philosophical concepts to management research. That said, the process has to be based on sound reasoning, which is obviously missing in the case of yin–yang theory. I agree with Li's (2016) view that Chinese philosophy has valuable wisdom, but I would also highlight that, unlike Western philosophy, Chinese philosophy has contributed little toward the development of natural science. Li (2016: 49) admits this contrast between Western and Chinese philosophies: "The West has tried to reduce and substitute complexity and uncertainty with simplicity and certainty, which has resulted in the dramatic advances in modern sciences in the West, while the East has attempted to embrace complexity and uncertainty with its own philosophical traditions." Contrary to Li's claim, the lack of modern sciences in China is not because its philosophical traditions embrace complexity and uncertainty. There are many Chinese superstition methods that claim to be able to predict the future as well as a person's fortune or even life profile. This fact indicates that people do not embrace uncertainty. Rather, the lack of modern sciences in China is because Chinese philosophy focuses on cultivation of the mind at the expense of studying nature. For instance, compared with dialectical thinking in other cultures, such as the Greek dialectic and the Hegelian dialectic, yin–yang theory "places more emphasis on a good/moral life on the basis of understanding the nature of the universe and the human world, whereas the Western dialectic strives for the ideal of truth" (Wong 2006: 246). In the Appendix, I discuss briefly the role of Chinese philosophy in the methodological development of natural science in pre-modern China. Since it has never been the intention of Chinese philosophy to shed light on natural science, it is unsurprising that scholars would find it hard to apply Chinese philosophical concepts, such as yin–yang, to a social science discipline like management. Isn't it commonsensical that a tool made for cutting trees won't do a good job in cutting hair?

CHAPTER 6

Multi-theoretical Explanation

Business phenomena are complex. For example, if one wants to know why Tesla has been so successful in the automobile industry, one can easily find more than a dozen reasons by searching the Internet. As the trend of globalization progresses, it is likely that complexity will further increase. Theories created by management researchers usually focus on certain aspects of a phenomenon only, and thus their explanatory power can be very limited. For instance, transaction cost economics (TCE) argues that managers make contracting decisions in a transaction-cost-economizing manner (Williamson 1985) while neglecting the value that can be generated by different governance modes (Zajac and Olsen 1993). Using data on the governance of 9 information services at 152 companies, Poppo and Zenger (1998) develop and test competing hypotheses from the TCE, knowledge-based, agency and measurement literatures concerning boundary choice and governance performance. Their results indicate that "a theory of the firm and a theory of boundary choice is likely to be complex, requiring integration of transaction cost, knowledge-based, and measurement reasoning" (853). Another example is that when Pouder and St. John (1996) discuss the competitive behavior of firms located in hot spots – fast-growing geographic clusters of competing firms – they identify six different theoretical perspectives, each of which focuses on different aspects of the phenomenon. There is little overlap between these perspectives in terms of what they focus on. A further example is an early experimental study of commitment in resource allocation conducted by Staw and Ross (1978). Subjects, who played the role of a decision maker in the World Bank, were asked to allocate resources to one of several courses of action. Their commitment to a previously chosen course of action was measured following a financial setback. Staw and Ross invoked six psychological theories: reinforcement, expectancy, dissonance, reactance, learned helplessness and illusion of invulnerability. Each of the six theories proposes a different mechanism underlying a model of commitment to a course of action, as elegantly summarized in their figure 1.

While there is often a need for using multiple theories in crafting explanations, there is no shortage of theories. More than a half-century ago, Koontz (1961) used the term "management theory jungle" to describe the proliferation of theories. The "jungle" surely has significantly expanded together with the growth in the number of management researchers. Concomitant with this development is the tendency that researchers work in silos, trying to protect the turf of their favorable theories (Donaldson, 1995). As Van de Ven (1989: 487) well says:

> we now have many theories competing with each other to explain a given phenomenon. Proponents for each theory engage in activities to make their theory better by increasing its internal consistency, often at the expense of limiting its scope.

Over time, boundaries between different camps of theorists become insurmountable (Aldrich 1992), resulting in the blind men and the elephant syndrome. These camps may even engage in debates concerning the explanatory power of their theories (e.g., Ghoshal and Moran 1996; Williamson 1996). In a sarcastic tone, McKinley and Mone (1998: 174) comment that "there is more consensus among organizational employees and other organizational participants about the nature of organizations than there is among organization theorists." One way to counter this unhealthly development is to encourage more studies that adopt a multi-theoretical approach, which is the focus of this chapter.

Relatively Few Multi-theoretical Studies

About two decades ago, in reviewing the research on the internationalization of smaller firms, Coviello and McAuley (1999) found that a single theoretical framework dominated the empirical studies they reviewed and concluded that in order to enhance our understanding of the phenomenon, scholars require a multi-theoretical approach. Yet, empirical studies on that topic in particular, and in the management field in general, very seldom adopt such an approach. There are at least three plausible reasons.

The first reason is related to the training of a management researcher. Although doctoral programs in North America usually require students to read major theories in management, which includes strategy, international business, entrepreneurship and organizational behavior, doctoral programs in Europe or Asia are often less extensive in this respect. Even in North

America, after students have passed their comprehensive exams, they start working on their dissertations usually based on one main theory only. Needless to say, it is a time-consuming endeavor to trace the development of a theory, understand the details of its arguments and generate sound hypotheses based on the theory. Within the time frame of finishing a dissertation while also submitting manuscripts to journals, it is much easier to master one theory than multiple theories. Economies of scale matter a great deal during this critical stage of doctoral training. Moreover, the saying "jack of all trades, master of none" often rings in students' ears. In fact, their dissertation committee chair may advise that in job interviews, they had better show that they are an expert of one theory rather than having shallow knowledge of various theories. Getting ahead in the job market is a primary concern of most doctoral students. Joining a research-oriented business school after graduation will benefit their career in the long run.

A related reason is that the tenure clock in North American business schools and some Asian and European business schools is not conducive to learning new theories or research methods. Junior scholars are under tremendous pressure to perform well in the classroom and to publish the required number of journal articles for obtaining tenure.[1] The dissertation is usually one main source of generating such journal submissions. That is to say, a single-theory researcher will remain as such during at least the first five to six years of that person's career. While this may be an astute career strategy for individuals, it hurts the management field as a whole. Having successfully overcome the tenure hurdle, scholars may not be motivated to work on other theories especially if they have already established their reputation as an expert of a particular theory. They may worry that diversifying into other theories will dilute their professional image. Some business schools prefer their faculty members to be recognized as some sort of expert.[2]

A third plausible reason is that promotion and tenure decisions are usually based on journal instead of book publications. Publishing in leading journals thus becomes more competitive over the years. Unlike books, journal articles are much shorter. Within the space constraint, authors have to clearly elaborate their arguments. Keeping other factors constant, it is usually easier to develop a coherent theoretical framework with in-depth discussions using one rather than multiple theories. Further, authors may deem it imprudent to cast the theoretical net too widely, fearing that reviewers would evaluate their manuscript as too broad and consisting of trivial results (St. John 2005). Many journal reviewers, including myself, consider incoherent arguments or trivial findings a valid reason for rejecting a manuscript. As such, authors may perceive that a multi-theoretical approach carries a higher risk.

Functions of a Multi-theoretical Approach

The above section discusses some of the difficulties faced by management researchers when adopting a multi-theoretical approach. Yet, the approach serves important functions that help advance the management field both empirically and conceptually. This section covers five such functions. The first two — capturing the essence of complex strategic decisions and providing a more complete explanation of outcomes — are specifically related to the complexity of phenomena, while the remaining three — compensating for the explanatory deficiency of a single theory, exploiting the complementarity of theories and testing conflicting explanations — are mostly concerned with the limited scope and focus of a theory.

Capturing the Essence of Complex Strategic Decisions

Most of the phenomena studied by management researchers are the result of complex decisions. When managers make such decisions, they naturally consider a variety of factors. Yet a theory is limited in scope and unable to cover most of these factors, implying that researchers have to bring in multiple theories in order to arrive at a more comprehensive explanation. For example, in their study of US executives' assessments of international joint venture (IJV) opportunities in China, Reuer et al. (2012) use four theories, namely resource-based view (RBV), TCE, real options theory (ROT) and information economics. They justify their approach by arguing that "managers are likely to draw upon decision criteria from multiple theories, although they are also boundedly rational, so what information they actually prioritize when assessing IJV partners is important to address" (312). In other words, given the multiplicity of factors that managers have to consider when evaluating IJV opportunities, adopting a single theoretical lens will likely miss some of these factors in their decision processes. Using an experimental technique known as policy capturing, they surveyed sixty top US executives to examine how executives cognitively weigh criteria from the four theories when assessing IJV opportunities in China. Their results indicate that all the four theories highlight criteria that are important for these executives' assessments of potential Chinese IJVs.

Reuer et al.'s (2012) collection of data directly from managers is an uncommon research method. A more common method used by management researchers is to use existing archival databases or compile their own databases. For instance, in their study of foreign market reentry commitment strategies, Surdu et al. (2019) constructed their database principally from two sources, namely Factiva (Dow Jones) and LexisNexis (Reed Elsevier). They make use of both organizational learning and institutional change theories to formulate their hypotheses. Their results suggest that both theories are explanatory relevant and complementary: (1) the experience of exit as a result of unsatisfactory performance affects how reentrants learn from their past experiences and subsequently adjust their reentry strategies and (2) institutional dynamics complement organizational learning considerations when firms formulate market reentry strategies.

A further example is Gaur et al.'s (2014) study of the shift from exporting to foreign direct investment (FDI) by emerging economy firms. Their sample consists of Indian firms derived from the Prowess database of the Center for Monitoring the Indian Economy. They integrate RBV and institutional theory to develop hypotheses concerning the conditions under which firms are more likely to make this shift and further internationalize their operations. Their results indicate that "both institutional and firm-specific resources, individually and jointly, help firms make the shift from exports to FDI" (18).

Providing a More Complete Explanation of Outcomes

In addition to studying phenomena related to strategic decisions, management researchers are often interested in explaining why certain outcomes of such decisions, such as profitability or survival of FDIs, occur. An excellent example is Child et al.'s (2003) survey study of Hong Kong firms managing operations in mainland China. They argue that there are two main kinds of factors affecting the performance of such cross-border units in a transition economy. The first kind consists of factors that are beyond managers' control, including underdeveloped institutions, fragmented markets, backward technologies and state interference, while the second refers to managerial action, such as selection of investment locations, transfer of resources, assignment of expatriates and development of trust with local partners. The former factors correspond to the natural selection view that performance is determined by environmental circumstances and, within that view, industrial organization (Porter 1980) and population ecology (Hannan and Freeman, 1989) are two of the most thoroughly researched theories. The latter factors constitute the core of strategic choice theory, which emphasizes the role played by managers in shaping conditions and processes both within and outside the firm (Child 1997). Child et al. also bring in contingency theory that attempts to resolve the tension between environment and managerial action as determinants of firm performance. Contingency theory is concerned with the "fit" between environmental conditions and the structures and strategies that managers adopt in their firms and proposes influence to both environment and managerial action through their congruence (Donaldson 2001).

Child et al. develop hypotheses based on each of the three theoretical perspectives, with the aim of providing a test of their relative explanatory power. Their results indicate that all three perspectives have significant explanatory power, supporting Capon et al.'s (1996) view that a more integrative framework consisting of a variety of factors is needed if business performance is to be better understood and more fully explained. There are many factors affecting a cross-border unit's performance through different causal mechanisms, which are usually considered to be theoretical building blocks (Mayntz 2004). For example, a strategy of assigning more expatriate managers to the unit will impact on performance in a way that is different from a host government policy of giving tax incentives to the unit. Since different theories include different sets of factors — such as managerial versus institutional factors — for constructing the explanans, it makes sense to employ more than one theory in order to arrive at a more complete explanation.

Another example is Watson and Hewett's (2006) survey study of intrafirm knowledge transfer. They argue that the effectiveness of intrafirm knowledge transfer depends on the reuse of existing knowledge, which is affected by two key factors: individuals' willingness to contribute their knowledge and the rate at which individuals access and reuse knowledge. Since the two factors are based on very different aspects of human psychology, Watson and Hewett apply a different theory to each. They use social exchange theory to develop a set of hypotheses concerning the frequency with which individuals contribute their valuable knowledge to the knowledge management system. For the other factor, they use expectancy theory and the technology acceptance model to generate a model that depicts how individuals access and reuse knowledge from the knowledge management system, with particular emphasis on how firms can increase the extent to which employees reuse knowledge. Watson and Hewett (2006: 146) consider their multi-theoretical model "a single, complex system, which models the flow of knowledge both *into* the system from individuals, and *out of* the system to other individuals." That is, the different theories together enable them to model the complicated outcome of intrafirm knowledge transfer.

Compensating for the Explanatory Deficiency of a Single Theory

The above two functions probably cover most of the multi-theoretical studies in the management literature. There are at least three additional functions. One is related to the limited explanatory scope of a theory. While a single theory is adequate for explaining one aspect the phenomenon, it may fail to explain another aspect. One major reason is that the plausible mechanisms related to the latter are not within the explanatory domain of the theory. For instance, Kogut (1991) develops a version of ROT that explains the formation of JVs as an option to expand in response to future market and technological developments. A JV partner possesses a real option because it is able to simultaneously limit its downside losses to an initial, limited investment amount and to position itself to expand in case circumstances turn out to be favorable. An acquisition of the venture indicates the exercise of the option, and the timing of the acquisition is triggered by a product market signal suggesting an increase in the venture's valuation.

From a real options perspective, Iriyama and Madhavan (2014) study the conditions under which an IJV partner is likely to acquire its counterpart's equity stake upon a market signal of more opportunities or sell its equity stake to the counterpart upon a market signal of fewer opportunities. Their dataset consists of longitudinal changes in equity share distributions in IJVs formed by Japanese automotive suppliers during the period of 1986–2003. A complication is that in a two-partner JV, each partner has the related real option and inter-partner equity shifts are basically a zero-sum game: one partner's equity acquisition is another partner's equity divestment (Iriyama and Madhavan 2014). ROT cannot provide an explanation for the dynamics of such equity shifts in IJVs, which are likely to be influenced by partners' characteristics. Iriyama and Madhavan incorporate the view of organizational learning theory, arguing that a partner's prior experience affects how likely the case that the multinational enterprise (MNE), or the local partner, can adjust its IJV ownership stake in its favor upon the emergence of market signals. During the initial stage of an IJV's operation, the local partner may be more capable in interpreting market signals and negotiating with its foreign counterpart favorable equity shifts. As the latter's experiential learning in the host country accumulates, it can more effectively evaluate market signals, bargain with the local partner and shift ownership in its favor. In sum, such learning-based mechanisms are outside the scope of ROT.

Another example is the study I worked on with two scholars – Bai et al. (2020) – concerning initial public offering (IPO) location choice between home country and foreign country based on the population of Chinese private issuers during the period from 2005 to 2014. The core research question is: How do CEOs' undergraduate educational experiences influence their firms' decision to list in a foreign or domestic capital market? A natural starting point is upper echelons theory. Yet, one serious limitation of the theory is that it does not take into account the fact that some experiences have longer-lasting influence on an individual than others. A unique characteristic of our study is that the time gap between a CEO's undergraduate education and his or her firm's IPO event can be more than three decades. In order to provide a mechanismic explanation that links the two events together, we bring in imprinting theory, arguing that CEOs' educational experiences have imprinting effects on their IPO location preferences. Our results indicate that CEOs with prestigious domestic degrees tend to list their firms in mainland China whereas CEOs with foreign degrees tend to list overseas (including Hong Kong).

Exploiting the Complementarity of Theories

Since theories usually focus on certain aspects of a phenomenon, there is a possibility that two theories may provide a more holistic explanation than either one in that the aspects covered by the theories are complementary to one another. For example, as mentioned at the beginning of this chapter, TCE focuses on the cost aspect of selecting governance modes. As such, the TCE logic explains the formation of JVs in terms of market failure for intermediate inputs, asset specificity and high uncertainty over specifying and monitoring performance. Putting more emphasis on the benefit side of a governance mode, RBV regards JVs as a means of exploiting and developing a firm's resources. Note that cost and benefit are complementary aspects of a governance mode. Ignoring either aspect may lead to flawed conclusions. For instance, an MNE may choose to form a JV with a local firm, instead of a wholly owned subsidiary, in a host country despite that the former option incurs significantly higher transaction costs than the latter. TCE scholars probably interpret this governance mode as inefficient and conclude that a decision error was made by the MNE. However, the local partner may be able to generate values, such as providing access to distribution channels, customer bases and connections with the host government, that are missing in the case of a wholly owned subsidiary. It is necessary to also take into account such values when evaluating the MNE's decision. In other words, both the mechanism driven by cost considerations and that driven by value considerations would affect the governance selection decision. In a conceptual essay (Tsang 2000), I exploit the complementarity of TCE and RBV. I first compare the two theories' rationales for forming JVs and then integrate both into a more holistic perspective with respect to explaining JV formation. By so doing, I produce a deeper explanation that "uncovers the inner workings of the relevant causal mechanism" (Marchionni 2008: 319–320).

Two theories may also be complementary with respect to explaining the same phenomenon by proposing different mechanisms. Unlike the case discussed above, here each theory is sufficient in explaining the phenomenon. Combining both theories shows the possibilities of different mechanisms at work. Using data from the global automotive industry from 2002 to 2008, Lampel and Giachetti (2013) study the performance of international manufacturing diversification. They identify the complementarity of TCE and RBV on this issue. Briefly stated, TCE scholars argue that internationally diversified manufacturing firms can gain competitive advantages by exploiting market imperfections (e.g., differences in national and human resources) and also gain the increased flexibility and greater bargaining power resulting from a multinational production network and from greater economies of scale and scope. However, spreading manufacturing operations over multiple countries will sooner or later lead to higher governance and transaction costs that gradually negate the advantage of internationalizing manufacturing. RBV, in contrast, suggests that firms pursuing international manufacturing diversification has the advantage of transferring their resources (e.g., engineering know-how and patented production processes) to new activities rather than selling or renting these resources on the open market. Yet, as firms continue the process of building their manufacturing operations globally, the whole value chain becomes increasingly complex. More managerial resources have to be spent on coordinating and monitoring these geographically dispersed manufacturing operations, resulting in reduced efficiency. In sum, both TCE and RBV predict that the relationship between such diversification and performance is curvilinear (i.e., inverted U-shaped) although each theory proposes a different mechanism. Lampel and Giachetti's results support the curvilinear relationship.

Testing Conflicting Explanations

The last function of a multi-theoretical approach is to resolve conflicting explanations. The causal mechanisms proposed by different theories may lead to contradicting predictions. This is not surprising since each theory proposes a somewhat distinct set of mechanisms, and some mechanisms of a theory may give rise to outcomes that are different from those derived from another theory under certain circumstances. There is a need to examine which theory's prediction is better supported in a specific context. Consider, for example, the study of international diversification and joint ownership control conducted by Chung et al. (2013). Their sample consists of Japanese subsidiaries located in the five countries directly impacted by the 1997 Asian Financial Crisis: Indonesia, Thailand, South Korea, Malaysia and the Philippines. The authors contrast between risk diversification theory (RDT) and ROT, each of which proposes distinct motivations for international diversification and for subsidiary divestment in crisis-stricken countries.

According to RDT, since countries have less than perfectly correlated economic cycles, investing in overseas operations enables an MNE to offset increased risk in one country by the potentially reduced risk in other countries, resulting in more stable corporate earnings (Rugman 1979). As an MNE's global portfolio of subsidiaries becomes more diversified, decision makers may believe the firm is close to being fully diversified internationally for maximum efficiency and be more prepared to divest its troubled subsidiaries. This divestment decision would be more easily justified for subsidiaries located in crisis-stricken countries. By contrast, ROT argues that MNEs benefit from internationally dispersed subsidiaries by having the right, but not the obligation, to shift value chain activities to countries that are more favorable when conditions in any one country become less favorable (Chung et al. 2010). In the case of competitive devaluation in crisis-stricken countries, like what happened in the Asian Financial Crisis, a globally diversified MNE can take advantage of its ability to shift value chain activities to these countries due to their exchange rate depreciation, lower factor costs and other favorable trade conditions. Thus, there is a real-options driven desire to retain ownership of overseas subsidiaries for their future flexibility. That is to say, the two theories generate opposite predictions based on the same initial conditions: RDT predicts that the greater the extent of an MNE's international diversification, the more likely the firm will divest its subsidiaries in crisis-stricken countries, whereas ROT predicts a lower likelihood of divestment. In addition to this pair of competing hypotheses, Chung et al. (2013) propose another pair with respect to the moderating effect of joint ownership control on subsidiary divestment. Their overall findings support the predictions of ROT.

Some Suggestions

Despite the empirical and conceptual functions of a multi-theoretical approach, studies based on more than one theory are still relatively few. This section offers several suggestions for not only promoting a multi-theoretical approach but also highlighting some precautions when researchers adopt the approach.

Promoting Multi-theoretical Studies

As discussed above, many management researchers are trained to be single-theory experts. If researchers are not well-versed in more than one theory, they are not likely to study phenomena through a multi-theoretical lens. Thus, there is a need to plant the seed in doctoral training so that a long-lasting imprinting effect can be made on the next generation of researchers (Marquis and Tilcsik 2013). To achieve this objective, one way of organizing doctoral seminars is that all students are required to attend the same set of seminars that cover the major areas of management research, regardless of a student's chosen major in his or her dissertation. This is the seminar arrangement of the doctoral program in my school. A key benefit is that students are not only exposed to a variety of theories but also required to have a reasonably good understanding of the theories in order to pass the seminars and the comprehensive exam that is based on the seminars. In addition to stressing multi-theoretical reasoning in doctoral seminars, dissertation committee chairs should encourage their students to practice it when conducing dissertation research. A dissertation committee may consist of experts of different theories. Like other skills, multi-theoretical reasoning can be difficult to learn but will improve with practice, as indicated by my own experience. It is a worthwhile investment by doctoral students before they embark on their academic career upon graduation.

If one is not familiar with a theory that is allegedly related to the phenomenon under study, learning the theory in a rush may not be a feasible option. Learning may also be constrained by the tenure clock. Collaboration with a scholar who is an expert of that theory is a better option. Such collaboration also helps to break down theoretical silos and stimulate integrative and holistic thinking, which benefits researchers in the long run. Researchers also become more familiar with different theories through discussion and mutual learning in the collaboration process.

As gatekeepers, journal editors and reviewers play a critical role in promoting multi-theoretical studies. Editors may explicitly state their preference for such studies. As the saying goes, "whenever there is demand, there will be supply." When reviewers evaluate a journal submission, whether conceptual or empirical, they may look out for multi-theoretical opportunities that will strengthen the theoretical foundation of the manuscript and encourage authors to think beyond the constraint of the theory proposed in the manuscript. For empirical papers, it is often an onerous task for authors to collect additional data in order to incorporate another theory into their study. That said, it is possible that they can add new variables to test an additional theory based on the data they have already collected. A caveat is that authors should by no means be coerced into adopting a multi-theoretical lens. Their intellectual autonomy and freedom should be respected (Tsang 2014a). If authors are able to provide sound reasons as to why a single theory is more appropriate in the context of their study, their view should be respected. In short, a frank and open-minded communication between editors, reviewers and authors is needed to sort out the matter.

Reconciling Inconsistent Core Assumptions

When researchers consider including more than one theory in their study, they should thoroughly understand not only each theory's proposed causal mechanism related to the phenomenon under investigation but also its core assumptions. Every management theory has some core assumptions of how people behave. Such behavioral assumptions are about the major causal relationships postulated by a theory (Mäki 2000) and are key elements of the mechanismic explanations offered by the theory (Tsang 2006b). For instance, a core behavioral assumption of TCE is opportunism, defined as "self-interest seeking with guile" (Williamson 1975: 6). The degree of opportunism manifested by the parties concerned affects the transaction costs associated with a governance mode, which in turn influence the choice of a governance arrangement (Wathne and Heide 2000).

When researchers attempt to use more than one theory in constructing their arguments, they first have to examine whether any of the theories have conflicting core assumptions. For instance, the agency and stakeholder views of the firm have significant differences along a number of dimensions, as shown in figures 1 and 2 of Shankman (1999). In particular, managers are perceived by agency theory as egoistic and morally hazardous but by stakeholder theory as enlightened self-interested with an objective of balancing the interests of all major stakeholders. Researchers who attempt to include these two theories in a single study will face an uphill task of reconciling their conflicting assumptions. They may have to argue, for example, that managers behave in accordance with agency theory in certain contexts and with stakeholder theory in others. Although this is a real possibility given the complexity of human psychology (Sternberg and Ben-Zeev 2001), how to put forward a convincing argument is a different matter. A similar caution applies to, say, TCE and stakeholder theory because like agency theory, the former has a far less charitable assumption about human nature than the latter. Unless one is an expert of multi-theoretical reasoning, this kind of theory combination had better be avoided by novices.

Instead of integrating theories that have conflicting core assumptions to explain a phenomenon, a better method may be to consider the explanatory power of each theory separately. For example, Ryan and Schneider (2003) examine the implications of the escalation in institutional investor power and heterogeneity for agency theory and stakeholder theory. They discuss the merits and limitations of each theory and summarize their analysis as follows:

> The simplicity of agency theory, although a virtue in terms of predictive power, is a weakness in terms of descriptive power. Our analysis, although it adds complexity to the theory, also increases its ability to account for real events facing practicing managers. Similarly, our analysis of stakeholder theory demonstrates its current lack of specificity. We propose that stakeholder theorists strengthen the theory by taking a deep view of stakeholder groups. (422)

Ryan and Schneider then briefly propose some future research opportunities concerning how escalated institutional investor power and heterogeneity affects the application of both theories.

Addressing Levels Issues

Business phenomena are multilevel, with individuals working in teams, teams working within organizations and organizations operating within an industry environment, which in turn is part of an even larger socio-political context of a country. International business studies also investigate phenomena within or across clusters of countries, such as Ronen and Shenkar's (1985) classification of eight clusters of culturally similar countries. The topic of levels issues is complicated and beyond the scope of this chapter (see Rousseau 1985; Klein et al. 1994; St. John 2005 for details). Suffice it to say, researchers adopting a multi-theoretical approach are more likely to encounter levels issues than those working with single theories because different theories aim at explaining phenomena at different levels. While some multi-theoretical studies manage to include theories, such as TCE and RBV (Tsang 2000) and RDT and ROT (Chung et al. 2013), which are at the same level, others do not.

When discussing mixed-level research, it is important to distinguish between three different levels, namely level of theory, level of measurement and level of statistical analysis. Level of theory refers to the target (e.g., individual, group, organization, country) that a researcher intends to describe or explain (Klein et al. 1994), and is "the level to which generalizations are made" (Rousseau 1985: 4). Level of measurement refers to the actual source of the data and "the unit to which data are directly attached" (Rousseau 1985: 4), such as psychological data being at the individual level and corporate cultural data at the firm level. Lastly, level of statistical analysis refers to the treatment of the data when statistical procedures are applied.

Although the definition of each of the three levels sounds clear and straightforward, ambiguities do arise occasionally. For example, while there is consensus that cultural distance is a country level construct, there are debates about the level of a closely related construct – psychic distance. Sousa and Bradley (2006: 51) argue that "it is the individual's perception of the differences between the home country and the foreign country that shapes the psychic distance concept." Different members of the same organization can perceive different degrees of psychic distance with respect to the same foreign country. Accordingly, psychic distance is an individual level construct and should be measured as such by, for example, cognitive mapping (Stöttinger and Schlegelmilch 1998). This argument has merit in that many management decisions associated with psychic distance, such as the decision to export to or set up an operation in a certain foreign country, are made based on the manager's perception at the moment of decision making (Dow and Karunaratna 2006). But there are thorny methodological difficulties, such as surveying a manager's perception immediately prior to the decision in question. To overcome these difficulties, Dow and Karunaratna (2006) propose to split psychic distance into a sequence of related macro-level factors, which are measured at the country level and are called "psychic distance stimuli." Examples of stimuli include culture, language, education and religion. The relationship between the two conceptualizations of psychic distance is that psychic distance stimuli "create the climate within which a manager's cognitive processes operate, and therefore frame the conditions within which managers form their perceptions and make their decisions" (Dow and Karunaratna 2006: 581). The choice between the two conceptualizations depends on whether the objective is to explain the behavior of a specific firm, a population of firms within a country or populations of firms in different countries.

Problems related to levels issues arise when any pair of the three levels is incongruent. In particular, difficulties often occur because of the misalignment between the theoretical level of a construct and the level that it is measured (St. John 2005). Consider, for instance, Child et al.'s (2003) study discussed above. The three theoretical perspectives are at the individual and environmental levels whereas the authors collected all their data through a survey of business executives. There is an inconsistency in terms of the levels of theories and the level of measurement. As Child et al. (2003: 253) acknowledge, "the measurement of the variables has been based on executives' perceptions." They admit this inconsistency as a major limitation of their study. A better alternative is that they supplement their survey data with objective measures of some environmental variables, such as market attractiveness, intensity of competition and legal support. The latter data should be available at the provincial or city level. This step will also address the problem of common method variance arising from the fact that each questionnaire was answered by only one representative of a sample firm. In contrast, Surdu et al.'s (2019) study of foreign market re-entry commitment strategies addresses levels issues more appropriately. The study employs organizational learning and institutional change theories, the former being at the firm level and the latter at the country level. They take host market-specific experience as an indicator of organizational learning and measure it at the firm level by the number of years the focal firm operated in the specific host market between initial entry and market exit. As to host country institutional change, they use the Economic Freedom of the World Index, which derives an overall institutional score for each of the approximately 100 nations and territories and measure institutional change by the difference of the indexes at $t - 1$ of exit and $t - 1$ of reentry. Therefore, each of the two variables is measured at the proper level.

Among the three levels, level of theory is more fundamental and determines the other two. For instance, if psychic distance is conceptualized as managerial perceptions that affect decisions, then the construct has to be operationalized at the individual level. This in turn determines the data collection and analysis procedures. The key is to align the three levels and check for any incongruence. When a study involves more than one theory, this step of alignment has to be conducted for each theory separately.

Beware of Ockham's Razor

Despite the valuable functions of a multi-theoretical approach, researchers should beware of the principle of parsimony, aka "Ockham's razor," which is often considered an important standard for judging the quality of a theory. Basically, parsimony is a theoretical virtue. Ockham's razor can be used not only in academic research but also in our daily lives, especially during the fast changing Covid-19 pandemic:

> As the Delta variant continues to sweep through countries around the world, including countries like Australia that were once poster children for a zero-COVID strategy, it's understandable that anxiety is on the rise. Is vaccine effectiveness waning so fast that we'll all need booster shots? Is Delta more dangerous to younger people? Do we all need to go back into lockdown? And the flip side to anxiety is fatalism: If vaccine effectiveness fades so fast, why bother getting the shot in the first place? (Millman 2021)

After analyzing the data, Millman (2021) argues that a simple and adequate explanation for the surge of infection cases is that the Delta variant is much more contagious than either Alpha or the original variant of Covid. It is not necessary to bring in new postulates such as Delta being vastly more dangerous and the vaccines not working well against it.

Barnes (2000) distinguishes between two different but interrelated principles of parsimony: the anti-quantity principle (AQP) and the anti-superfluity principle (ASP). The AQP stipulates that theorists "posit as few theoretical components as possible in the construction of explanations of phenomena" while the ASP advises theorists to "avoid positing superfluous components – components which are not required for the purpose of explaining the relevant data" (354). The two principles seem to be the same, but they are not:

> The two principles are clearly not equivalent: consider two competing theories, *A* and *B*, which both fit the relevant data equally well. Theory *A*

contains more components than B, and is thus less parsimonious than B by the lights of the AQP. But while A contains no components that are not required (within A) to explain the data, theory B posits one or more superfluous components – i.e., one or more components which could be deleted from B without impairing B's ability to explain the data. Thus B is less parsimoinious than A by the ASP.[3] (Barnes 2000: 354)

Although Ockham's razor is usually used to evaluate competing theories, it sheds light on multi-theoretical studies. According to the two principles of parsimony, when including more than one theory in a single study, researchers should try to minimize the number of theories used to arrive at an adequate explanation and to make sure that none of the theories are superfluous in terms of explaining their data.

Lampel and Giachetti's (2013) study is problematic in this respect. As discussed, they draw on both TCE and RBV to derive the main hypothesis about the curvilinear relationship between manufacturing diversification and firm performance and arrive at a conclusion that both theories predict an inverted U-shaped relationship. They also derive two hypotheses about the moderating effects of product diversification and co-location of manufacturing and sales activities in the same geographic market based on the two theories. By so doing, they provide richer conceptual arguments proposing multiple causal mechanisms. However, a serious problem is that the empirical part of their study does not test any of these mechanisms. They used archival data that consist of the number of vehicles produced and sold in fifty-eight countries by thirty-eight automakers with headquarters in fifteen different countries from 2002 to 2008. Their statistical analysis is based on a reduced model format (see Chapter 7), excluding the variables related to the causal mechanisms that link the independent variables and the dependent variable together. It serves little purpose for them to use both theories to develop their hypotheses because none of the mechanisms proposed by either theory are tested in the empirical part. Since either theory is good enough to explain their data and using both does not improve their empirical results, either of the two theories is superfluous, violating the ASP. One way they may show the necessity of using both theories is that they adopt a structural model (see Chapter 7) in their empirical part by adding two sets of variables: one directly related to TCE and the other directly related to RBV. Then they show that including both sets in their statistical analysis generates better results in terms of, say, variance explained or model fitting than just including either set. For instance, Child et al. (2003) clearly show in their table 4 that adding each of the three theoretical perspectives to their analysis significantly increases the variance explained, providing a sound empirical justification for using all three perspectives.

In conclusion, the complexity of business phenomena and the limited scope of a management theory indicate the potential of multi-theoretical approaches for offering more comprehensive explanations of these phenomena. However, multi-theoretical studies are relatively few due to deficient doctoral training, individual career considerations and constraints of the journal review process. This is an unfortunate situation because multi-theoretical approaches have at least five useful functions that together will significantly advance management research. Needless to say, multi-theoretical reasoning is not easy and is often a challenging task.

CHAPTER 7

Research Methods

The explanation of a phenomenon depends on the nature of the data collected on the phenomenon and the analysis of the collected data. How data are collected and analyzed in turn depends on the research method. In other words, research methods have a crucial impact on the nature and quality of an explanation. Since in the management field alone there exists already a huge literature on research method, my discussion in this chapter will focus on the topic of explanation.

To start with, the following view that qualitative and quantitative methods – the two major categories of research method – play different explanatory roles seems to have persisted for decades:

> Until recently, the dominant view was that field studies should busy themselves with description and leave the explanations to people with large quantitative data bases. Or perhaps field researchers, as is now widely believed, can provide "exploratory" explanations – which still need to be quantitatively verified. (Miles and Huberman 1984: 132)

This view, which is what Maxwell (2004: 8) calls "a hierarchical prioritizing of quantitative and experimental methods for explanatory purposes," is simplistic. As the following discussions indicate, qualitative and quantitative methods can produce explanations that are different in nature without implying that one method must have greater explanatory power than the other.

It is imperative to clarify the meaning of qualitative research, as the term has been used loosely in the literature and means different things to different people. Here, qualitative research means "any kind of research that produces findings not arrived at by means of statistical procedures or other means of quantification" (Strauss and Corbin 1990: 17); it is research that generates findings from investigating real-world settings where the phenomenon of interest unfolds naturally (Patton 2002). The emphasis is on the absence of quantitative analysis, except simple statistical tabulation. In contrast, quantitative research refers to studies that focus on quantitative analysis of data, although such studies may also contain, as supplementary information, some qualitative data, such as interviews with managers.

Structural versus Reduced Models

A good example demonstrating the relationship between research methods and explanation is the core behavioral assumption of transaction cost economics (TCE) – opportunism. Many empirical studies on TCE are based on quantitative data. As elaborated later in this chapter, these studies may not be able to directly examine opportunism, which is used in formulating some of the hypotheses. For instance, Coff's (2003) study exploring the implications of knowledge intensity in the market for corporate control emphasized the strategic importance of knowledge-based assets, with a focus on opportunism. Following a multi-theoretical approach (discussed in Chapter 6), he compared the explanatory power of TCE versus knowledge-based theory as the R&D intensity of the target firm in a merger and acquisition (M&A) increased. The opportunistic behavior of managers in the target firm is the conceptual backbone of his hypothesis stating, "as R&D intensity increases, knowledge management dilemmas and the threat of opportunism rise in concert, since information asymmetries enable opportunistic behavior" (75). However, opportunism was not measured. In fact, even if he wanted to measure it, he couldn't because the Securities Data Corporation's M&A database that he used would not have such data.

In order to study the effects of opportunism directly, other research methods, such as case study, are needed, as illustrated by Pathak et al.'s (2020) recent study of value co-creation and value co-destruction in the business-to-business (B2B) context. Pathak et al. adopted an in-depth case study–based approach using data triangulation, where multiple sources of information (interviews, conference audio recordings and documents) were collected from the case organization (a vendor) and its service ecosystem partners in the information and communications technology sector. The partners included in the study were distributors, channel partners, competitors and customers. The results revealed that all actors in the vendor's ecosystem displayed opportunistic behavior, which hurt partner relationships and diminished co-created value. The impact of actors' opportunism on value co-destruction can be categorized under three key themes: termination of relationship, conflict and business liquidation. Each of the first two themes consists of sub-themes, which are actually mechanisms linking actors' opportunism with the outcome of value co-destruction. For instance, a sub-theme of termination of relationship is misuse of resources. In the ecosystem, actors' capabilities in the form of resources were a fundamental building block for value co-creation. When actors adopted self-promoting strategies, this led to misuse of resources and thus value co-destruction. Pathak et al. list several quotes from their interviews to support each theme or sub-theme in their table 3. A quote related to misuse of resources is: "There have been occasions where those [marketing] funds have been misused. Sometimes that's just gone directly to the company's bottom line as a way of making extra profit on a deal or over the course of the year." In short, Pathak et al.'s (2020) study provides a better mechanismic explanation of the effects of opportunism than Coff's (2003) because the former shows directly the mechanisms through which these effects take place whereas the latter only describes the mechanisms in the hypothesis development section. A major difference between the two studies is that they are based on different models of empirical analysis.

There is a distinction between structural and reduced models in econometrics (Chow 1983; Johnston 1991). Structural models consist of formulas that represent the relation of every dependent variable to its independent variables on various levels, whereas reduced models exhibit the net or overall relation between the dependent variable and the ultimate independent variables. Consider a structural model of the form

$$z = f(x, y) \qquad (1a)$$

where

$$x = g(u), \text{ and } y = h(v) \qquad (1b)$$

Substituting Equations 1b into Equation 1a results in the corresponding reduced model

$$z = \varphi(u, v) \qquad (2)$$

The variables x, y, z, u and v represent constructs — such as firm performance, employee morale and entrepreneurial orientation — in the empirical domain. There are two key methodological differences between the two models (Bunge 1997). First, Equations 1b "explain" (in the sense of computing) the intermediary variables x and y but Equation 2 does not even contain these variables. That is to say, the reduced model is simpler yet shallower than the structural model because it skips one level of empirical relation, represented by x and y. In other cases, the structural model may consist of more than two levels. Second, the reduced model can be derived from the structural model but not the other way round for the simple reason that the task of constructing the structural model based on the reduced model is an inverse problem with an indefinite number of solutions. There are many empirically possible structural models corresponding to one reduced model.

Bunge (1997: 430) calls the reduced model "the black box model" and offers this advice to researchers: "apply your talent to building structural models, leaving the reduced ones to computer-aided curve fitting." Referring to quantitative studies in general, Hedström and Swedberg (1998: 7) provide a cautionary note: "we are not satisfied with merely establishing systematic covariation between variables or events; a satisfactory explanation requires that we are also able to specify the social 'cogs and wheels.'" Similarly, Davis and Marquis (2005: 341) argue that "the quality of explanation is enhanced by an explicit focus on the cogs and wheels behind the regression coefficients." While these scholars' focus on specifying the mechanism in question is commendable, they have to distinguish between reduced- and structural-model studies because the latter provide a more direct test of the mechanisms (or cogs and wheels) related to the covariation between independent and dependent variables.

Returning to Coff's (2003) study, his first hypothesis is: "The likelihood that targets will grant lockup agreements increases with target R&D intensity" (77). The core of his argument is that in an M&A bidding war, the highest bidder may not be the one managers in the target firm prefer, although shareholders of the target firm usually welcome the purchase price proposed by such a bidder. Therefore, there is a conflict of interest between target managers and shareholders. Target managers may signal their preference for avoiding a bidding war by granting a lockup agreement with their favored bidder. Since information asymmetry between bidders and target managers increases with R&D intensity of the target firm, it is more likely that target managers act opportunistically:

> At the extreme, managers may threaten that they and the rest of the firm's core assets will quit rather than be acquired. This can be a very effective "scorched earth" defense – a hostile bidder is unlikely to realize value if the primary assets cannot be transferred. As such, the signal that management will not cooperate with other bidders may carry more weight and may be more effective at deterring rival bidders. (Coff 2003: 77)

In other words, when R&D intensity is high, a lockup agreement becomes more effective in deterring bidders that target managers do not prefer and thus is more likely to be used by these managers. Coff's argument underlying the first hypothesis describes a structural model with a mechanism that links R&D intensity and the likelihood of granting lockup agreements through opportunistic behavior of target managers. However, what he actually tested empirically is a reduced model consisting of variables at the two ends of the mechanism: R&D intensity and likelihood of lockup agreements. "Correlation is not the same as causation; statistical technique, alone, does not make the connection" (Freedman 1991: 301).[1] Even if a statistical correlation is found to hold between these two variables, there are possible mechanisms other than the one proposed by Coff that connect the variables together, including mechanisms that involve back-door paths (see Chapter 2). As discussed above, constructing a structural model based on a reduced model is an inverse problem with an indefinite number of solutions. Thus, Coff's proposed explanation has not been tested directly. The distinction between reduced and structural models is not applicable to Pathak et al.'s (2020) case study; the study does, however, present evidence for the existence of their proposed mechanisms in their case company.

While Coff's (2003) study uses quantitative data, this does not imply that all quantitative studies must be of the reduced-model type. This depends on how data are collected. For instance, Judge and Dooley (2006) analyzed factors associated with opportunistic behavior and strategic alliance performance, collecting data from the US healthcare industry through a questionnaire survey. They measured opportunistic behavior directly via four questionnaire items, one of which was "The actions of their TMT are fully consonant with executing strategic decisions of the alliance" (31). This item was about the respondent's assessment of the opportunistic behavior displayed by the top management team (TMT) of the strategic alliance partner. Opportunistic behavior was at the center of Judge and Dooley's theoretical model (shown in their figure 1) that was tested empirically. As such, the mechanisms associated with opportunistic behavior were tested more directly by Judge and Dooley (2006) than by Coff (2003).

Quantitative studies can also be in the form of experiments. For instance, using an experimental research method, Pilling et al. (1994) asked midlevel purchasing personnel from aerospace, electronics and defense contracting firms to examine the effects of different levels of asset specificity, uncertainty and frequency on transaction costs and relational closeness in the context of manufacturer-supplier relationships. They used TCE reasoning to formulate hypotheses about the costs of guarding against opportunism, which are regarded as one type of transaction cost.

They also hypothesized the impact of transaction costs on the preference for relational governance. Similar to Judge and Dooley's (2006) survey study, Pilling et al.'s (1994: 248) experiment sheds light on the effects of opportunism directly: "the transaction cost of guarding against opportunistic behavior had a negative impact on both relationship focus and willingness to share benefits and burdens." This discussion shows that there is a variety of quantitative studies and that we have to read a study before we can conclude whether its empirical analysis is based on a structural or a reduced model.

Post Hoc Hypothesizing

The practice of post hoc hypothesizing by quantitative researchers has been a topic of discussion in recent times. Most quantitative studies published in management journals are presumed to follow the method of null hypothesis statistical testing (NHST) – to test a hypothesis (and its underlying theory) by checking whether its null counterpart can be rejected at a certain level of significance (usually $p < 0.05$). A typical approach to these studies is for authors to first conduct a literature review and then derive several hypotheses from one or more theories. The next section describes the sample, the data collection method and the statistical modeling, followed by the presentation of results. The paper then ends with a discussion of the contributions and limitations of the study and points to future research directions. In terms of the timing of the steps, the order of presentation indicates that hypotheses are formulated before data are collected. However, this positivist hypothetico-deductive approach promoted by Hempel (1965) often does not reflect actual practice.

Bettis (2012) recounts an incident during his visit to a top twenty-five business school in which he asked a second-year doctoral student, "So what are you studying?":

> His reply of "I look for asterisks" momentarily confused me. He proceeded to tell me how as a research assistant under the direction of two senior faculty members he searched a couple of large databases for potentially interesting regression models within a general topical area with "asterisks" (10% or better significance levels) on some variables. When such models were found, he helped his mentors propose theories and hypotheses on the basis of which the "asterisks" could be explained. (108–109)

The student's reply that confused Bettis indicates the practice of what Kerr (1998) labels as "HARKing" (Hypothesizing After the Results are Known).

The practice presents "post hoc hypotheses in a research report as if they were, in fact, a priori hypotheses" (Kerr 1998: 197). The student focused on finding statistically significant relationships because journals tend to accept papers in which hypotheses are supported (i.e., the "file drawer problem," see Rosenthal 1979). The student's mentioning of "potentially interesting regression models" reflects the management field's obsession with interestingness (see Chapter 1).

Instead of formulating hypotheses *before* data collection and analysis, HARKing practitioners actually develop hypotheses *after* they have obtained the results of data analysis; that is, they reverse the order of the steps presented in their papers. HARKing is more common among studies using archival databases, which may be publicly available or compiled by researchers themselves, than those using questionnaire surveys or experiments. This is because researchers have to have some sort of hypothesis and related variables in mind when they design their questionnaires or experiments. HARKing is practiced to a varying extent by many researchers: "primary-level and meta-analysis estimates based on self-reports indicate that 30–40% of researchers engage in HARKing" (Aguinis et al. 2017: 657). The doctoral student's reply to Bettis's question is a more extreme form of HARKing. Rather than going on a "fishing expedition," researchers often have some rough idea of several plausible relationships between key variables. They focus on analyzing such relationships and adjust their analysis as they progress.

It is impossible for readers to know for certain whether or not the authors of a research paper engaged in HARKing because readers do not have knowledge of either when the hypotheses were formulated or when the data were collected and analyzed; only the authors themselves have this knowledge. Here, I share my own HARKing experience in developing the study — Bai et al. (2020) — that I worked with two scholars discussed in Chapter 6. The first two hypotheses are the base hypotheses of our study:

> Hypothesis 1. CEOs who have prestigious Chinese degrees are more likely to list their firms in China than CEOs who do not have such degrees.

> Hypothesis 2. CEOs who have foreign degrees are more likely to list their firms in foreign markets than CEOs who do not have such degrees.

These two hypotheses were not formulated before we started compiling the dataset from initial public offering (IPO) prospectuses and other sources. That said, for a long time we observed the phenomenon that the IPOs of some private Chinese firms were launched inside mainland China while others were launched outside (including in Hong Kong). We were interested in studying the key factors affecting the listing decision. Upper echelons theory suggested that the CEO should be a key figure in the decision-making process.

We noticed that some of the CEOs of Chinese firms received their undergraduate education inside mainland China while others received their education outside of that country. We suspected that this could be a key factor affecting the listing decision. For CEOs who graduated from, say, prestigious Chinese universities, such as Peking, Tsinghua and Fudan, they would probably have cultivated valuable social ties – guanxi (關係) – because of their undergraduate education. Given the institutional environment in China, such guanxi could help them get through the IPO approval process (Tsang 1998). Thus, these CEOs might like to exploit this competitive edge and choose to list their firms on the stock exchange of Shanghai or Shenzhen. In contrast, CEOs who received their undergraduate education outside mainland China would probably have a higher level of English proficiency and be more familiar with how a capitalist economy works. Thus, they might be more willing to take on the challenges associated with foreign listing, such as being questioned by journalists and potential investors during IPO roadshows. Luckily, our hunch turned out to be supported strongly by the data, to an extent much greater than we expected. We then formulated the argument underlying the first two hypotheses, which in effect explains our findings. We also revised our argument substantially during the journal review process. Speaking frankly, if our hunch had been rejected by the data, we would not have developed the hypotheses, simply because of the "file drawer problem." I believe this study represents an approach to HARKing that is followed rather commonly by quantitative researchers, while the doctoral student's reply mentioned above refers to a more extreme approach.

In addition to the different time ordering of hypothesis development and data analysis, another key difference between NHST and HARKing, which has been largely neglected by the HARKing literature, is the intellectual activities that each represents. Using mostly deductive reasoning, NHST practitioners derive hypotheses from one or more theories with the intention of testing the hypotheses using empirical data. As such, they face uncertainty concerning the results of hypothesis testing; the hypotheses may or may not be supported by the data. That is to say, the *prediction* embedded in a hypothesis may be rejected. In contrast, employing one or more theories, HARKing practitioners explain statistically significant relationships written in the form of hypotheses without citing their results as supporting evidence. Unlike their NHST peers, HARKing practitioners face no uncertainty. As mentioned above concerning Bai et al. (2020), the argument underlying the first two hypotheses is in fact an *explanation* of the phenomenon represented by the hypotheses.

Needless to say, HARKing is a questionable research practice, although there is disagreement concerning the extent to which the practice is detrimental to the progress of management research (e.g., Aguinis et al. 2017; Hollenbeck and Wright 2017; Rubin 2022). At the very least, HARKing practitioners present their post hoc hypotheses as if they were a priori hypotheses, violating the norm of academic honesty. Yet HARKing practitioners alone should not be blamed for this "crime" because few journals offer them the channel to report honestly their research procedures. Virtually all journals follow a structural format based on NHST. Hence, journal editors should share the blame.

Since related significant statistical relationships identified in a study may indicate the presence of a phenomenon, such findings call for an explanation. The situation is similar to case study researchers discovering new phenomena in their fieldwork (see my discovery of organizational unlearning in the "A Multi-method Approach" section below). Putting aside the issue of misrepresenting an explanation as a hypothesis, HARKing may not be as bad as it appears, at least from an explanatory point of view. What *is* really bad is the lack of replications, despite Tsang and Kwan's (1999) explanation more than two decades ago of why replications are critical for the development of the management discipline.

Replication

When HARKing practitioners develop hypotheses based on their findings, they engage in accommodation (Lipton 1991). In the process, they are motivated to force their arguments to make the accommodation. Sometimes a theory seems so vague and elastic that it can be fudged to accommodate even irrelevant observations. Thus, an explanation derived from HARKing may be a fudged one and so is not likely to be robust. The best way to check whether an explanation and its associated findings are valid in another context is to replicate the study. A replication avoids all the shortcomings of HARKing because its hypotheses, which are the hypotheses of the original study, preexist data collection and analysis.

To illustrate some of the functions of replication, I discuss briefly here two of the replications I conducted. The original study associated with the first replication is Barkema and Vermeulen's (1998) investigation, based on a dataset from 1966 to 1994 compiled by the authors, of international expansion by Dutch firms. The study went on to win the Academy of Management Journal Best Article Award and so is supposedly an exemplary quantitative study. Junichi Yamanoi and I replicated the study using a comparable dataset for Singapore firms from 1980 to 2000 (see Tsang and Yamanoi 2016). We found that Barkema and Vermeulen misinterpreted their regression coefficients for hypothesis testing and that thus only two of their four hypotheses were actually tested. Of these two hypotheses, one was supported in neither their study nor ours and the other was supported in their study but not ours. As to the remaining two hypotheses that were not tested in their study, we found only partial support for one of them. In sum, although Barkema and Vermeulen *claimed* that all four hypotheses were supported, only one was (partially) supported in our replication.

The discrepancy in the results from testing the original study's Hypothesis 3, which is the most complicated hypothesis among the four in terms of the relationship depicted among the variables concerned, motivated me to search for an explanation for the discrepancy. In addition to the usual steps of examining sample characteristics along with differences in measurement and data analysis, I studied Barkema and Vermeulen's argument for justifying that hypothesis and discovered possible signs of HARKing. For the sake of discussion, let us assume that the data from both the original study and our replication had few errors, that the methods of measurement and analysis were basically sound and that the results were reported accurately. Given these assumptions, one may ask: Why was Hypothesis 3 not supported in the replication? In order to answer that question, I first answer a related one: Why was Hypothesis 3 supported in the original study? HARKing is one plausible answer to the latter question.[2] As mentioned above, only the authors of a research paper know whether HARKing was involved in the research process. Yet it is possible to pick up some clues from reading the paper's hypothesis development section carefully. I present below a few clues in Barkema and Vermeulen's (1998) arguments for their hypotheses. I stress here that the discussion of Barkema and Vermeulen's probable act of HARKing is a purely academic endeavor and should by no means be perceived as a personal attack. As I admit above, I have also engaged in what could be described as HARKing at some points in my career.

When searching for signs of HARKing in a paper, one must bear in mind the question: Does a hypothesis follow naturally from the literature that existed at the time the paper was written? The answer is likely "no" for Hypothesis 3, which is the most complicated hypothesis. It is unlikely that one can derive the complicated relationship among variables based on even the current literature, let alone the literature of the late 1990s, without any knowledge of the related findings. I quote verbatim below Barkema and Vermeulen's (1998: 11) complete discussion preceding the hypothesis:

> The above theory implies that intermediately product-diversified firms have relatively strong technological capabilities because they benefit from multiple learning opportunities while staying within cognitive and organizational limits on information sharing between divisions and between divisions and headquarters (cf. Hitt et al., 1994; Tallman & Li, 1996). Such firms are thus more likely than both single-business firms and highly product-diversified firms to set up new ventures in foreign countries.
>
> However, our reasoning also suggests that intermediately product-diversified firms have relatively little cognitive capacity left with which to handle the further complexities of increasing multinational diversity. In contrast, single-business firms and the rather independent divisions of highly product-diversified firms (Hitt et al., 1994) are less complex and can thus better benefit from expansions into a number of countries (cf. Kim, Hwang, & Burgers, 1989; Tallman & Li, 1996): their specific organizational configuration makes them more likely to benefit from the learning opportunities that multinational diversity offers. In sum, firms with either very low or very high product diversity may reap learning benefits beyond the point where they occur for intermediately diversified firms that already combine several divisions and therefore reach their organizational limits more quickly.
>
> Consequently, we expected multinational diversity to have a relatively strong positive effect on the technological capabilities of single-business firms and on highly product-diversified firms and, thus, on their propensity to set up new ventures in foreign countries. That is, we expected the curvilinear relationship between product diversity and the propensity to start new ventures (an inverted U-shape) to become weaker (cf. Tallman & Li, 1996) at higher levels of multinational diversity.

The first and the last paragraphs are elaborated restatements of Hypotheses 2 and 3, respectively, and add little substance to the argument for the latter hypothesis. The essence of Barkema and Vermeulen's argument is contained in the middle paragraph, which consists of three sentences. Contrary to their claim, the first sentence does not follow from the reasoning in either the first paragraph or the preceding discussion. It is unclear why intermediately product-diversified firms are constrained in their cognitive capacities to handle the further complexities of increasing multinational diversity. The second sentence concerning single-business firms and highly product-diversified firms contradicts their own arguments elsewhere. According to their first core argument mentioned earlier, learning is enhanced by diversity in experience. Single-business firms are therefore generally not good at learning, due to their homogeneous experience of operating mostly within one industry. As to highly product-diversified firms, the multidivisional structure adopted by these firms "constrains learning and innovation" (Barkema and Vermeulen 1998: 11). Barkema and Vermeulen's last sentence mainly recapitulates their argument, adding virtually no new information. Finally, their descriptions in the first two paragraphs of intermediately product-diversified firms' learning capabilities are confusing, if not self-contradictory. On the one hand, these firms "benefit from multiple learning opportunities while staying within cognitive and organizational limits on information sharing between divisions and between divisions and headquarters" (first paragraph). On the other hand, these firms "already combine several divisions and therefore reach their organizational limits more quickly" (second paragraph). To summarize, it is more reasonable to believe that Barkema and Vermeulen (1998) worked out their argument in order to fit their findings than to believe that they first proposed an argument that their subsequent findings supported.

Returning to the first question posed above, why was Hypothesis 3 not supported in the replication? The signs of HARKing identified in the original study suggest that the authors fudged their hypothesis (and the associated argument) in order to accommodate their findings. It is therefore not surprising that the hypothesis was not supported in our study; the opposite (i.e., that our study supported the hypothesis) would actually be surprising because it was likely that Barkema and Vermeulen's findings with respect to the hypothesis were idiosyncratic to their sample of Dutch firms. Further replications are clearly needed in order to test the conjecture of idiosyncrasy.

This replication suggests that there will be a much higher chance of discovering errors made by the authors of a study when the study is scrutinized for the purpose of replication than when the study is read casually. While this outcome sounds commonsensical, it highlights the error identification function of replication that has been neglected by the replication literature. A side effect of this function is that if replication is conducted regularly, management researchers will be under greater pressure to ensure that their data analysis and interpretation of results are error-free. This, in turn, will improve the quality of empirical studies on which future research is based.

My second replication repeated Bettman and Weitz's (1983) study of self-serving attributions (see Tsang 2002). To compile their dataset,

Bettman and Weitz conducted a content analysis of letters to shareholders in US corporate annual reports in 1972 and 1974. Their study tested the theory of self-serving bias in the attribution of causality – individuals tend to attribute favorable results to internal causes and to attribute unfavorable results to external causes. I applied Bettman and Weitz's coding method to letters to shareholders in the 1985 and 1994 annual reports of listed companies in Singapore and used the same statistical analysis in the replication. In contrast to the first replication (of Barkema and Vermeulen's study), this one managed to replicate the hypothesis testing results for six of the eight hypotheses. The general self-serving pattern of attributions found in Bettman and Weitz's original study was also identified in my replication. More specifically, four of the six hypotheses were supported in both studies.

Let's assume that Bettman and Weitz developed those four hypotheses largely through HARKing and thus the theoretical arguments underlying the hypotheses were obtained by accommodation. When my replication generated results that supported the four hypotheses, this was a case of successful prediction. Lipton (1991: 133) argues eloquently that "a theory deserves more inductive credit when data are predicted than when they are accommodated." As discussed, when data need to be accommodated, researchers are motivated to fudge a theoretical argument to make the accommodation. That is, by looking at the data, researchers know exactly the result that the argument has to support and so they might do whatever it takes to arrive at the argument. With special clauses incorporated to deal with particular accommodations, the argument may become more like an arbitrary conjunction, such as Barkema and Vermeulen's (1998) Hypothesis 3, than a unified explanation. A theoretical argument that is compatible with most of the background beliefs of a discipline is more credible than one that contradicts many of these beliefs. The need for accommodation may force researchers to construct an argument that fits poorly into the background. Hence, fudging often weakens a theoretical argument. On the other hand, in the case of prediction, the argument comes into existence before the data and fudging is out of the question. "So there is reason to suspect accommodations that does not apply to predictions, and this makes predictions better" (Lipton 1991: 140).

Miller (1987: 308) argues similarly that "when a hypothesis is developed to explain certain data, this can be grounds for a charge that its explanatory fit is due to the ingenuity of the developer in tailoring hypotheses to data, as against the basic truth of the hypothesis." However, if a hypothesis predicts successfully some phenomena in a replication, the above charge is not relevant because the "ingenuity in the investigators implies nothing about the presence of the alleged regularity in the world" (Miller 1987: 193–194). In sum, the first confirmatory replication of a study represents a quantum leap in credibility for the theoretical arguments of the study. If the four supported hypotheses of Bettman and Weitz were really based on accommodation, the credibility of the arguments underlying these hypotheses would be boosted tremendously by my replication, which was the first successful attempt to retest the hypotheses.

The key discrepancy between Bettman and Weitz (1983) and my replication was that the data of Bettman and Weitz did not support unequivocally either the motivational or informational explanation for the existence of self-serving attributions, whereas my data supported strongly the latter explanation. By following their research method closely, I minimized the methodological variations between the two studies. This, in turn, helped me work out a likely explanation for the differing results: cultural differences between the United States and Singapore. My results were consistent with the growing evidence provided by cross-cultural psychological studies on East Asians' greater sensitivity to situational influences when making causal attributions (Choi et al. 1999). My replication contributes to the theory of self-serving bias by suggesting that cross-cultural differences in sensitivity to situational influences could be an important factor that has been neglected thus far by the literature. While the first replication mainly identified errors in Barkema and Vermeulen's analysis and cast doubt on their results, this second replication confirmed most of Bettman and Weitz's results and made one additional theoretical contribution to the topic in question. The two replications demonstrate that replication can serve a variety of functions, one of which is to counter-check the results of quantitative studies that may be based on HARKing.

A Multi-method Approach

It goes without saying that each research method, whether qualitative or quantitative, has its own merits and shortcomings. Miller and Tsang (2011) advocate a four-step approach for theory testing that identifies and tests for the presence and effects of hypothesized causal mechanisms. Their approach involves both quantitative and qualitative methods, which play distinct roles in theory testing. As indicated by the quote from Miles and Huberman (1984) at the beginning of this chapter, the dominant view seems to prioritize quantitative methods at the expense of qualitative ones. Bryman (2006: 111) presents a more balanced view:

Qualitative research is often depicted as a research strategy whose emphasis on a relatively open-ended approach to the research process frequently produces surprises, changes of direction and new insights. However, quantitative research is by no means a mechanical application of neutral tools that results in no new insights. In quantitative data analysis, the imaginative application of techniques can result in new understandings. If the two are conducted in tandem, the potential – and perhaps the likelihood – of unanticipated outcomes is multiplied.

The multi-method approach advocated by Bryman refers to a study that includes both quantitative and qualitative methods. It should be noted that a multi-method approach may involve only quantitative or qualitative methods of different types; for example, an analysis of archival data may be followed by an experiment. A multi-method approach should be distinguished from a multi-study approach, the latter referring to inclusion of more than one study in a research paper, which is quite popular in organizational behavior research. But these different studies may use the same method, such as experiment. Instead of summarizing the multi-method approach literature, I illustrate below, based on my doctoral research, how the multi-method approach may lead to what Bryman calls "an unanticipated outcome".

I conducted the fieldwork for my doctoral dissertation in the mid-1990s. My research question was: How do Singaporean companies learn from their joint venturing experience in China? The research was in the domain of organizational learning and strategic alliances. (Chapter 4 discusses briefly the concept of organizational learning.) I adopted a multi-method research design by starting with a case study of multiple Singapore companies that had set up joint ventures in China, followed by a questionnaire survey based on the data collected as part of the case study. A key objective of the survey was to examine the extent to which some of the relationships observed in the case study could be generalized to other Singapore companies that also had joint ventures in China. I interviewed fourteen Singapore companies and visited some of their joint ventures in China. For these visits, my original plan was to study how Singapore parent companies transferred their organizational routines to the joint ventures and how the latter learned to implement the routines.

Although I had done a thorough literature review before the visits, I was surprised to discover that the literature did not cover an important issue – that a joint venture could be established from scratch or be based on an existing state enterprise. I labeled the former a greenfield joint venture and the latter an acquisition joint venture. In an acquisition joint venture, the

Chinese partner, which was a state enterprise, usually contributed its factory (or one of its factories) and machinery to the venture, while the foreign partner injected capital, technology and new machinery. Most of the Chinese employees, who had been hired originally by that state enterprise, continued to work in the venture. In contrast, a greenfield joint venture was based on a factory built on a new site, with most of its Chinese employees recruited from the labor market. The two types of joint venture differed only in terms of how they were established; they were exactly the same in all other aspects. As such, the setting was similar to a natural experiment with, say, greenfield joint ventures serving as the control group.

I observed that when transferring organizational routines to the ventures, expatriate managers from Singapore working in acquisition joint ventures often encountered more obstacles than their counterparts in greenfield joint ventures. A key reason was that acquisition joint ventures had to go through an additional step of organizational unlearning – discarding old routines inherited from the original state enterprises — whereas greenfield joint ventures only had to deal with organizational learning. An expatriate manager in one acquisition joint venture summarized aptly the difficulties of unlearning:

> People are very resistant to change . . . . If we say, "The production flow will be this: we'll put this coating on before that coating," they (the Chinese employees) don't like that because change in the system of the factory changes the routine of the factory. The change makes their life more complicated.

Subsequently, I tested the finding concerning organizational unlearning using a questionnaire survey in Singapore and Hong Kong; the results indicated that the existence of old routines, which had to be discarded, affected adversely the absorption of new ones (Tsang 2016). In short, my multi-method approach contributed to the empirical foundation of organizational unlearning. The unanticipated discovery of unlearning in my case study also motivated me to develop the concept (Tsang and Zahra 2008). The term "unlearn" first appeared in Hedberg's (1981) seminal article "How Organizations Learn and Unlearn" and was then mentioned mostly in a casual manner in the literature, researchers devoting little effort to articulating the conceptual domain and conducting few empirical studies of organizational unlearning. I believe my empirical and conceptual contributions to the development of the concept subsequently aroused management researchers' attention and interest; there has been a steady stream of empirical and simulation research on unlearning since my 2008 conceptual paper (e.g., Wensley and Navarro 2015; Martignoni and Keil 2021; Zhang et al. 2021).

There is some consensus in the literature that case studies enable researchers to tease out ever-deepening layers of reality when searching for mechanisms and contingencies that could explain the phenomenon under study (Gerring 2007) and that case studies thus provide "an in-depth understanding of contextualized human experience" (Carminati 2018: 2099). This refers mainly to the situation where researchers have a clear idea of the phenomenon they are going to study. For Pathak et al.'s (2020) TCE study discussed above, they had two research questions in mind when embarking on their fieldwork: "How do organisations and their ecosystem actors co-create value in the B2B context?" and "What is the impact of actors' opportunistic behaviour on value co-creation/destruction in the B2B context?" (3). What has been discussed much less by the literature is that case studies provide the opportunity to discover new phenomena that have important theoretical and managerial implications. The phenomenon of unlearning that I discovered in acquisition joint ventures was surely not captured by archival data. Since the literature at that time did not cover the phenomenon, I would have missed the phenomena if I had conducted a questionnaire survey alone. My questionnaire items would not even have distinguished between the two types of joint venture. Without the distinction, a similar problem would have occurred if I had conducted an experiment with joint venture managers as subjects. Only when I visited the joint ventures and interviewed both expatriate and local managers did the phenomenon reveal itself. Having the opportunity of detailed discussion with these managers, I could figure out the mechanisms and contingencies related to learning and unlearning and explain the greater difficulties of transferring routines to acquisition joint ventures than to greenfield joint ventures (see Tsang 2008). To summarize, the case study enabled me to gain an in-depth understanding of the phenomenon. However, case study as a major research method is often criticized for generating results that are less generalizable than those of large-sample, quantitative methods (Tsang 2014b). The questionnaire survey enabled me to check the generalizability of some of my case findings.

In spite of the benefits of a multi-method approach, it is uncommon in the management field. Two of the three reasons that account for relatively few multi-theoretical studies discussed in Chapter 6 also apply here. It takes time to learn and be proficient in using even one research method.

A multi-method approach is thus inconsistent with the principle of economies of scale that is often followed by doctoral students who compete for jobs in research-oriented schools and by junior scholars who are under the pressure of the tenure clock. Unlike a multi-theoretical study, a multi-method study is less likely to fit into the space of a journal article. For my study of organizational unlearning, the case study and survey results were published in separate journal papers. Therefore, a multi-method approach's strength in explaining a phenomenon cannot be demonstrated in a single journal submission. Unfortunately, books are often not well received when it comes to tenure evaluation, especially in North American and some Asian business schools. Despite these difficulties, I hope management researchers will take up the challenge and improve the quality of their explanations by collecting data using more than one method.

CHAPTER 8

Explanation as Science (or Art?)

It has been a long journey to get to this concluding chapter. The previous chapters as a group suggested that providing an explanation for an event or a phenomenon can be a complex task. Yet people seldom lack the creativity for coming up with explanations even though these explanations turn out to be false. For example, just before the burst of the 2008 housing bubble in the United States, there were explanations by analysts and scholars (including Eugene Fama, a Nobel Laureate in economics) as to why housing prices were not excessive and a housing bubble didn't exist (Krugman 2020). Without doubt, providing an explanation is a core element of the work of scientific researchers in general and management researchers in particular. Explaining clearly relationships between the concepts, constructs or variables used in a study is often a prerequisite for publishing in management journals (Thomas et al. 2011). As such, readers may wonder whether there is any systematic method that enables one to arrive at the best explanation based on a given set of data. As elaborated in the following section, one may form a wrong impression that the answer to this question is "yes" when hearing of a mode of inference called "inference to the best explanation."

Inference to the Best Explanation

The term "inference to the best explanation" was first used in the title of Harman's classic 1965 paper, in which he described the distinctive character of such explanatory inference:

> In making this inference one infers, from the fact that a certain hypothesis would explain the evidence, to the truth of that hypothesis. In general, there will be several hypotheses which might explain the evidence, so one must be able to reject all such alternative hypotheses before one is warranted in making the inference. Thus one infers, from the premise that a given hypothesis would provide a "better" explanation for the evidence than would any other hypothesis, to the conclusion that the given hypothesis is true. (89)

In essence, the task of inference to the best explanation (IBE) is to identify the hypothesis that, if true, would provide a "better" explanation than any of its competitors. This task turns out to be extraordinarily difficult because what exactly makes one hypothesis a significantly better explanation than another hypothesis remains elusive. Harman admitted this problem and proposed that hypotheses be evaluated along several dimensions of goodness, such as "which hypothesis is simpler, which is more plausible, which explains more, which is less *ad hoc*, and so forth" (89). Yet simplicity, plausibility, explanatory power and the absence of ad hoc elements are also familiar criteria of theory choice in the philosophy of science (Gelfert 2010). As such, Harman did not provide any additional guidance beyond what had been discussed in the philosophy of science literature.

A complication is that IBE is often treated by philosophers as synonymous with Charles S. Peirce's term "abduction," causing confusion about the nature of IBE. Abduction is a third mode of inference, alongside deduction and induction. The confusion was initiated by Harman (1965: 88–89) himself: "'The inference to the best explanation' corresponds approximately to what others have called 'abduction,' 'the method of hypothesis,' 'hypothetic inference,' 'the method of elimination,' 'eliminative induction,' and 'theoretical induction.'" Sometimes, the confusion was propagated when scholars cited Harman's arguments. Peirce's conception of abduction evolved over several decades and he gave no systematically coherent account of abduction. Thus, the concept of abduction itself is rather ambiguous (see Niiniluoto 1999). A good starting point, though, is Peirce's (1986: 325–326) concise illustration of deduction, induction and abduction (which he also termed "hypothesis") in the following example involving a Barbara syllogism.

Deduction is the inference of a result from a rule and a case:

> Rule – All the beans from this bag are white.
>
> Case – These beans are from this bag.
>
> ∴ Result – These beans are white.

Induction is the inference of the rule from the case and result:

> Case – These beans are from this bag.
>
> Result – These beans are white.
>
> ∴ Rule – All the beans from this bag are white.

Abduction is the inference of the case from the rule and result:

Rule — All the beans from this bag are white.

Result — These beans are white.

∴ Case — These beans are from this bag.

In essence, Peirce characterized abduction as the operation of adopting an explanatory hypothesis. In the above example, abduction attempts to explain why the beans are white. McAuliffe (2015) provides a detailed discussion of the distinction between abduction and IBE, which can be summarized as follows:

> Peirce's notion of abduction does not address how to choose one theory over others given a body of evidence. Rather, abduction is best interpreted as a method for arriving at hypotheses and selecting a hypothesis to test. Put another way, inference to the best explanation is supposed to be the *last* stage of inquiry, whereas abduction corresponds to the *first* stage of inquiry. (301)

Inferring from McAuliffe's distinction, IBE is concerned mostly with the choice of theoretical or atheoretical explanations by researchers based on their findings generated from data. In contrast, abduction is about formulating hypotheses and selecting the more promising ones to test before or after data collection. It addresses such philosophy of science questions as "what constitutes a scientific explanation?" and "what theories are, even in principle, untestable?" (McAuliffe 2015: 314). When such rather subtle differences as these are neglected, it is not surprising then that IBE and abduction are considered to be synonymous.

Peter Lipton was the most notable advocate of IBE.[1] Lipton (1991) first distinguishes between actual and potential explanations: an actual explanation "must be (at least approximately) true" (59). He then construes IBE as "Inference to the Best Potential Explanation" (59). That is, from a pool of potential explanations, we infer the best one. According to IBE, "we do not infer the best actual explanation; rather we infer that the best of the available potential explanations is an actual explanation" (60). There are two senses in which a potential explanation may be the best among competing ones. On the one hand, it may be the most probable explanation; on the other hand, we may characterize the best explanation as the one that, if true, would provide the most understanding (see Chapter 1 for a discussion of the understanding provided by explanation). Lipton (1991) labels the two senses of best explanation as the "likeliest" explanation and the "loveliest" explanation, respectively. Likeliness is concerned with truth whereas loveliness is about potential understanding.

Given a body of evidence, the loveliest explanation may not coincide with the likeliest explanation. A good example is the abrupt downturn of Dell Computer's performance between around 2005 and 2007, discussed in Chapter 5. Some of the theoretical explanations proposed by the media or scholars may significantly increase understanding of the performance downturn even though these explanations are less likely to be true than the explanation based on regression to the mean. Yet that latter explanation is less lovely in that it attributes Dell's superior performance in 2005 to extreme luck and its subsequent downturn to regression to the mean. There is no tangible causal mechanism linking the two events. In particular, citing luck as the cause of an event seldom improves one's understanding of why the event occurred; it is somewhat akin to saying that the event occurred by chance. One reason for the divergence between likeliness and loveliness is that "likeliness is relative to the total available evidence, while loveliness is not, or at least not in the same way" (Lipton 1991: 62). Returning to the Dell example, each of the explanations proposed by the media or scholars focused on a certain aspect of Dell's operations. For instance, *Business Week* commented that "Dell succumbed to complacency in the belief that its business model would always keep it far ahead of the pack" (Rosenzweig 2007: 6). That is, Dell stuck to the same business model and failed to adapt to market changes. This explanation is lovely in that it enhances understanding by relating poor performance to a rather common cause: failure to adapt. In contrast, the regression-to-the-mean explanation considers the overall performance of Dell relative to its competitors during that period of time. When a company has extremely good performance in a year, luck is likely to be a major cause unless other specific causes can be found. Statistically speaking, the company's performance was bound to drop toward a level approximating the average performance of its competitors.

IBE had been commonly practiced in the history of science long before Harman's (1965) coining of the term. Thagard (1978: 77) mentions Charles Darwin's theory of the evolution of species as one of several examples of IBE application:

> In his book *The Origin of Species* he cites a large array of facts which are explained by the theory of evolution but which are inexplicable on the then-accepted view that species were independently created by God. Darwin gives explanations of facts concerning the geographical distribution of species, the existence of atrophied organs in animals, and many other phenomena.

In the natural sciences, a phenomenon such as the one studied by Darwin is often explained by one theory. IBE is concerned with choosing the best theory among competing theories. In the case of Darwin, the choice was between the creation theory held by the church and his own theory of evolution.

As suggested by the discussion of multi-theoretical explanation in Chapter 6, a management phenomenon may not be explained adequately by a single theory. Thus, IBE cannot be applied to the entire phenomenon. Consider my co-authored study (Bai et al. 2020) – discussed in Chapters 6 and 7 – in which we investigated the initial public offering (IPO) location choice between home country and foreign country made by private Chinese firms The phenomenon in question was IPO location choice, which was the outcome of the IPO firm's decision making. The decision was likely affected by a number of factors. While our study focused on just one factor – the CEO's undergraduate education – the statistical modeling results showed that other factors, such as IPO size, profitability and technological level of the IPO firm, as well as venture capital investment in the firm, also significantly affected IPO location choice. For this study, IBE would have involved choosing the best theoretical explanation for the impact of CEO undergraduate education on IPO location choice; the explanation would not be applicable to other factors affecting the choice. During our research process, we unconsciously used IBE, reviewing various management theories and settling on upper echelons theory for the simple reason that the theory describes how CEO characteristics affect firm decisions. Since the time gap between a CEO's undergraduate education and his or her firm's IPO event can be more than three decades, we supplemented upper echelons theory with imprinting theory to explain the long-lasting influence of undergraduate education.

For our study, few other theories were relevant. Although signaling theory is often used in IPO studies, such studies are about how signals sent by the IPO firm affect investors' decisions (e.g., Cohen and Dean 2005; Heeley et al. 2007; Arthurs et al. 2009), rather than what affects IPO location decisions. Instead, upper echelons theory and social identity theory together constitute a potential explanation for location decisions. Put simply, CEOs who have an undergraduate degree from a prestigious Chinese institution identify themselves as local elites. Consistent with that social identity, they prefer to list their firms inside China. In contrast, CEOs who have an undergraduate degree from a foreign institution identify themselves as members of an emerging group of overseas college graduates in China and tend to distinguish themselves from local graduates by listing their firms overseas. One difficulty, among others, that can arise with this characterization is when a CEO has undergraduate and post-graduate degrees from both foreign and prestigious Chinese universities and so acquires more than one social identity in this domain. Our explanation deals with the case of multiple college degrees by focusing on undergraduate education only. (One rarely has more than one under-graduate degree.) According to imprinting theory, experiences gained during sensitive periods of an individual's life will have more persistent effects on the individual's subsequent decisions than experiences gained in other periods. We argue that undergraduate education occurs during one such sensitive period, being the transition from teenager to young adult. Therefore, the impact of undergraduate education is more long-lasting than that of postgraduate education. In sum, among the few potential explanations, ours is the loveliest in that it enables the greatest understand-ing of the impact of CEO undergraduate education on IPO location choice. I believe this explanation is also the likeliest, given that it is derived from upper echelons theory and imprinting theory, both of which have substantial empirical support. It should be noted that "likeliest" means our explanation is most likely to be true among competing explanations; it could still turn out to be false. After all, IBE is "a defeasible, limited argument strategy" (Day and Kincaid 1994: 275).

Some Suggested Heuristics

In spite of Lipton's insightful distinction between likeliness and loveliness, IBE may still sound too abstract to many management scholars and pro-vides few concrete guidelines for explaining their research results. Management is a practical subject; some management researchers, includ-ing myself, come to academia with industry experience. From time to time, management researchers may engage in practical reasoning, which is to select a contemplated action as a hypothesis from a set of available alternative actions in a given research setting. Once the hypothesis is selected as the most practical in that setting relative to the researcher's goals, the researcher will go ahead with the chosen action. Like IBE, practical reasoning is defeasible. The researcher may learn that the circum-stances have changed or have been misperceived and thus another action might then become the best one available (Walton 2007). My own empirical research experience indicates that I am a follower of such practical reasoning. For example, the questionnaire survey for my doctoral research was conducted in Singapore. After I finished my doctoral study,

I had more free time and so repeated the survey in Hong Kong to fulfill, at least partially, my goal of obtaining a more generalizable set of results. Conducting the survey simultaneously in Singapore and Hong Kong during my doctoral research had not been practical due to time and other resource constraints.

In line with the spirit of practical reasoning, I suggest below several heuristics, derived from Chapters 5 to 7, aimed at assisting management researchers to explain their findings.

(1) *Don't rush to provide theoretical explanations.* My study of superstitious decision making (discussed in Chapter 5) shows that when investigating a relatively new phenomenon or a phenomenon that has not been studied before, researchers should avoid the temptation to come up with a theoretical explanation by creating a new theory or using an existing theory. The focus should be on understanding the phenomenon itself and the embedded causal mechanisms. An adequate explanation need not be theory-based. Patience is golden. Only recently — about two decades after my initial study — did I begin working with other researchers to develop a theoretical foundation for superstitious decision making.

(2) *Don't fudge theoretical explanations.* This heuristic is related to the preceding one. When researchers try to construct a theoretical explanation in post hoc hypothesis development — especially an explanation that is interesting in Davis's (1971) sense (Chapter 1) — they may consciously or unconsciously fudge the explanation to fit the results (Chapter 7). Seriously fudged explanations lack the conceptual and empirical backing of the theory concerned and so are less likely to be true. As such, these explanations are like viruses: they spread in the literature when other researchers read and cite the explanations in their own studies.

(3) *Having a flawed explanation is worse than having no explanation.* This heuristic follows from the preceding two. Flawed explanations, which include seriously fudged explanations, are detrimental to the general body of knowledge. An illustrative example of a flawed explanation is Cohen and Dean's (2005) use of signaling theory to explain IPO underpricing. Their central argument was that the higher the information asymmetry between an IPO firm and its potential investors, the greater the underpricing. They constructed a top management team (TMT) legitimacy score for each IPO firm in their sample and then argued that it was a valid signal of value to investors,

with TMT legitimacy relating negatively to information asymmetry and thus implying that the higher the legitimacy score, the lower the extent of underpricing. However, a fatal flaw in their explanation was that while different legitimacy scores may signal different levels of TMT quality, a high score does not reduce more information asymmetry than a low score (see Tsang and Blevins 2015). Assuming that their data and analysis were error free, their argument fails to explain the relationship between TMT legitimacy scores and underpricing.

(4) *If possible, start with qualitative methods.* Compared to quantitative studies, qualitative methods such as case study, enable researchers to examine more directly the mechanisms and contingencies associated with a phenomenon. Such information is critical for constructing high-quality explanations. In particular, a longitudinal case design allows researchers to observe in real time how a casual mechanism unfolds and thus provides stronger empirical evidence than a cross-sectional design (Tsang 2014b). My doctoral research (presented in Chapter 7) indicates that qualitative methods also have a neglected yet useful function, which is to discover new phenomena, as illustrated by my identification of organizational unlearning in acquisition joint ventures.

(5) *Be prepared to adopt a multi-method approach.* As discussed in Chapter 7, quantitative methods are often in the form of reduced models, which fail to test mechanisms directly. Unless there have been a number of studies of the focal phenomenon and the research stream is at a mature stage, the preceding heuristic recommends the use of qualitative methods first. Kent Miller and I proposed a roadmap for testing mechanisms using different methods (Miller and Tsang 2011). In contrast to a single research method, a multi-method approach usually offers a more rigorous test and produces more generalizable results. This heuristic applies more to a research project than to a journal manuscript because journal space seldom allows for the presentation of results generated by multiple methods.

(6) *Be prepared to adopt a multi-theoretical approach.* For the study of IPO location choice presented above, neither upper echelons theory nor imprinting theory alone can explain the effect of CEO undergraduate education on the choice. Chapter 6 includes a thorough discussion of the functions of a multi-theoretical approach. This does not imply that the approach is needed often. According to Ockham's razor, if a single theory is adequate for explaining results, adding one more

theory serves little purpose, as illustrated by Lampel and Giachetti's (2013) study (also discussed in Chapter 6). That said, researchers should avoid fudging a single-theory explanation in order to save themselves the trouble of bringing in other theories.

(7) *Don't forget replication.* Recent years have seen an increasing awareness of a reproducibility crisis in management (Bergh et al. 2017; Hensel 2021) as well as in other social science disciplines. That is to say, results of many published studies have been found to be non-replicable. Likely due to this crisis, journals are more receptive to publishing replications than before. For example, the 2016 *Strategic Management Journal* had a special issue dedicated to replications, and my co-authored replication (Tsang and Yamanoi 2016) was published there. That replication and my other replication (discussed in Chapter 7) suggested that replicating prior studies can reveal errors in an explanation, identify the boundary of an explanation and even enrich an explanation.

The Craft of Explanation

Explanations, whether scientific or otherwise, are answers to why-questions. Pearl and Mackenzie (2018) present in *The Book of Why* the new science of causal inference. Yet they caution that in a certain sense, science can never be objective because causal inference essentially involves making causal claims that go beyond the data. Causal information cannot be dug out from our observations by any purely data-driven process. In fact, "the ideal technology that causal inference strives to emulate resides in our own minds" (Pearl and Mackenzie 2018: 1).

The above discussion of IBE shows that given a set of data collected on a phenomenon, there are no systematic steps for reaching the best explanation for the phenomenon. Similarly, my suggested heuristics are only broad guidelines short of listing any such steps. My own research experience indicates that constructing a satisfactory explanation, which hopefully will be the best explanation in the IBE sense, involves a great deal of judgement and decision making as well as requires imagination (e.g., using counterfactuals) and intuition (e.g., drawing on experience). For example, a certain degree of creativity on the part of the researcher is needed for conjuring a causal mechanism based on collected data (Chapter 2). The process of explaining arouses a variety of feelings and emotions: frustration, doubt, disappointment, surprise, excitement, joy and so on. As such, explaining management phenomena is not just a scientific endeavor but also an art (in the meaning of its Latin root *artem* — a form of skill). As the saying goes, practice makes perfect. To improve the craft of explanation, management researchers have to engage in learning-by-doing. I hope this book will be a helpful companion in this learning process.

Chinese Philosophy and Scientific Research

> The Chinese mind therefore cannot be accused of lacking originality or creativeness. Its inventiveness has been equal to the handicraft stage in which Chinese industries have always remained. Because of the failure to develop a scientific method and because of the peculiar qualities of Chinese thinking, China has been backward in natural science.
>
> Lin Yutang (1977: 75)

The above quote by noted scholar Lin Yutang (林語堂) highlights China's "failure to develop a scientific method." In this appendix, I look into what Lin called "the peculiar qualities of Chinese thinking" and other related issues that led to the failure. Before I proceed further, I first define the domain of my discussion by distinguishing between the methodology and the object of an empirical study. The former refers to the principles and/or procedures of conducting the study while the latter concerns the issues or phenomenon investigated by the study. I argue that Chinese philosophy contributes virtually nothing to the *methodology* of empirical management research; my argument does not apply to the *object of research*.

The study by Pan and Sun (2018) that examined the mechanism through which zhong yong (中庸) thinking influences employee adaptive performance, using data collected from 361 subordinates and their 62 team supervisors in multiple manufacturing firms in two Chinese cities, illustrates well this distinction. Their study is an example of exploring the effects of a key construct drawn from Confucianism — zhong yong thinking — in the context of a firm. While zhong yong thinking influences the norms and coping behaviors of people in Chinese society, its managerial effects remain under-researched and so Pan and Sun surely contribute to addressing this literature gap. Yet their study has nothing to do with the contribution of Chinese philosophy to methodology: their sampling, data collection, measurement of variables and data analysis follow the standard procedures of an academic study. In other words, zhong yong thinking is the object of their study and does not contribute to their research methodology.

Science in Ancient and Medieval China

This is admittedly a complex and controversial topic. On the one hand, about a century ago, there was a famous scholar of Chinese philosophy, Fung Yu-Lan (馮友蘭), who held an even more radical view than that of Lin (1977) quoted above. Fung (1922: 238) argued that "China has no science, because according to her own standard of value she does not need any." Similarly, John Fairbank (1983: 75), a renowned Sinologist, argued that China never created "science as a persisting institution, a system of theory and practice socially transmitted, consciously developed and used." On the other hand, the publication in 1954 of the first of the seven volumes of Joseph Needham's mammoth work, *Science and Civilisation in China*, saw the rather common impression that China had been backward in science throughout its history despite its admirable civilization start to change. Needham and his team provided voluminous amounts of evidence in support of their claim that ancient Chinese scientists, engineers and artisans had achieved significant advances in a variety of fields, such as astronomy, medicine, pharmacology, chemistry, geology and mathematics. Most famous among these advances were the "Four Great Inventions" – the compass, gunpowder, papermaking and printing – that had become known in Europe by the end of the Middle Ages. The isolated situation of scientific development in China ended when the Jesuit China missions introduced Western science to China in the sixteenth and seventeenth centuries.

While the country's achievements were remarkable, the mode of scientific development in ancient and medieval China was very different from that of its Western counterparts. In China, innovation and inventions were used mainly for solving problems encountered in everyday life or at work. For example, Chinese dynasties had specific institutions that were in charge of astronomical observation and calendar compilation. Astronomical observations were an essential part of imperial court rituals because they were used to determine auspicious times for a wide variety of important events, such as coronations, praying to heaven and military maneuvers, while the calendar guided the scheduling of agricultural activities by peasants. Some of these functions of astronomy created an interesting tension between astronomy and astrology (Sivin 1988). In China, astronomy had a practical focus and was not engaged in simply for the sake of satisfying intellectual curiosity about the motion of heavenly bodies. In contrast, ancient Greek civilization had a strong sense of wonder about the universe and presumed that nature could be understood by the discovery of laws. Even Needham questioned why modern science had developed in Europe but not in Chinese civilization — the well-known Needham problem or question.

Related to its focus on practical functionality was China's interest in the "how" and the "what" rather than the "why." For example, the oldest known book on Chinese herbal medicine, *Shennong's Materia Medica* (神農本草經), classifies 365 species of roots, grasses, woods, furs, animals and stones into three categories:

- those effective for treating multiple diseases and maintaining and restoring the body balance, with few negative side effects;
- those whose consumption should be constrained and must not be prolonged; and
- those for treating specific diseases, in small doses only.

The book describes the therapeutic and side effects of each species. Since it was compiled in the third century, it is understandable that it does not explain why a species had certain effects. However, in subsequent centuries, Chinese physicians' attention rarely shifted to this issue, focusing instead on examining whether the described effects were accurate and on identifying new effects. On the other hand, the drive to answer why-questions has always been much stronger in Western science. For instance, penicillin was discovered accidentally by Alexander Fleming in 1928 and saved many lives during World War II. Yet scientists were not content to stop there and continued to study the compound; its molecular structure was identified by Dorothy Hodgkin in 1945 and this helped further development of the drug. The chemical composition of Chinese herbal medicine, in contrast, started to be analyzed only in recent times.

As a result of pre-modern Chinese science downplaying the "why," science in China developed precariously, without a solid theoretical foundation (Huff 2017). Even when theory *was* proposed, it was drawn from Chinese philosophy, as discussed in the next section. Notable figures similar to Aristotle and Descartes, who excelled in both science (in its modern sense) and philosophy, did not exist in Chinese history and a title similar to "natural philosopher" was also nonexistent. Moreover, those conducting science and technology research received much lower social recognition than their counterparts in the West. While prominent scientists, such as Descartes and Newton, were well respected celebrities of their time in the West, in medieval and ancient China, "the celebrities were the amateurs who had made their reputations as statesmen or poets ... or the learned teachers who had founded well-populated lineages of practice" (Sivin 1988: 55). In short, compared to its Western counterpart, Chinese philosophy played a less engaging role in the development of science.

The Role of Philosophy

Fung (1922: 259–260) stated succinctly the reason why China failed to develop a scientific method, pinpointing the nature of Chinese philosophy:

> Bergson says in Mind Energy that Europe discovered the scientific method, because modern European science started from matter . . .. So China has not discovered the scientific method, because Chinese thought started from mind, and from one's own mind.

In other words, Chinese philosophy devoted itself to the cultivation of the mind (xin 心), which overrode or replaced interest in studying nature. Among the three major philosophical perspectives molding Chinese civilization — Confucianism, Buddhism and Taoism, Confucianism was the one adopted by rulers of most dynasties. Cultivation of the mind is clearly reflected in Confucianism. Mencius (孟子), a key scholar of Confucianism, said:

> He who has exhausted all his mind, knows his nature. Knowing his nature, he knows Heaven. To preserve one's mind and nourish one's nature, is the way to serve Heaven. When neither a premature death nor a long life makes any difference, but he waits in the cultivation of his character for whatever comes; this is the way in which he establishes his Heaven-ordained being.

> 盡其心者，知其性也。知其性，則知天矣。存其心，養其性，所以事天也。殀壽不貳，修身以俟之，所以立命也。《盡心上》

Since it is a lifelong endeavor to properly cultivate one's mind in order to be a virtuous person, exploring nature has to take a backseat. This Confucian focus on ethics at the expense of ontology and epistemology is not conducive to the development of science because ontology and epistemology are intimately related to scientific research. A researcher's ontological commitment influences their epistemological orientation and, together, their ontological and epistemological stances affect which methods they consider to be legitimate and appropriate in conducting empirical research (Tsang 2017). On the other hand, the relationship of ethics to science is mainly about how research can be conducted ethically or how research results should be used (e.g., Einstein's most famous equation, $E = mc^2$ can be used to make atomic bombs or to generate electricity).

Medicine is one major domain where there is a substantial degree of engagement between science and philosophy. *Yellow Emperor's Classic of Internal Medicine* (黃帝內經) is an ancient medical text that for over two millennia has been considered the authoritative source on Chinese medicine. A key characteristic of the book is its departure from the popular yet simplistic shamanistic belief in ancient time that disease was caused by demonic influences. Instead, it uses the Taoist theory of yin and yang (陰陽) and five phrases (五行) – gold, wood, water, fire and earth – to express the correspondence between the articulations of the cosmos and the body, specifically between heaven and earth. on the one hand. and the upper and lower parts of the body. on the other. Yin and yang are in constant flux and follow a pattern of five phases, which shows when and how yang will shift to yin and vice versa. Diseases are understood as states of yin and yang imbalance in the body. A doctor should focus on his patient's balance of bodily functions and the propagation of functional imbalance. Unlike Western medical theory, such as the blood circulation theory, methodologically speaking, this theory of yin–yang and five phrases is very broad and has not been used to derive hypotheses for empirical testing in a scientific way. It is no wonder that a 2007 editorial essay in *Nature* stated that traditional Chinese medicine "is fraught with pseudoscience" (106).

Needham (1954) argued that Taoism, to which the theory of yin–yang and five phrases belongs, is both naturalistic and interested in natural phenomena. Also in the 1950s, Welch (1957: 134) provided a more specific description of the relation between Taoism and science:

> to a large extent the Taoists practiced experimental science. They were reluctant to alter their premises in the light of logic and experimentation, but they did at least experiment. They were ultimately responsible for the development of dyes, alloys, porcelains, medicines, the compass, and gunpowder. They would have developed much more if the best minds in China had not been pre-empted by Confucian orthodoxy.

Taoism is an extreme "nature" philosophy whose teachings can be summarized in a single phrase: "returning to nature." This is because people are mostly happy in the state of nature. "The omnipotent Tao gives everything its own nature, in which it finds its own satisfaction"

(Fung 1922: 241). Since Tao (道) is already within us, what we need and ought to do is to understand and control ourselves. This inward-looking orientation corresponds to the cultivation of the mind mentioned above. Here, knowledge of the external world is of little use and can in fact do harm, as aptly pointed out by Zhuangzi (莊子):

> Our life is limited, but knowledge is not limited. With what is limited to pursue what is not limited is a perilous thing.
>
> 吾生也有涯，而知也无涯。以有涯隨无涯，殆已。《養生主》

Such a life attitude is clearly antithetical to scientific research, which aims to understand, explain and sometimes control nature.

Sivin (1978) offers a detailed and trenchant rebuttal of the view held by Needham, Welch and others that Taoism favored or promoted science. One reason Sivin gives for this disagreement is that the terms "Taoism" and "Taoist" are vague and have been used to cover cases that do not in fact belong to the philosophy; another is the confusion between Taoism as a philosophy and Taoism as a religion. Sivin's (1978: 310) assessment is as follows:

> As for the beginnings of a scientific movement, the theoretical and practical work of disparate individuals who may be called Taoist in one sense or another does not warrant generalizations about Taoism as either a religion or a philosophy. It remains to be proved through close study of each individual that these accomplishments were in some special sense due to Taoist connections or sentiments. It also has yet to be demonstrated that these associations and feelings formed a consistent pattern more significant for scientific accomplishment than that formed by the intellectual and social allegiances of equally important scientists who were in no sense Taoists.

Concluding Remarks

Chinese philosophers in general played a detached and somewhat aloof role in the development of science in ancient and medieval China due to their focus on the cultivation of the mind at the expense of exploring nature. It is thus unsurprising that a discipline similar to philosophy of science never emerged in China even after Western science had been introduced to the country in the sixteenth and seventeenth centuries. As such, unlike its Western counterpart, Chinese philosophy is not well positioned to shed light on management research methodology. As for me, while I have learned a great deal from Confucian teachings about how to be a morally upright person (with implications for being an ethical researcher), I cannot, unfortunately, see how Confucian wisdom could help my research.

Although the above discussion may be disappointing to fans of Chinese philosophy, such as Peter Ping Li (who applies yin–yang theory to management research, as discussed in Chapter 5), it should not be interpreted to mean that I consider Western philosophy to be superior or more useful. My own experience of reading Western and Chinese philosophy is that they serve somewhat complementary functions for our intellectual and spiritual development, as suggested by Lin's (1977: 85–86) comparison:

> It was Aristotle, I believe, who said that man is a reasoning, but not a reasonable being. Chinese philosophy admits this, but adds that man should try to be a reasonable, and not a merely reasoning, being. By the Chinese, reasonableness is placed on a higher level than reason.

Notes

Chapter 1

1 I presume in this book that management researchers consider themselves to be doing science. As elaborated in Chapter 8 of my book *The Philosophy of Management Research*, this presumption is highly reasonable. A simple piece of supporting evidence is the names of some leading academic journals such as *Administrative Science Quarterly, Management Science, Organization Science,* and *Strategy Science.*

2 Faye (1999) raises a valid point that why-questions are not the only explanation seeking questions. Certain kinds of questions may also be considered as serious requests for explanation. While simple fact-finding questions like "What time is it?" do not involve explanation, a question like "How did life begin on earth?" surely requires the respondent to put in a substantive explanatory effort. This question should be distinguished from the corresponding why-question "Why did life begin on earth?" that demands a completely different answer. For simplicity of presentation, I presume in this book that why-questions are the only explanation seeking questions. My treatment is reasonable, as Jenkins (2008: 62) argues that answering why-questions "is a central use of explanation talk, and one that has attracted a lot of attention from philosophers."

3 The profitability requirement is for business opportunities. In social entrepreneurship, the corresponding requirement depends on the nature of the social enterprise in question. For instance, if one thinks of a new way to improve the livelihood of the residents in a community, the requirement could be a reduction of the poverty rate in the community. Again, the opportunity has to result in a positive outcome; it simply makes no sense for one to claim exploiting an opportunity that leads to a higher poverty rate in the community as the objective of establishing a social enterprise.

4 Since this book focuses on management phenomena, I skip the complicated debate about whether evolutionary theory is tautological. Interested readers may refer to Peters (1976), who holds an affirmative position, as well as Ferguson (1976), Caplan (1977), Castrodeza (1977), and Stebbins (1977), who hold the opposite position.

5 Another definition of firm resources used by Barney (1991: 101) is: "all assets, capabilities, organizational processes, firm attributes, information, knowledge, etc. controlled by a firm that enable the firm to conceive of and implement strategies that improve its efficiency and effectiveness." Priem and Butler (2001a) use this definition to carve out their more convoluted challenge. The two definitions are consistent, although this one is narrower in scope because improving efficiency and effectiveness is just one form of value creation. It should also be noted that Barney (1991) focuses on the value-creating attributes of firm resources and, as such, firm resources and valuable firm resources refer to the same thing — as shown by these two sentences: "However, those attributes of a firm's physical, human, and organizational capital that do enable a firm to conceive of and implement strategies that improve its efficiency and effectiveness are, for the purpose of this discussion, firm resources" (102) and "As suggested earlier, resources are valuable when they enable a firm to conceive of and implement strategies that improve its efficiency and effectiveness" (106).

6 Here I regard "organizational resources" and "firm resources" as equivalent because Barney (1991) uses the two terms interchangeably.

7 I am not arguing that Barney's (1991) paper does not have any useful insights. In fact, when I analyzed the role played by guanxi (關係) in doing business in China, I used value, rarity and imperfect imitability as three key conditions for guanxi to provide a sustained competitive advantage (Tsang 1998).

8 The contrastive approach to explanation should be distinguished from van Fraassen's (1980) pragmatic theory of explanation, which regards explanations as answers to contrastive why-questions. As such, what counts as explanatory depends on context, which includes the background knowledge and the interest of the inquirer. If an explanation provides the missing piece of the puzzle of an inquirer's background knowledge, the explanation will improve the inquirer's understanding. My discussion focuses on the nature of contrastive questions with the purpose of showing that an explanation only covers a certain aspect of a phenomenon. In contrast, van Fraassen (1980) goes beyond that and develops a theory of explanation to address some deficiencies of existing theories such as the deductive-nomological model presented in Chapter 3.

9 To illustrate the "weak" end of their "causal explanation" dimension, Welch et al. (2011) claim that Eisenhardt's (1989) case study method represents "a weak form of causality, in that it seeks to establish regularities rather than the reasons behind them" (746). I refute their claim by presenting solid contradicting evidence (Tsang 2013). Somewhat surprisingly, in their retrospective paper, Welch et al. (2022: 7) stick to their claim: "according to Eisenhardt, understanding 'why' is secondary to the main theoretical output: the potentially generalizable constructs 'linked together in relationships' (Eisenhardt, 2021, p. 148) during the analysis." Nevertheless, the full sentence containing the phrase "linked together in relationships" in Eisenhardt (2021) and two preceding sentences on the same page are as follows: "The 'Eisenhardt

Method' (the Method) is first and foremost about theory building. So while it relies on Yin's work (1984) on cases (and replication logic) and Glaser and Strauss' (1967) iterative process of constant comparison of data and theory (and theoretical sampling and saturation), the Method's unique contribution is theory building from multiple cases (with particular emphasis on theoretical arguments). By theory, I simply mean a set of constructs linked together in relationships that are supported by theoretical arguments (i.e. mechanisms) that seek to explain a focal phenomenon." It is crystal clear that Eisenhardt (2021) emphasizes theory building that aims at causal explanation (in the form of mechanismic explanation discussed in Chapter 3), again contradicting Welch et al.'s claim.

10 In addition to this problem, there are errors that are philosophical in nature. One such error is in endnote 5 where Welch et al. (2011) claim that Popper's falsificationism is a variant of positivism; they therefore classify the philosophical orientation of the natural experiment method as "positivist (falsificationist)" in their table 1. This is a blunder in that Popper (2002: 99) claimed responsibility for killing logical positivism: "Everybody knows nowadays that logical positivism is dead. But nobody seems to suspect that there may be a question to be asked here—the question 'Who is responsible?' or, rather, the question 'Who has done it?' . . . I fear that I must admit responsibility." Welch et al. do not seem to be aware of this simple fact, which is well known in philosophy of science and will be revealed by a quick literature search. Owing to Popper's complex relationship with the Vienna Circle that founded logical positivism, he was sometimes mistaken for a positivist. Popper (1994, 2002) provided a first-person account of the relationship, while Edmonds and Eidinow (2001), Naraniecki (2010) and Sigmund (2017) offered a third-person description. Popper (1994: 133) considered himself "a metaphysical realist." Welch et al.'s error suggests that when management scholars who are not familiar with philosophy include substantive philosophical elements in their papers, they have to first conduct a thorough literature review. Given the complexity of philosophy as a subject, I have to say that this is by no means an easy task.

11 Interested readers may read my detailed critique of Davis's article in Tsang (2022b), which includes a table showing that management is the field that contributes the largest number of citations to the article. When I read the article, the most surprising finding was its large number of errors, both logical and factual. The article simply lacks the rigor normally found in an academic paper, not to mention a supposedly philosophy-based academic paper; after all, it was published in the journal *Philosophy of the Social Sciences*.

Chapter 2

1 Although this relationship is related to the resource-based view of the firm, it is different from Barney's (1991: 107) tautological proposition that "valuable

and rare organizational resources can be a source of competitive advantage" discussed in Chapter 1. The relationship is about firm performance, not competitive advantage.

2 The term "agent" used here should be distinguished from that used in the principal–agent relationship depicted by agency theory in which "one party (the principal) delegates work to another (the agent), who performs that work" (Eisenhardt 1989: 58). These two meanings of "agent" are obviously very different.

3 Related to the concept of entities is the concept of sociomateriality, which originates from the domain of information systems research and has also generated substantial interest in management studies. The sociomaterial perspective conflates the social and the material into the same ontological assemblage, as suggested by Orlikowski's (2007: 1437) claim that "the social and the material are considered to be inextricably related – there is no social that is not also material, and no material that is not also social." Her claim is bold but flawed. If it is legitimate to merge the social with the material ontologically, why can't we do the same for the psychological and the material to create the concept of psychomateriality? Consider Orlikowski's (2007) empirical example of Google's information search technology. When someone uses Google's search capabilities, the activity involves the search technology (i.e., the material) and the person's psychology. Or, taking one step further, why shouldn't we create the concept of psychosociomateriality? No wonder the sociomaterial perspective has been rather severely criticized by Mutch (2013) and Tunçalp (2016). In brief, my use of "entities" has nothing to do with sociomateriality.

4 The section "Mechanismic Explanation" of Chapter 3 discusses the explanatory function of mechanisms. The current section presents the nature of mechanism itself and its relationship to causation.

5 If Y is temporally prior to X, there are no plausible mechanisms that depict X as the cause of Y. Yet, this is due to the principle that an effect cannot happen before its cause rather than any conviction regarding mechanisms. In other words, this reasoning does not belong to the no-plausible-mechanism strategy.

Chapter 3

1 To avoid repetition, I do not compare and contrast the major philosophical perspectives in this book. Interested readers may refer to Chapter 1 of my book *The Philosophy of Management Research*. Personally I subscribe to a realist philosophical perspective that a mind-independent reality, which has its own inherent order, exists (Fay 1996). For example, in management research, the "realist asserts that organizations are real. They have form, structures, boundaries, purposes and goals, resources, and members whose behaviors result from structured relations among them" (Dubin 1982: 372). A realist thesis is reflected in some of my arguments in this book.

Chapter 4

1 There is a typo here: "statures" should be "statues."

Chapter 5

1 In early 2005, a graduate student of library science at a major university in the mid-west of the United States searched the English literature for me and did not find any academic studies on the topic, other than the two papers I published from my research of the phenomenon (Tsang 2004a, 2004b). Upon my request, two management scholars, Chi-Nien Chung and Chung-Ming Lau, kindly searched the Chinese academic literature in Taiwan. They also failed to identify any such academic studies.

2 I have some reservations, though, about this reviewer's stress on the interest-ingness of my study. As discussed in Chapter 1, whether an explanation is interesting has little relevance as far as scientific research is concerned.

3 Other than this serious problem, Li's arguments often lack the precision and rigor I would expect to find in philosophical discussions. Consider, for example, this point: "I posit that paradox is never fully resolvable, neither spatially nor temporally; if it is fully resolvable, it is a fake paradox" (Li 2021: 60). His point is tautological in the sense that he implicitly defines a genuine paradox as being never fully resolvable. I am also astounded by his biased caricatures of Western philosophy, such as "The West has tried to reduce and substitute complexity and uncertainty with simplicity and certainty" (Li 2016: 49) and "the Western philosophical tendency to favor consistency at the expense of completeness" (Li 2021: 55).

Chapter 6

1 I was fortunate that I followed a career path very different from those of my peers who are at research-oriented business schools in North America. I did not face much tenure pressure and could freely explore different research topics and theories – including even philosophy– early in my academic career (see Tsang 2006a for details). This freedom enables me to share my own multi-theoretical experience in this chapter.

2 When I attended my first ever Academy of Management Annual Meeting in 1999 (two years after receiving my PhD), I was interviewed by a research-oriented US business school for an assistant professor position. To my surprise, I was asked, "When people think of Eric Tsang, what will they associate with your name?" During the subsequent conversation, I realized that it was intended as a mild criticism of my "fragmented" publication record rather than a job interview question. Without any surprise this time, I was not hired.

3 There is a typo: "parsimoinious" should be "parsimonious."

Chapter 7

1 This point is based on classical statistics founded by R. A. Fisher and Karl Pearson, which maintains that correlation is not causation. Most empirical studies in management use classical statistics. Pearl and Mackenzie (2018) present a ladder of knowledge with three levels: association, causation and counterfactuals, differentiated in terms of the kind of statements that can be asked and answered at each level. While classical statistics belongs to the association level, causal graph modeling (discussed in Chapter 2) belongs to the causation level. Empirical analysis based on the latter is in a better position than the former to allow for causal inference.

2 One may tend to think that only papers with all hypotheses supported, such as what Barkema and Vermeulen (1998) claimed, are likely to involve HARKing. This may not be the case. Authors usually try to make sure that all hypotheses form a coherent theoretical framework. This constraint sometimes results in some only partially supported or fully unsupported hypotheses. However, if most of the hypotheses in a paper are not supported it is fairly likely that HARKing is absent. That said, such a paper is also not likely to be accepted for publication due to the "file drawer problem."

Chapter 8

1 I sat in Lipton's philosophy of science lectures in 1994 when I studied for my PhD at Cambridge. I recall that he gave one-hour lectures from memory, without referring to lecture notes or using transparencies. He showed beautifully how profound philosophical concepts and arguments could be presented with little pedantic pretense and, in the process, managed to capture students' attention for the entire lecture. While attending his lectures. I purchased and read the first edition of his book *Inference to the Best Explanation*, which became unquestionably the most important IBE reference in philosophy. The book reflects the lucidity of his lecture style. Sadly, he passed away unexpectedly in November 2007, aged only 53.

References

Abbott, K. W., Green, J. F. and Keohane, R. O. 2016. Organizational ecology and institutional change in global governance. *International Organization*, 70: 247–277.

Adomako, S. and Amankwah-Amoah, J. 2021. Managerial attitude towards the natural environment and environmental sustainability expenditure. *Journal of Cleaner Production*, 326: 129384.

Agassi, J. 1960. Methodological individualism. *British Journal of Sociology*, 11: 244–270.

1971. Tautology and testability in economics. *Philosophy of the Social Sciences*, 1: 49–63.

Aguinis, H., Cascio, W. F. and Ramani, R. S. 2017. Science's reproducibility and replicability crisis: International business is not immune. *Journal of International Business Studies*, 48: 653–663.

Alchian, A. A. and Demsetz, H. 1972. Production, information costs, and economic organization. *American Economic Review*, 62: 777–795.

Aldrich, H. E. 1992. Incommensurable paradigms? Vital signs from three perspectives. In M. Reed and M. Hughes (Eds.), *Rethinking organization: New directions in organization theory and analysis*: 17–45. London: Sage.

Alexander, S. 1920. *Space, time, and deity: The Gifford Lectures at Glasgow 1916–1918*. Vol. II. London: Macmillan.

Alvarez, M. and Hyman, J. 1998. Agents and their actions. *Philosophy*, 73: 219–245.

Alvarez, S. A., Barney, J. B., and Anderson, P. 2013. Forming and exploiting opportunities: The implications of discovery and creation processes for entrepreneurial and organizational research. *Organization Science*, 24: 301–317.

Alvarez, S. A., Barney, J. B., McBride, R. and Wuebker, R. 2014. Realism in the study of entrepreneurship. *Academy of Management Review*, 39: 227–233.

Amihud, Y. and Lev, B. 1981. Risk reduction as a managerial motive for conglomerate mergers. *Bell Journal of Economics*, 12: 605–617.

1999. Does corporate ownership structure affect its strategy towards diversification? *Strategic Management Journal*, 20: 1063–1069.

Anderson, P. J., Blatt, R., Christianson, M. K., Grant, A. M., Marquis, C., Neuman, E. J., Sonenshein, S. and Sutcliffe, K. M. 2006. Understanding mechanisms in organizational research: Reflections from a collective journey. *Journal of Management Inquiry,* 15: 102–113.

Andrews, T. G., Nimanandh, K., Htun, K. T. and Santidhirakul, O. 2022. MNC response to superstitious practice in Myanmar IJVs: Understanding contested legitimacy, formal–informal legitimacy thresholds, and institutional disguise. *Journal of International Business Studies,* 53: 1178–1201.

Arntzenius, F. 1992. The common cause principle. In D. Hull and K. Okruhlik (Eds.), *Proceedings of the 1992 biennial meeting of the Philosophy of Science Association.* Vol. 2: 227–237. East Lansing, MI: Philosophy of Science Association.

Arthurs, J. D., Busenitz, L. W., Hoskisson, R. E. and Johnson, R. A. 2009. Signaling and initial public offerings: The use and impact of the lockup period. *Journal of Business Venturing,* 24: 360–372.

Ayer, A. J. 1959. Editor's introduction. In A. J. Ayer (Ed.), *Logical positivism:* 3–28. New York: Free Press.

Baetu, T. M. 2015. The completeness of mechanistic explanations. *Philosophy of Science,* 82: 775–786.

Bai, X., Tsang, E. W. K. and Xia, W. 2020. Domestic versus foreign listing: Does a CEO's educational experience matter? *Journal of Business Venturing,* 35: 105906.

Bandura, A. 1977. *Social learning theory.* Englewood Cliffs, NJ: Prentice-Hall.

Barkema, H. G. and Vermeulen, F. 1998. International expansion through start-up or acquisition: A learning perspective. *Academy of Management Journal,* 41: 7–26.

Barnes, E. 1994. Why P rather than Q? The curiosities of fact and foil. *Philosophical Studies,* 73: 35–53.

Barnes, E. C. 2000. Ockham's razor and the anti-superfluity principle. *Erkenntnis,* 53: 353–374.

Barney, J. 1991. Firm resources and sustained competitive advantage. *Journal of Management,* 17: 99–120.

Barney, J. B. 2001. Is the resource-based "view" a useful perspective for strategic management research? Yes. *Academy of Management Review,* 26: 41–56.

Bartlett, C. A. and Ghoshal, S. 1989. *Managing across borders: The transnational solution.* Boston, MA: Harvard Business School Press.

Beach, D. 2016. It's all about mechanisms – What process-tracing case studies should be tracing. *New Political Economy,* 21: 463–472.

Beach, D. and Pedersen, R. B. 2019. *Process-tracing methods: Foundations and guidelines.* Ann Arbor, MI: University of Michigan Press.

Beauchamp, T. and Rosenberg, A. 1981. *Hume and the problem of causation.* New York: Oxford University Press.

Bechtel, W. 2005. Explanation: A mechanistic alternative. *Studies in the History and Philosophy of Biology and Biomedical Sciences,* 36: 421–441.

Beebee, H. 2006. *Hume on causation.* New York: Routledge.

Bennett, A. 2010. Process tracing and causal inference. In H. E. Brady and D. Collier (Eds.), *Rethinking social inquiry: Diverse tools, shared standards* (2nd ed.): 207–220. Lanham, MD: Rowman and Littlefield.

Bennett, J. 1988. *Events and their names*. Indianapolis, IN: Hackett.

Bergh, D. D., Sharp, B. M., Aguinis, H. and Li, M. 2017. Is there a credibility crisis in strategic management research? Evidence on the reproducibility of study findings. *Strategic Organization*, 15: 423–436.

Bergmann, C. 1957. *Philosophy of science*. Madison, WI: University of Wisconsin Press.

Berry, M. W. and Young, P. G. 1995. Using latent semantic indexing for multilanguage information retrieval. *Computers and Humanities*, 29: 413–429.

Bettis, R. A. 2012. The search for asterisks: Compromised statistical tests and flawed theories. *Strategic Management Journal*, 33: 108–113.

Bettman, J. R. and Weitz, B. A. 1983. Attributions in the board room: Causal reasoning in corporate annual reports. *Administrative Science Quarterly*, 28: 165–183.

Bhaskar, R. 1978. *A realist theory of science*. Hassocks: Harvester Press.

Bilton, N. 2016. How Elizabeth Holmes's House of Cards came tumbling down. *Vanity Fair*, September 6. [www.vanityfair.com/news/2016/09/elizabeth-holmes-theranos-exclusive].

Bingham, C. B. and Kahl, S. J. 2013. The process of schema emergence: Assimilation, deconstruction, unitization and the plurality of analogies. *Academy of Management Journal*, 56: 14–34.

Bishop, C. M. 2006. *Pattern recognition and machine learning*. New York: Springer.

Bishop, J. 1983. Agent-causation. *Mind*, 92: 61–79.

Blei, D. M., Ng, A. Y. and Jordan, M. I. 2003. Latent Dirichlet allocation. *Journal of Machine Learning Research*, 3: 993–1022.

Block, L. and Kramer, T. 2009. The effect of superstitious beliefs on performance expectations. *Journal of the Academy of Marketing Science*, 37: 161–169.

Blumberg, A. E. and Feigl, H. 1931. Logical positivism. *Journal of Philosophy*, 28: 281–296.

Borgatti, S. P., Mehra, A., Brass, D. J. and Labianca, G. 2009. Network analysis in the social sciences. *Science*, 323: 892–895.

Boudon, R. 1998. Social mechanisms without black boxes. In P. Hedström and R. Swedberg (Eds.), *Social mechanisms: An analytical approach to social theory*: 172–203. Cambridge: Cambridge University Press.

Bowden, B. 2021. The historic (wrong) turn in management and organizational studies. *Journal of Management History*, 27: 8–27.

Braithwaite, R. B. 1946. Teleological explanation. *Proceedings of the Aristotelian Society*, 47: i–xx.

Brewer, W. F. and Chinn, C. A. 1994. The theory-ladenness of data: An experimental demonstration. In A. Ram and K. Eiselt (Eds.), *Proceedings of the sixteenth annual conference of the Cognitive Science Society*: 61–65. Hillsdale, NJ: Lawrence Erlbaum.

Brewer, W. F. and Lambert, B. L. 2001. The theory-ladenness of observation and the theory-ladenness of the rest of the scientific process. *Philosophy of Science*, 68: S176–S186.

Brock, D. M. and Hydle, K. M. 2018. Transnationality – Sharpening the integration-responsiveness vision in global professional firms. *European Management Journal*, 36: 117–124.

Bromberger, S. 1966. Why-questions. In R. Colodny (Ed.), *Mind and cosmos*: 86–111. Pittsburgh, PA: University of Pittsburgh Press.

Bryman, A. 2006. Integrating quantitative and qualitative research: How is it done? *Qualitative Research*, 6: 97–113.

Buchanan, D. and Dawson, P. M. 2007. Discourse and audience: Organizational change as multi-story process. *Journal of Management Studies*, 44: 669–686.

Buckley, P. J. and Chapman, M. 1997. The perception and measurement of transaction costs. *Cambridge Journal of Economics*, 21: 127–145.

Bulcão-Neto, R. F., Camacho-Guerrero, J. A., Dutra, M., Barreiro, A., Parapar, J. and Macedo, A. A. 2011. The use of latent semantic indexing to mitigate OCR effects of related document images. *Journal of Universal Computer Science*, 17: 64–80.

Bunge, M. 1997. Mechanism and explanation. *Philosophy of the Social Sciences*, 27: 410–465.

2004. How does it work? The search for explanatory mechanisms. *Philosophy of the Social Sciences*, 34: 182–210.

Burrell, G. and Morgan, G. 1979. *Sociological paradigms and organizational analysis*. Hants: Ashgate.

Caldwell, B. 1980. Positivist philosophy of science and the methodology of economics. *Journal of Economic Issues*, 14: 53–76.

Campbell, C. 1982. A dubious distinction? An inquiry into the value and use of Merton's concepts of manifest and latent function. *American Sociological Review*, 47: 29–44.

Caplan, A. L. 1977. Tautology, circularity, and biological theory. *American Naturalist*, 111: 390–393.

Capon, N., Farley, J. U. and Hoenig, S. 1996. *Toward an integrative explanation of corporate financial performance*. Boston, MA: Kluwer.

Cappelli, P. and Sherer, P. D. 1991. The missing role of context in OB: The need for a meso-level approach. *Research in Organizational Behavior*, 13: 55–110.

Carminati, L. 2018. Generalizability in qualitative research: A tale of two traditions. *Qualitative Health Research*, 28: 2094–2101.

Carnap, R. 1936. Testability and meaning. *Philosophy of Science*, 3: 419–471.

Carreyrou, J. 2020. *Bad blood: Secrets and lies in a Silicon Valley startup*. New York: Vintage Books.

Cartwright, N. 1999. *The dappled world: A study of the boundaries of science*. Cambridge: Cambridge University Press.

Castrodeza, C. 1977. Tautologies, beliefs, and empirical knowledge in biology. *American Naturalist*, 111: 393–394.

Chandler, A. D. 1977. *The visible hand: The managerial revolution in American business*. Cambridge, MA: Belknap.

Chang, W. L. and Lii, P. 2010. Feng Shui and its role in corporate reputation and image: A review from business and cultural perspectives. *Journal of Architectural and Planning Research*, 27: 1–14.

Checkel, J. T. 2006. Tracing causal mechanisms. *International Studies Review*, 8: 362–370.

Child, J. 1997. Strategic choice in the analysis of action, structure, organizations and environment: Retrospect and prospect. *Organization Studies*, 18: 43–76.

Child, J., Chung, L. and Davies, H. 2003. The performance of cross-border units in China: A test of natural selection, strategic choice and contingency theories. *Journal of International Business Studies*, 34: 242–254.

Chiles, T. H. and McMackin, J. F. 1996. Integrating variable risk preferences, trust, and transaction cost economics. *Academy of Management Review*, 21: 73–99.

Choi, I., Nisbett, R. E. and Norenzayan, A. 1999. Causal attribution across cultures: Variation and universality. *Psychological Bulletin*, 125: 47–63.

Chow, G. C. 1983. *Econometrics*. Singapore: McGraw-Hill.

Chung, C. C., Lee, S. H., Beamish, P. W., Southam, C. and Nam, D. D. 2013. Pitting real options theory against risk diversification theory: International diversification and joint ownership control in economic crisis. *Journal of World Business*, 48: 122–136.

Clark, P. and Rowlinson, M. 2004. The treatment of history in organisation studies: Towards an "historic turn?". *Business History*, 46: 331–352.

Coase, R. H. 1937. The nature of the firm. *Economica*, 4: 386–405.

1988. The nature of the firm: Meaning. *Journal of Law, Economics, and Organization*, 4: 19–32.

Coff, R. 2003. Bidding wars over R&D-intensive firms: Knowledge, opportunism, and the market for corporate control. *Academy of Management Journal*, 46: 74–85.

Cohen, B. A. 2017. How should novelty be valued in science? *Elife*, 6: e28699.

Cohen, B. D. and Dean, T. J. 2005. Information asymmetry and investor valuation of IPOs: Top management team legitimacy as a capital market signal. *Strategic Management Journal*, 26: 683–690.

Cohen, W. M. and Levinthal, D. A. 1990. Absorptive capacity: A new perspective on learning and innovation. *Administrative Science Quarterly*, 35: 128–152.

Coleman, J. 1990. *Foundations of social theory*. Cambridge, MA: Belknap.

Collier, D. 2011. Understanding process tracing. *PS: Political Science & Politics*, 44: 823–830.

Collins, J., Hall, N. and Paul, L. A. 2004. Counterfactuals and causation: History, problems, and prospects. In J. Collins, N. Hall and L. A. Paul (Eds.), *Causation and counterfactuals*: 1–57. Cambridge, MA: MIT Press.

Colquitt, J. A. and George, G. 2011. Publishing in *AMJ* – Part 1: Topic choice. *Academy of Management Journal*, 54: 432–435.

Colvin, G. 2020. Coming out of a crisis, the boldest companies win. *Fortune*, June 25. [https://fortune.com/2020/06/25/coronavirus-business-opportunities-spending-mergers-acquisitions-research-development-recruiting/]

Copi, I. M. and Cohen, C. 1998. *Introduction to logic* (10th ed.). Upper Saddle River, NJ: Prentice Hall.

Corbett, A. C. 2007. Learning asymmetries and the discovery of entrepreneurial opportunities. *Journal of Business Venturing*, 22: 97–118.

Cornelissen, J. and Durand, R. 2012. More than just novelty: Conceptual blending and causality. *Academy of Management Review*, 37: 152–154.

Coviello, N. E. and McAuley, A. 1999. Internationalization and the smaller firm: A review of contemporary empirical research. *Management International Review*, 39: 223–256.

Craik, K. 1943. *The nature of explanation*. Cambridge: Cambridge University Press.

Craver, C. 2007. *Explaining the brain*. Oxford: Oxford University Press.

Crick, F. 1989. *What mad pursuit: A personal view of scientific discovery*. London: Penguin Books.

Crossan, M. M., Lane, H. W. and White, R. E. 1999. An organizational learning framework: From intuition to institution. *Academy of Management Review*, 24: 522–537.

Csibra, G. and Gergely, G. 2007. "Obsessed with goals": Functions and mechanisms of teleological interpretation of actions in humans. *Acta Psychologica*, 124: 60–78.

Currie, G. 1984. Individualism and global supervenience. *British Journal for the Philosophy of Science*, 35: 345–358.

Danermark, B., Ekström, M., Jakobsen, L. and Karlsson, J. C. 2002. *Explaining society: Critical realism in the social sciences*. London: Routledge.

Darden, L. 2006. *Reasoning in biological discoveries: Essays on mechanisms, interfield relations, and anomaly resolution*. Cambridge: Cambridge University Press.

Davidson, D. 1963. Actions, reasons, and causes. *Journal of Philosophy*, 60: 685–700.

   1980. *Essays on actions and events*. Oxford: Oxford University Press.

Davidsson, P. and Wiklund, J. 2009. Scott A. Shane: Winner of the global award for entrepreneurship research. *Small Business Economics*, 33: 131–140.

Davis, G. F. and Marquis, C. 2005. Prospects for organization theory in the early twenty-first century: Institutional fields and mechanisms. *Organization Science*, 16: 332–343.

Davis, M. E., Barber, W. P., Finelli, J. J. and Klem, W. 1952. *Report of committee on new recording means and computing devices*. Chicago, IL: Society of Actuaries.

Davis, M. S. 1971. That's interesting! Towards a phenomenology of sociology and a sociology of phenomenology. *Philosophy of the Social Sciences*, 1: 309–344.

Davis, T. R. and Luthans, F. 1980. A social learning approach to organizational behavior. *Academy of Management Review*, 5: 281–290.

Day, M. and Botterill, G. S. 2008. Contrast, inference and scientific realism. *Synthese*, 160: 249–267.

Day, T. and Kincaid, H. 1994. Putting inference to the best explanation in its place. *Synthese*, 98: 271–295.

De Massis, A. and Foss, N. J. 2018. Advancing family business research: The promise of microfoundations. *Family Business Review*, 31: 386–396.

Demeulenaere, P. 2011. Introduction. In P. Demeulenaere (Ed.), *Analytical sociology and social mechanisms*: 1–30. Cambridge: Cambridge University Press.

Denis, D. J., Denis, D. K. and Sarin, A. 1999. Agency theory and the influence of equity ownership structure on corporate diversification strategies. *Strategic Management Journal*, 20: 1071–1076.

Dicker, G. 1998. *Hume's epistemology and metaphysics: An introduction*. New York: Routledge.

Doll, R., Peto, R., Wheatley, K., Gray, R. and Sutherland, I. 1994. Mortality in relation to smoking: 40 years' observations on male British doctors. *British Medical Journal*, 309: 901–911.

Donaldson, L. 1995. *American anti-management theories of organization: A critique of paradigm proliferation*. Cambridge: Cambridge University Press.

　1998. The myth of paradigm incommensurability in management studies: Comments by an integrationist. *Organization*, 5: 267–272.

　2001. *The contingency theory of organizations*. Thousand Oaks, CA: Sage.

Dore, R. P. 1961. Function and cause. *American Sociological Review*, 26: 843–853.

Douglas, H. E. 2009. Reintroducing prediction to explanation. *Philosophy of Science*, 76: 444–463.

Dow, D. and Karunaratna, A. 2006. Developing a multidimensional instrument to measure psychic distance stimuli. *Journal of International Business Studies*, 37: 578–602.

Downing, P. B. 1959. Subjunctive conditionals, time order, and causation. *Proceedings of the Aristotelian Society*, 59: 125–140.

Dretske, F. I. 1977. Referring to events. *Midwest Studies of Philosophy*, 2: 90–99.

Dretske, F. 1989. Reasons and causes. *Philosophical Perspectives*, 3: 1–15.

Dubin, R. 1978. *Theory building* (Revised ed.). New York: Free Press.

　1982. Management: Meanings, methods, and moxie. *Academy of Management Review*, 7: 372–379.

Duch, W., Swaminathan, K. and Meller, J. 2007. Artificial intelligence approaches for rational drug design and discovery. *Current Pharmaceutical Design*, 13: 1497–1508.

Dunlop, C. A. and Radaelli, C. M. 2017. Learning in the bath-tub: The micro and macro dimensions of the causal relationship between learning and policy change. *Policy and Society*, 36: 304–319.

Durand, R. and Vaara, E. 2009. Causation, counterfactuals and competitive advantage. *Strategic Management Journal*, 30: 1245–1266.

Eden, D. and Rynes, S. 2003. Publishing across borders: Furthering the internationalization of *AMJ*. *Academy of Management Journal*, 46: 679–683.

Edmonds, D. and Eidinow, J. 2001. *Wittgenstein's poker: The story of a ten-minute argument between two great philosophers*. New York: HarperCollins.

Eisenhardt, K. M. 1989. Agency theory: An assessment and review. *Academy of Management Review*, 14: 57–74.

2021. What is the Eisenhardt Method, really? *Strategic Organization*, 19: 147–160.

Elder-Vass, D. 2007. For emergence: Refining Archer's account of social structure. *Journal for the Theory of Social Behaviour*, 37: 25–44.

2014. Social entities and the basis of their powers. In J. Zahle and F. Collin (Eds.), *Rethinking the individualism-holism debate*: 39–53. Cham: Springer.

Elgin, C. 2007. Understanding and the facts. *Philosophical Studies*, 132: 33–42.

Elster, J. 1984. *Ulysses and the sirens: Studies in rationality and irrationality* (Revised ed.). Cambridge: Cambridge University Press.

1989. *Nuts and bolts for the social sciences*. Cambridge: Cambridge University Press.

1994. Functional explanation: In social science. In M. Martin and L. C. McIntyre (Eds.). *Readings in the philosophy of social science*: 403–414. Cambridge, MA: MIT Press.

Emmet, D. 1962. "That's that"; or some uses of tautology. *Philosophy*, 37: 15–24.

Epstein, B. 2009. Ontological individualism reconsidered. *Synthese*, 166: 187–213.

Fairbank, J. K. 1983. *The United States and China* (4th ed.). Cambridge, MA: Harvard University Press.

Fay, B. 1996. *Contemporary philosophy of social science: A multicultural approach*. Oxford: Blackwell.

Faye, J. 1999. Explanation explained. *Synthese*, 120: 61–75.

Feldman, M. S. and Pentland, B. T. 2003. Reconceptualizing organizational routines as a source of flexibility and change. *Administrative Science Quarterly*, 48: 94–118.

Felin, T., Foss, N. J. and Ployhart, R. E. 2015. The microfoundations movement in strategy and organization theory. *Academy of Management Annals*, 9: 575–632.

Ferguson, A. 1976. Can evolutionary theory predict? *American Naturalist*, 110: 1101–1104.

Fetzer, J. H. 1974. Grünbaum's "defense" of the symmetry thesis. *Philosophical Studies*, 25: 173–187.

Feyerabend P. K. 1987. *Farewell to reason*. London: Verso.

Fortin, N. M., Hill, A. J. and Huang, J. 2014. Superstition in the housing market. *Economic Inquiry*, 52: 974–993.

Francis, J. R. 1994. Auditing, hermeneutics, and subjectivity. *Accounting, Organizations and Society*, 19: 235–269.

Franklin, A. 2015. The theory-ladenness of experiment. *Journal for General Philosophy of Science*, 46: 155–166.

Freedman, D. A. 1991. Statistical models and shoe leather. *Sociological Methodology*, 21: 291–313.

Friedman, M. 1953. *Essays in positive economics*. Chicago, IL: University of Chicago Press.

Friedman, M. 1974. Explanation and scientific understanding. *Journal of Philosophy*, 71: 5–19.

2000. Hempel and the Vienna Circle. In J. H. Fetzer (Ed.), *Science, explanation, and rationality: Aspects of the philosophy of Carl G. Hempel*: 39–64. New York: Oxford University Press.

Fung, Y.-L. 1922. Why China has no science – An interpretation of the history and consequences of Chinese philosophy. *International Journal of Ethics*, 32: 237–263.

Gadamer, H.-G. 1975. *Truth and method*. Translated by G. Barden and J. Cumming. New York: Seabury.

Gaddis, J. L. 2002. *The landscape of history: How historians map the past*. Oxford: Oxford University Press.

Galton, F. 1886. Regression towards mediocrity in hereditary stature. *Journal of the Anthropological Institute of Great Britain and Ireland*, 15: 246–263.

Gambetta, D. 1998. Concatenations of mechanisms. In P. Hedström and R. Swedberg (Eds.), *Social mechanisms: An analytical approach to social theory*: 102–124. Cambridge: Cambridge University Press.

Gandjour, A. and Lauterbach, K. W. 2003. Inductive reasoning in medicine: Lessons from Carl Gustav Hempel's "inductive-statistical" model. *Journal of Evaluation in Clinical Practice*, 9: 161–169.

Garfinkel, A. 1981. *Forms of explanation: Rethinking the questions in social theory*. New Haven, CT: Yale University Press.

Gaur, A. S., Kumar, V. and Singh, D. 2014. Institutions, resources, and internationalization of emerging economy firms. *Journal of World Business*, 49: 12–20.

Gelfert, A. 2010. Reconsidering the role of inference to the best explanation in the epistemology of testimony. *Studies in History and Philosophy of Science*, 41: 386–396.

Gerring, J. 2007. The case study: What it is and what it does. In C. Boix and S. C. Stokes (Eds.), *Oxford handbook of comparative politics*: 90–122. New York: Oxford University Press.

2008. The mechanismic worldview: Thinking inside the box. *British Journal of Political Science*, 38: 161–179.

2010. Causal mechanisms: Yes, but … *Comparative Political Studies*, 43: 1499–1526.

Ghoshal, S. and Moran, P. 1996. Bad for practice: A critique of the transaction cost theory. *Academy of Management Review*, 21: 13–47.

Giddens, A. 1976. *New roles in sociological methods*. London: Hutchinson.

1984. *The constitution of society: Outline of the theory of structuration*. Cambridge: Polity Press.

Glaser, B. G. and Strauss, A. L. 1967. *The discovery of grounded theory: Strategies of qualitative research*. Chicago, IL: Aldine.

Glennan, S. S. 1996. Mechanisms and the nature of causation. *Erkenntnis*, 44: 49–71.

Glennan, S. 2010. Ephemeral mechanisms and historical explanation. *Erkenntnis*, 72: 251–266.

Görling, S. and Rehn, A. 2008. Accidental ventures: A materialist reading of opportunity and entrepreneurial potential. *Scandinavian Journal of Management*, 24: 94–102.

Greenwood, J. D. 1990. Two dogmas of neo-empiricism: The "theory-informity" of observation and the Quine-Duhem thesis. *Philosophy of Science*, 57: 553–574.

Griffin, M. A. 2007. Specifying organizational contexts: Systematic links between contexts and processes in organizational behavior. *Journal of Organizational Behavior*, 28: 859–863.

Gruner, R. 1966. Teleological and functional explanations. *Mind*, 75: 516–526.

Gunstone, R. F. and White, R. T. 1981. Understanding of gravity. *Science Education*, 65: 291–299.

Gurd, B. and Or, F. K. H. 2011. Attitudes of Singaporean Chinese towards retirement planning. *Review of Pacific Basin Financial Markets and Policies*, 14: 671–692.

Haller, R. 1982. New light on the Vienna Circle. *Monist*, 65: 25–37.

Hannan, M. T. and Freeman, J. 1989. *Organizational ecology*. Cambridge, MA: Harvard University Press.

Hanson, N. R. 1969. *Perception and discovery: An introduction to scientific inquiry*. San Francisco, CA: Freeman, Cooper & Company.

Harbers, H. and de Vries, G. 1993. Empirical consequences of the "double hermeneutic." *Social Epistemology*, 7: 183–192.

Harima, A. and Freudenberg, J. 2020. Co-creation of social entrepreneurial opportunities with refugees. *Journal of Social Entrepreneurship*, 11: 40–64.

Harman, G. H. 1965. The inference to the best explanation. *Philosophical Review*, 74: 88–95.

Harman, G. 1986. *Change in view: Principles of reasoning*. Cambridge, MA: MIT Press.

Harré, R. 1970. *The principles of scientific thinking*. Chicago, IL: University of Chicago Press.

   1988. Modes of explanation. In D. J. Hilton (Ed.), *Contemporary science and natural explanation*: 129–144. Brighton: Harvestor Press.

Harré, R. and Madden, E. H. 1975. *Causal powers: A theory of natural necessity*. Oxford: Basil Blackwell.

Harré, R. and Second, P. F. 1972. *The explanation of social behavior*. Oxford: Basil Blackwell.

Hartley, J. 1997: *The representative agent in macroeconomics*. London: Routledge.

Hassard, J. 1988. Overcoming hermeticism in organization theory: An alternative to paradigm incommensurability. *Human Relations*, 41: 247–259.

Hausman, D. M. 1998. *Causal asymmetries*. Cambridge: Cambridge University Press.

Hayek, F. A. 1967. *Studies in philosophy, politics and economics*. London: Routledge and Kegan Paul.

Hayes, D. 2020. Zoom booms due to COVID-19, with Q1 revenue nearly tripling, stock at new high. *Deadline*, June 2. [https://deadline.com/2020/06/zoom-video-communication-revenue-rises-q1-1202949506/]

Hedberg, B. 1981. How organizations learn and unlearn. In P. C. Nystrom and W. H. Starbuck (Eds.), *Handbook of organizational design*. Vol. 1: 3–27. Oxford: Oxford University Press.

Hedström, P. and Swedberg, R. 1996. Social mechanism. *Acta Sociologica*, 39: 281–308.

1998. Social mechanisms: An introductory essay. In P. Hedström and R. Swedberg (Eds.), *Social mechanisms: An analytical approach to social theory*: 1–31. Cambridge: Cambridge University Press.

Hedström, P. and Ylikoski, P. 2010. Causal mechanisms in the social sciences. *Annual Review of Sociology*, 36: 49–67.

Heeley, M. B., Matusik, S. F. and Jain, N. 2007. Innovation, appropriability, and the underpricing of initial public offerings. *Academy of Management Journal*, 50: 209–225.

Heller, M. 1985. Non-backtracking counterfactuals and the conditional analysis. *Canadian Journal of Philosophy*, 15: 75–85.

Helm, P. 1971. Manifest and latent functions. *Philosophical Quarterly*, 21: 51–60.

Hempel, C. G. 1942. The function of general laws in history. *Journal of Philosophy*, 39(2): 35–48.

1950. Problems and changes in the empiricist criterion of meaning. *Revue Internationale de Philosophie*, 4(11): 41–63.

1965. *Aspects of scientific explanation and other essays in the philosophy of science*. New York: Free Press.

1970. Fundamentals of concept formation in empirical science. In O. Neurath, R. Carnap and C. Morris (Eds.), *Foundations of the unity of science*. Vol. 2: 651–745. Chicago, IL: University of Chicago Press.

Hempel, C. G. and Oppenheim, P. 1948. Studies in the logic of explanation. *Philosophy of Science*, 15: 135–175.

Hennig, B. 2009. The four causes. *Journal of Philosophy*, 106: 137–160.

Hensel, P. G. 2021. Reproducibility and replicability crisis: How management compares to psychology and economics – A systematic review of literature. *European Management Journal*, 39: 577–594.

Hintikka, J. 1988. On the incommensurability of theories. *Philosophy of Science*, 55: 25–38.

Hitchcock, C. R. 1995. Salmon on explanatory relevance. *Philosophy of Science*, 62: 304–320.

1996. Farewell to binary causation. *Canadian Journal of Philosophy*, 26: 267–282.

Hitt, M. A., Hoskisson, R. E. and Ireland, R. D. 1994. A mid-range theory of the interactive effects of international and product diversification on innovation and performance. *Journal of Management*, 20: 297–326.

Hodgson, G. M. 2007. Meanings of methodological individualism. *Journal of Economic Methodology*, 14: 211–226.

Hollenbeck, J. R. and Wright, P. M. 2017. Harking, sharking, and tharking: Making the case for post hoc analysis of scientific data. *Journal of Management*, 43: 5–18.

Hong, J. F. L., Easterby-Smith, M. and Snell, R. S. 2006. Transferring organizational learning systems to Japanese subsidiaries in China. *Journal of Management Studies*, 43: 1027–1058.

Huang, L. S. and Teng, C. I. 2009. Development of a Chinese superstitious belief scale. *Psychological Reports*, 104: 807–819.

Huff, T. E. 2017. *The rise of early modern science: Islam, China, and the West* (3rd ed.). Cambridge: Cambridge University Press.

Hume, D. 1999. *An enquiry concerning human understanding* (Edited by T. L. Beauchamp). Oxford: Oxford University Press.

2007. *A treatise of human nature*. Vol. 1 (Edited by D. F. Norton and M. J. Norton). Oxford: Oxford University Press.

Humphreys, P. 1989. *The chances of explanation*. Princeton, NJ: Princeton University Press.

Hunt, S. D. 1994. A realist theory of empirical testing resolving the theory-ladenness/objectivity debate. *Philosophy of the Social Sciences*, 24: 133–158.

Ilgen, D. R., Major, D. A. and Tower, S. L. 1994. The cognitive revolution in organizational behavior. In J. Greenberg (Ed.), *Organizational behavior: The state of the science*: 1–22. Hillsdale, NJ: Erlbaum.

Illari, P. 2013. Mechanistic explanation: Integrating the ontic and epistemic. *Erkenntnis*, 78: 237–255.

Illari, P. and Williamson, J. 2011. Mechanisms are real and local. In P. Illari, F. Russo and J. Williamson (Eds.), *Causality in the sciences*: 818–844. Oxford: Oxford University Press.

Iriyama, A. and Madhavan, R. 2014. Post-formation inter-partner equity transfers in international joint ventures: The role of experience. *Global Strategy Journal*, 4: 331–348.

Jackson, N. and Carter, P. 1991. In defence of paradigm incommensurability. *Organization Studies*, 12: 109–127.

Janssen, M. C. and Tan, Y. H. 1991. Why Friedman's non-monotonic reasoning defies Hempel's covering law model. *Synthese*, 86: 255–284.

Jansson, L. 2015. Explanatory asymmetries: Laws of nature rehabilitated. *Journal of Philosophy*, 112: 577–599.

Jenkins, C. 2008. Romeo, René, and the reasons why: What explanation is. *Proceedings of the Aristotelian Society*, 108: 61–84.

Jenkins, C. S. and Nolan, D. 2008. Backwards explanation. *Philosophical Studies*, 140: 103–115.

Jenson, J. C. 2015. The belief illusion. *British Journal for the Philosophy of Science*, 67: 965–995.

Johnston, J. 1991. *Econometric methods* (3rd ed.). Singapore: McGraw-Hill.

Jones, G. and Perry, C. 1982. Popper, induction and falsification. *Erkenntnis*, 18: 97–104.

Judge, W. Q. and Dooley, R. 2006. Strategic alliance outcomes: A transaction-cost economics perspective. *British Journal of Management*, 17: 23–37.

Kahneman, D. 2011. *Thinking, fast and slow*. New York: Farrar, Straus and Giroux.

Kao, J. 1993. The worldwide web of Chinese business. *Harvard Business Review*, 71(2): 24–36.

Kerr, N. L. 1998. HARKing: Hypothesizing after the results are known. *Personality and Social Psychology Review*, 2: 196–217.

Kieser, A. 1994. Why organization theory needs historical analyses – and how this should be performed. *Organization Science*, 5: 608–620.

Kim, W. C., Hwang, P. and Burgers, W. P. 1989. Global diversification strategy and corporate profit performance. *Strategic Management Journal*, 10: 45–57.

Kincaid, H. 1986. Reduction, explanation and individualism. In M. Martin and L. C. McIntyre (Eds.), *Readings in the philosophy of social science*: 497–513. Cambridge, MA: MIT Press.

   1990. Assessing functional explanations in the social sciences. In A. Fine, M. Forbes and L. Wessels (Eds.), *Proceedings of the 1990 biennial meeting of the Philosophy of Science Association*. Vol. 1: 341–354. East Lansing, MI: Philosophy of Science Association.

King, G., Keohane, R. O. and Verba, S. 1994. *Designing social inquiry*. Princeton, NJ: Princeton University Press.

Klein, B. 1988. Vertical integration as organizational ownership: The Fisher Body-General Motors relationship revisited. *Journal of Law, Economics, and Organization*, 4: 199–213.

Klein, B., Crawford, R. G. and Alchian, A. A. 1978. Vertical integration, appropriable rents, and the competitive contracting process. *Journal of Law and Economics*, 21: 297–326.

Klein, K. J., Dansereau, F. and Hall, R. J. 1994. Levels issues in theory development, data collection, and analysis. *Academy of Management Review*, 19: 195–229.

Klein, P. G. 2008. The make-or-buy decision: Lessons from empirical studies. In C. Menard and M. M. Shirley (Eds.), *Handbook of new institutional economics*: 435–464. Berlin: Springer.

Kogut, B. 1991. Joint ventures and the option to expand and acquire. *Management Science*, 37: 19–33.

Koontz, H. 1961. The management theory jungle. *Academy of Management Journal*, 4: 174–188.

Korman, J. and Khemlani, S. 2020. Explanatory completeness. *Acta Psychologica*, 209: 103139.

Korsgaard, S. T. 2011. Entrepreneurship as translation: Understanding entrepreneurial opportunities through actor-network theory. *Entrepreneurship & Regional Development*, 23: 661–680.

Krugman, P. 2020. *Arguing with zombies: Economics, politics, and the fight for a better future*. New York: W. W. Norton.

Kuhn, T. S. 1970. *The structure of scientific revolutions* (2nd ed.). Chicago, IL: University of Chicago Press.

   1990. Dubbing and redubbing: The vulnerability of rigid designation. In C. W. Savage (Ed.), *Minnesota studies in the philosophy of science. Vol. XIV: Scientific theories*: 298–318. Minneapolis, MN: University of Minnesota Press.

Kvanvig, J. 2003. *The value of knowledge and the pursuit of understanding.* Cambridge: Cambridge University Press.

Lampel, J. and Giachetti, C. 2013. International diversification of manufacturing operations: Performance implications and moderating forces. *Journal of Operations Management,* 31: 213–227.

Lane, P. J., Cannella, A. A. and Lubatkin, M. H. 1999. Ownership structure and corporate strategy: One question viewed from two different worlds. *Strategic Management Journal,* 20: 1077–1086.

Lane, S. M. 1981. Mathematical models: A sketch for the philosophy of mathematics. *American Mathematical Monthly,* 88: 462–472.

Langley, A. 1999. Strategies for theorizing from process data. *Academy of Management Review,* 24: 691–710.

Langley, A., Smallman, C., Tsoukas, H. and Van de Ven, A. H. 2013. Process studies of change in organization and management: Unveiling temporality, activity, and flow. *Academy of Management Journal,* 56: 1–13.

Langley, A. and Tsoukas, H. 2010. Introducing "Perspectives on process organization studies." In T. Hemes and S. Maitlis (Eds.), *Process, sensemaking and organizing:* 1–26. Oxford: Oxford University Press.

Laudan, L. 1996. *Beyond positivism and relativism: Theory, method, and evidence.* Boulder, CO: Westview Press.

Lebow, R. N. and Stein, J. G. 1996. Back to the past: Counterfactuals and the Cuban missile crisis. In P. Tetlock and A. Belkin (Eds.), *Counterfactual thought experiments in world politics: Logical, methodological and psychological perspectives:* 119–148. Princeton, NJ: Princeton University Press

Leonard-Barton, D. 1992. Core capabilities and core rigidities: A paradox in managing new product development. *Strategic Management Journal,* 13 (S1): 111–125.

Lester, R. A. 1946. Shortcomings of marginal analysis for wage-employment problems. *American Economic Review,* 36: 63–82.

Levinthal, D. and March, J. G. 1993. Myopia of learning. *Strategic Management Journal,* 14: 95–112.

Levitt, B. and March, J. G. 1988. Organizational learning. *Annual Review of Sociology,* 14: 319–340.

Lewis, D. 1973. Causation. *Journal of Philosophy,* 70: 556–567.

1979. Counterfactual dependence and time's arrow. *Noûs,* 13: 455–476.

1983. New work for a theory of universals. *Australasian Journal of Philosophy,* 61: 343–377.

1986. *Philosophical papers.* Vol. II. New York: Oxford University Press.

Lewis, M. W. and Smith, W. K. 2014. Paradox as a metatheoretical perspective: Sharpening the focus and widening the scope. *Journal of Applied Behavioral Science,* 50: 127–149.

Lewis, P. 2012. Emergent properties in the work of Friedrich Hayek. *Journal of Economic Behavior & Organization,* 82: 368–378.

Li, P. P. 1998. Towards a geocentric framework of organizational form: A holistic, dynamic and paradoxical approach. *Organization Studies,* 19: 829–861.

2014. The unique value of Yin-Yang balancing: A critical response. *Management and Organization Review*, 10: 321–332.

2016. Global implications of the indigenous epistemological system from the East: How to apply Yin-Yang balancing to paradox management. *Cross Cultural & Strategic Management*, 12: 42–77.

2021. The meta-perspective of Yin-Yang balancing: Salient implications for organizational management. *Research in the Sociology of Organizations*, Part 73A: 51–74.

Li, P. P., Li, Y. and Liu, H. 2012. The exploration-exploitation link reframed from paradox into duality. Working Paper, Copenhagen Business School.

Lin, Y. 1977 [1936] *My country and my people*. Hong Kong: Heinemann.

Lindenberg, S and Foss, N. J. 2011. Managing joint production motivation: The role of goal framing and governance mechanisms. *Academy of Management Review*, 36: 500–525.

Lipton, P. 1990. Contrastive explanation. In D. Knowles (Ed.), *Explanation and its limits*: 247–266. Cambridge: Cambridge University Press.

1991. *Inference to the best explanation*. London: Routledge.

1993. Making a difference. *Philosophica*, 51: 39–54.

2009. Understanding without explanation. In H. W. de Regt, S. Leonelli and K. Eigner (Eds.), *Scientific understanding: Philosophical perspectives*: 43–63. Pittsburgh, PA: University of Pittsburgh Press.

Little, D. 1991. *Varieties of social explanation: An introduction to the philosophy of social science*. Boulder, CO: Westview Press.

1998. *Microfoundations, method, and causation*. New Brunswick, NJ: Transaction.

2012. Explanatory autonomy and Coleman's boat. *Theoria*, 27: 137–151.

Liu, C. and de Rond, M. 2016. Good night, and good luck: Perspectives on luck in management scholarship. *Academy of Management Annals*, 10: 409–451.

Locke, J. 1975. *An essay concerning human understanding* (4th ed.). P. H. Nidditch (Ed.). Oxford: Clarendon Press.

Losee, J. 2005. *Theories on the scrap heap: Scientists and philosophers on the falsification, rejection, and replacement of theories*. Pittsburgh, PA: University of Pittsburgh Press.

Lukes, S. 1968. Methodological individualism reconsidered. *British Journal of Sociology*, 19: 119–129.

Lyngaas, S. 2021. Apple sues NSO Group over spyware. *CNN Business*, November 23. [www.cnn.com/2021/11/23/tech/apple-nso-spyware-law suit/index.html]

Mach, E. 1883. *Die mechanik in ihrer entwicklung*. Leipzig: Brockhaus. Translated by T. J. McCormick, 1960. *The science of mechanics*. Chicago, IL: Open Court.

Machamer, P., Darden, L. and Craver, C. F. 2000. Thinking about mechanisms. *Philosophy of Science*, 67: 1–25.

Mackie, J. L. 1974. *The cement of the universe*. Oxford: Clarendon Press.

Madeddu, M. and Zhang, X. 2017. Harmonious spaces: The influence of Feng Shui on urban form and design. *Journal of Urban Design*, 22: 709–725.

Mahoney, J. 2001. Beyond correlational analysis: Recent innovations in theory and method. *Sociological Forum,* 16: 575–593.

Maiocchi, R. 1990. The case of Brownian motion. *British Journal for the History of Science,* 23: 257–283.

Mäki, U. 2000. Kinds of assumptions and their truth: Shaking an untwisted F-twist. *Kyklos,* 53: 317–336.

2004. Theoretical isolation and explanatory progress: Transaction cost economics and the dynamics of dispute. *Cambridge Journal of Economics,* 28: 319–346.

March, J. G. 1991. Exploration and exploitation in organizational learning. *Organization Science,* 2: 71–87.

March, J. G. and Simon, H. A. 1958. *Organizations.* New York: Wiley.

Marchionni, C. 2006. Contrastive explanation and unrealistic models: The case of the new economic geography. *Journal of Economic Methodology,* 13: 425–446.

2008. Explanatory pluralism and complementarity. *Philosophy of the Social Sciences,* 38: 314–333.

Marquis, C. and Tilcsik, A. 2013. Imprinting: Toward a multilevel theory. *Academy of Management Annals,* 7: 195–245.

Martignoni, D. and Keil, T. 2021. It did not work? Unlearn and try again – Unlearning success and failure beliefs in changing environments. *Strategic Management Journal,* 42: 1057–1082.

Masterman, M. 1970. The nature of a paradigm. In I. Lakatos and A. Musgrave (Eds.), *Criticism and the growth of knowledge:* 59–89. Cambridge: Cambridge University Press.

Maxwell, J. A. 2004. Causal explanation, qualitative research, and scientific inquiry in education. *Educational Researcher,* 33(2): 3–11.

Mayntz, R. 2004. Mechanisms in the analysis of social macro-phenomena. *Philosophy of the Social Sciences,* 34: 237–259.

McAuliffe, W. H. 2015. How did abduction get confused with inference to the best explanation? *Transactions of the Charles S. Peirce Society,* 51: 300–319.

McBreen, B. 2007. Realism and empiricism in Hume's account of causality. *Philosophy,* 82: 421–436.

McCain, K. 2015. Explanation and the nature of scientific knowledge. *Science & Education,* 24: 827–854.

McGuire, J. M. 2007. Actions, reasons, and intentions: Overcoming Davidson's ontological prejudice. *Dialogue,* 46: 459–479.

McKelvey, B. 1978. Organizational systematics: Taxonomic lessons from biology. *Management Science,* 24: 1428–1440.

McKinley, W. and Mone, M. A. 1998. The re-construction of organization studies: Wrestling with incommensurability. *Organization,* 5: 169–189.

McMullin, E. 2008. The virtues of a good theory. In S. Psillos and M. Curd (Eds.), *The Routledge companion to philosophy of science:* 498–508. New York: Routledge.

McMullen, J. S., Plummer, L. A. and Acs, Z. J. 2007. What is an entrepreneurial opportunity? *Small Business Economics*, 28: 273–283.

Merton, R. K. 1948. The self-fulfilling prophecy. *Antioch Review*, 8: 193–210.

1957. *Social theory and social structure* (Enlarged and revised ed.). New York: Free Press.

1967. *On theoretical sociology*. New York: Free Press.

1968. *Social theory and social structure* (Enlarged ed.). New York: Free Press.

Miles, M. B. and A. M. Huberman. 1984. *Qualitative data analysis: A sourcebook of new methods*. Newbury Park, CA: Sage.

Mill, J. S. 1973. *System of logic*, Books I–III. In J. M. Robson (Ed.), *The collected works of J. S. Mill*. Toronto: University of Toronto Press.

Miller, K. D. and Tsang, E. W. K. 2011. Testing management theories: Critical realist philosophy and research methods. *Strategic Management Journal*, 32: 139–158.

Miller, R. W. 1987. *Fact and method: Explanation, confirmation and reality in the natural and social sciences*. Princeton, NJ: Princeton University Press.

Millman, N. 2021. The simplest explanation for the Delta surge is still the best one. *Yahoo News*, August 31. [www.yahoo.com/news/simplest-explanation-delta-surge-still-095512097.html]

Mohr, L. B. 1982. *Explaining organizational behavior*. San Francisco, CA: Jossey-Bass.

Moravcsik, J. M. 1974. Aristotle on adequate explanations. *Synthese*, 28: 3–17.

Murphey, M. G. 1986. Explanation, cause, and covering laws. *History and Theory*, 25: 43–57.

Mutch, A. 2013. Sociomateriality — Taking the wrong turning? *Information and Organization*, 23: 28–40.

Nagel, E. 1979. *The structure of science: Problems in the logic of scientific explanation*. Indianapolis, IN: Hackett.

Naraniecki, A. 2010. Neo-positivist or neo-Kantian? Karl Popper and the Vienna Circle. *Philosophy*, 85: 511–530.

Nature. 2007. Hard to swallow: Is it possible to gauge the true potential of traditional Chinese medicine? *Nature*, 448: 106.

Neander, K. 1991. The teleological notion of "function." *Australasian Journal of Philosophy*, 69: 454–468.

Needham, J. 1954. *Science and civilisation in China*. Vol. 1. Cambridge: Cambridge University Press.

Niiniluoto, I. 1999. Defending abduction. *Philosophy of Science*, 66: S436–S451.

2000. Hempel's theory of statistical explanation. In J. H. Fetzer (Ed.), *Science, explanation, and rationality: Aspects of the philosophy of Carl G. Hempel*: 138–163. New York: Oxford University Press.

Nobel, W. S. 2006. What is a support vector machine? *Nature Biotechnology*, 24: 1565–1567.

Numagami, T. 1998. The infeasibility of invariant laws in management studies: A reflective dialogue in defense of case studies. *Organization Science*, 9: 2–15.

O'Connor, T. 1996. Why agent causation? *Philosophical Topics*, 24: 143–158.

Oremus, W. 2021. Elizabeth Holmes's trial spotlights Silicon Valley's thin line between hype and deceit. *Washington Post*, September 1. [www .washingtonpost.com/technology/2021/09/01/elizabeth-holmes-theranos-trial-analysis-silicon-valley/]

Orlikowski, W. 2007. Sociomaterial practices: Exploring technology at work. *Organization Studies*, 28: 1435–1448.

Østergaard, C. R., Timmermans, B. and Kristinsson, K. 2011. Does a different view create something new? The effect of employee diversity on innovation. *Research Policy*, 40: 500–509.

Pan, W. and Sun, L. Y. 2018. A self-regulation model of Zhong Yong thinking and employee adaptive performance. *Management and Organization Review*, 14: 135–159.

Pathak, B., Ashok, M. and Tan, Y. L. 2020. Value co-destruction: Exploring the role of actors' opportunism in the B2B context. *International Journal of Information Management*, 52: 102093.

Patton, M. Q. 2002. *Qualitative evaluation and research methods* (3rd ed.). Thousand Oaks, CA: Sage.

Pearl, J. 1998. Graphs, causality, and structural equation models. *Sociological Methods & Research*, 27: 226–284.

2009. *Causality: Models, reasoning, and inference* (2nd ed.). New York: Cambridge University Press.

Pearl, J. and Mackenzie, D. 2018. *The book of why: The new science of cause and effect*. New York: Basic Books.

Peirce, C. S. 1908. A neglected argument for the reality of God. *Hibbert Journal*, 7: 90–112.

1986. *The writings of Charles S. Peirce – A chronological edition*. Vol. 3 (1872–1878) (Edited by M. H. Fisch). Bloomington, IN: Indiana University Press.

Perrin, J. 1913. *Les atomes*. Paris: Alcan. Translated by D. Hammick, 1923. *Atoms*. London: Constable.

Perrow, C. 1994. Pfeffer slips! *Academy of Management Review*, 19: 191–194.

Peters, R. H. 1976. Tautology in evolution and ecology. *American Naturalist*, 110: 1–12.

Pettit, P. 2003. Groups with minds of their own. In F. F. Schmitt (Ed.), *Socializing metaphysics*: 167–193. Lanham, MD: Rowman and Littlefield.

Pfeffer, J. 1993. Barriers to the advance of organizational science: Paradigm development as a dependent variable. *Academy of Management Review*, 18: 599–620.

Phillips, D. C. 1990. Subjectivity and objectivity: An objective inquiry. In E. W. Eisner and A. Peshkin (Eds.), *Qualitative inquiry in education: The continuing debate*: 19–37. New York: Teachers College Press.

Pilling, B. K., Crosby, L. A. and Jackson, D. W. 1994. Relational bonds in industrial exchange: An experimental test of the transaction cost economic framework. *Journal of Business Research*, 30: 237–251.

Podsakoff, P. M., Podsakoff, N. P., Mishra, P. and Escue, C. 2018. Can early-career scholars conduct impactful research? Playing "small ball" versus "swinging for the fences." *Academy of Management Learning & Education*, 17: 496–531.

Popper, K. R. 1959. *The logic of scientific discovery*. London: Hutchinson.

1994. *The myth of the framework: In defense of science and rationality*. M. A. Notturno (Ed.). London: Routledge.

Popper, K. 2002. *Unended quest*. New York: Routledge.

Poppo, L. and Zenger, T. 1998. Testing alternative theories of the firm: Transaction cost, knowledge-based, and measurement explanations for make-or-buy decisions in information services. *Strategic Management Journal*, 19: 853–877.

Porter, M. E. 1980. *Competitive strategy*. New York: Free Press.

Pouder, R. and St. John, C. H. 1996. Hot spots and blind spots: Geographical clusters of firms and innovation. *Academy of Management Review*, 21: 1192–1225.

Prasad, A. 2002. The contest over meaning: Hermeneutics as an interpretive methodology for understanding texts. *Organizational Research Methods*, 5: 12–33.

Pratt, S. and Kirillova, K. 2019. Are hotel guests bothered by unlucky floor or room assignments? *International Journal of Hospitality Management*, 83: 83–94.

Priem, R. L. and Butler, J. E. 2001a. Is the resource-based "view" a useful perspective for strategic management research? *Academy of Management Review*, 26: 22–40.

2001b. Tautology in the resource-based view and the implications of externally determined resource value: Further comments. *Academy of Management Review*, 26: 57–66.

Qui, J., Donaldson, L. and Luo, B. N. 2012. The benefits of persisting with paradigms in organizational research. *Academy of Management Perspectives*, 26: 93–104.

Radcliffe-Brown, A. R. 1935. On the concept of function in social science. *American Anthropologist*, 37: 394–402.

Rainsford, K. D. (Ed.). 1995. *Progress in drug research*. Basel: Springer.

Raisch, S. and Birkinshaw, J. 2008. Organizational ambidexterity: Antecedents, outcomes, and moderators. *Journal of Management*, 34: 375–409.

Ramoglou, S. and Tsang, E. W. K. 2016. A realist perspective of entrepreneurship: Opportunities as propensities. *Academy of Management Review*, 41: 410–434.

2017. In defense of common sense in entrepreneurship theory: Beyond philosophical extremities and linguistic abuses. *Academy of Management Review*, 42: 736–744.

Ramsey, F. P. 1925. The foundations of mathematics. *Proceedings of the London Mathematical Society*, 2: 338–384.

Ravichandran, H. 2021. Business opportunity where you least expect it. *Forbes*, June 9. [www.forbes.com/sites/forbestechcouncil/2021/06/09/business-opportunity-where-you-least-expect-it/]

Reece, B. C. 2019. Aristotle's four causes of action. *Australasian Journal of Philosophy*, 97: 213–227.

Reichenbach H. 1956. *The direction of time.* Berkeley, CA: University of California Press.

Reiss, J. 2009. Counterfactuals, thought experiments, and singular causal analysis in history. *Philosophy of Science*, 76: 712–723.

Reuer, J. J., Tyler, B. B., Tong, T. W. and Wu, C. W. 2012. Executives' assessments of international joint ventures in China: A multi-theoretical investigation. *Management and Organization Review*, 8: 311–340.

Reuters. 2020. Samsung to relocate Chinese display production to Vietnam. June 19. [www.reuters.com/article/vietnam-samsung-idUSL4N2DW2CV]

Reydon, T. A. and Scholz, M. 2009. Why organizational ecology is not a Darwinian research program. *Philosophy of the Social Sciences*, 39: 408–439.

Ricoeur, P. 1971. The model of the text: Meaningful action considered as a text. *Social Research*, 38: 529–562.

Ritzer, G. 1990. Metatheorizing in sociology. *Sociological Forum*, 5: 3–15.

Roberts, C. 1996. *The logic of historical explanation.* University Park, PA: Pennsylvania State University Press.

Robins, J. A. 1987. Organizational economics: Notes on the use of transaction-cost theory in the study of organizations. *Administrative Science Quarterly*, 32: 68–86.

Ronen, S. and Shenkar, O. 1985. Clustering countries on attitudinal dimensions: A review and synthesis. *Academy of Management Review*, 10: 435–454.

Rosenthal, R. 1979. The file drawer problem and tolerance for null results. *Psychological Bulletin*, 86: 638–641.

Rosenzweig, P. 2007. Misunderstanding the nature of company performance: The halo effect and other business delusions. *California Management Review*, 49(4): 6–20.

Ross, W. D. (Ed.). 1936. *Aristotle's Physics.* Oxford: Oxford University Press.
(Ed.). 1948. *Aristotle's Metaphysics.* Oxford: Clarendon Press.

Roth, G. 1976. History and sociology in the work of Max Weber. *British Journal of Sociology*, 27: 306–318.

Rousseau, D. M. 1985. Issues of level in organizational research: Multi-level and cross-level perspectives. *Research in Organizational Behavior*, 7: 1–37.

Roy, W. G. 1990. Functional and historical logics in explaining the rise of the American industrial corporation. *Comparative Social Research*, 12(20): 19–44.

Ruben, D.-H. 1990. *Explaining explanation.* London: Routledge.

Rubin, M. 2022. The costs of HARKing. *British Journal for the Philosophy of Science*, 73: 535–560.

Rugman, A. 1979. *International diversification and the multinational enterprise.* Lexington, MA: Lexington Books.

Runde, J. and de Rond, M. 2010. Evaluating causal explanations of specific events. *Organization Studies*, 31: 431–450.

Ryan, L. V. and Schneider, M. 2003. Institutional investor power and heterogeneity: Implications for agency and stakeholder theories. *Business & Society*, 42: 398–429.

Salmon, W. C. 1975. Theoretical explanation. In S. Körner (Ed.), *Explanation*: 118–145. Oxford: Basil Blackwell.

1984. *Scientific explanation and the causal structure of the world*. Princeton, NJ: Princeton University Press.

1990. Scientific explanation: Causation and unification. *Critica: Revista Hispanoamericana de Filosofia*, 22(66): 3–23.

Salmon, W. 1998. *Causality and explanation*. Oxford: Oxford University Press.

1999. The spirit of logical empiricism: Carl G. Hempel's role in twentieth-century philosophy of science. *Philosophy of Science*, 66: 333–350.

2006. *Four decades of scientific explanation*. Pittsburgh, PA: University of Pittsburgh Press.

Salvato, C. and Aldrich, H. E. 2012. "That's interesting!" in family business research. *Family Business Review*, 25: 125–135.

Sankey, H. 1993. Kuhn's changing concept of incommensurability. *British Journal for the Philosophy of Science*, 44: 759–774.

Sarkar, S. 1996. (Ed.) *The emergence of logical empiricism: From 1900 to the Vienna Circle*. New York: Garland.

Sawyer, R. K. 2002. Nonreductive individualism: Part I – Supervenience and wild disjunction. *Philosophy of the Social Sciences*, 32: 537–559.

Sayer, A. 1992. *Method in social science: A realist approach* (2nd ed.). London: Routledge.

2000. *Realism and social science*. London: Sage.

Scheffler, I. 1957. Explanation, prediction and abstraction. *British Journal for the Philosophy of Science*, 7: 293–309.

Scherer, A. G. 1998. Pluralism and incommensurability in strategic management and organization theory: A problem in search of a solution. *Organization*, 5: 147–168.

Scherer, A. G., Does, E. and Marti, E. 2016. Epistemology: Philosophical foundations and organizational controversies. In R. Mir, H. Willmott and M. Greenwood (Eds.), *The Routledge companion to philosophy in organization studies*: 33–50. New York: Routledge.

Schumpeter, J. 1909. On the concept of social value. *Quarterly Journal of Economics*, 23: 213–232.

Scriven, M. 1959. Explanation and prediction in evolutionary theory. *Science*, 130: 477–482.

1962. Explanations, predictions, and laws. In H. Feigl and G. Maxwell (Eds.), *Minnesota studies in the philosophy of science*. Vol. III: 170–230. Minneapolis, MN: University of Minnesota Press.

Searle, J. R. 1990. Collective intentions and actions. In P. R. Cohen, J. Morgan and M. Pollack (Eds.), *Intentions in communication*: 401–415. Cambridge, MA: MIT Press.

1991. Intentionalistic explanations in the social sciences. *Philosophy of the Social Sciences*, 21: 332–344.

2006. Social ontology: Some basic principles. *Anthropological Theory*, 6: 12–29.

2007. *Freedom & neurobiology: Reflections on free will, language, and political power*. New York: Columbia University Press.

Shane, S. and Venkataraman, S. 2000. The promise of entrepreneurship as a field of research. *Academy of Management Review*, 25: 217–226.

Shankman, N. A. 1999. Reframing the debate between agency and stakeholder theories of the firm. *Journal of Business Ethics*, 19: 319–334.

Shevrin, H. and Dickman, S. 1980. The psychological unconscious: A necessary assumption for all psychological theory? *American Psychologist*, 35: 421–434.

Short, J. 2009. The art of writing a review article. *Journal of Management*, 35: 1312–1317.

Siggelkow, N. 2007. Persuasion with case studies. *Academy of Management Journal*, 50: 20–24.

Sigmund, K. 2017. *Exact thinking in demented times: The Vienna Circle and the epic quest for the foundations of science*. New York: Basic Books.

Simon, H. A. 1991. Bounded rationality and organizational learning. *Organization Science*, 2: 125–134.

Sindo, T. 1973. Allergy: Concept and history. *Journal of Asthma Research*, 10: 141–155.

Sivin, N. 1978. On the word "Taoist" as a source of perplexity. With special reference to the relations of science and religion in traditional China. *History of Religions*, 17: 303–330.

1988. Science and medicine in imperial China – The state of the field. *Journal of Asian Studies*, 47: 41–90.

Skinner, B. F. 1953. *Science and human behavior*. New York: Free Press.

1985. Cognitive science and behaviourism. *British Journal of Psychology*, 76: 291–301.

Smith, A. 1776. *An inquiry into the nature and causes of the wealth of nations*, reprinted in R. H. Campbell, A. S. Skinner and W. B. Todd (Eds.). 1976. *Glasgow edition of the works and correspondence of Adam Smith*. Vol. II. Oxford: Oxford University Press.

Sousa, C. M. and Bradley, F. 2006. Cultural distance and psychic distance: Two peas in a pod? *Journal of International Marketing*, 14: 49–70.

Spirtes, P., Glymour, C. and Schein, R. 1993. *Causation, prediction and search*. New York: Springer.

St. John, C. H. 2005. Multi-theoretical mixed-level research in strategic management. *Research Methodology in Strategy and Management*, 2: 197–223.

Staw, B. M. and Ross, J. 1978. Commitment to a policy decision: A multi-theoretical perspective. *Administrative Science Quarterly*, 23: 40–64.

Stebbins, G. L. 1977. In defense of evolution: Tautology or theory? *American Naturalist*, 111: 386–390.

Steel, D. 2004. Social mechanisms and causal inference. *Philosophy of the Social Sciences*, 34: 55–78.

2005. Mechanisms and functional hypotheses in social science. *Philosophy of Science*, 72: 941–952.

2008. *Across the boundaries. Extrapolation in biology and social Sciences*. Oxford: Oxford University Press.

Stephan, A. 1992. Emergence – A systematic view on its historical facets. In A. Beckermann, H. Flohr and J. Kim (Eds.), *Emergence or reduction? Essays on the prospects of nonreductive physicalism*: 25–48. Berlin: Walter de Gruyter.

Sternberg, R. J. and Ben-Zeev, T. 2001. *Complex cognition: The psychology of human thought*. New York: Oxford University Press.

Stinchcombe, A. L. 1968. *Constructing social theories*. Chicago, IL: University of Chicago Press.

Stöttinger, B. and Schlegelmilch, B. B. 1998. Explaining export development through psychic distance: Enlightening or elusive? *International Marketing Review*, 15: 357–372.

Stouffer, S. A., Suchman, E. A., Devinney, L. C., Star, S. A. and Williams, R. M., Jr. 1949. *The American soldier: Adjustment during army life*. Princeton, NJ: Princeton University Press.

Strauss, A. and Corbin, J. 1990. *Basics of qualitative research: Grounded theory procedures and techniques*. Newbury Park, CA: Sage.

Strevens, M. 2004. The causal and unification accounts of explanation unified – Causally. *Noûs*, 38: 154–179.

2013. No understanding without explanation. *Studies in History and Philosophy of Science*, 44: 510–515.

Stroud, B. 1977. *Hume*. London: Routledge & Kegan Paul.

Su, W. and Tsang, E. W. K. 2015. Product diversification and financial performance: The moderating role of secondary stakeholders. *Academy of Management Journal*, 58: 1128–1148.

Suppes, P. 1970. *A probabilistic theory of causality*. Amsterdam: North-Holland.

Surdu, I., Mellahi, K. and Glaister, K. W. 2019. Once bitten, not necessarily shy? Determinants of foreign market re-entry commitment strategies. *Journal of International Business Studies*, 50: 393–422.

Susman, G. I. and Evered, R. D. 1978. An assessment of the scientific merits of action research. *Administrative Science Quarterly*, 23: 582–603.

Sutton, R. I. and Staw, B. M. 1995. What theory is not. *Administrative Science Quarterly*, 40: 371–384.

Swanson, D. 1988. Migraine and magnesium: Eleven neglected connections. *Perspectives in Biology and Medicine*, 31: 526–557.

Tallman, S. and Li, J. 1996. Effects of international diversity and product diversity on the performance of multinational firms. *Academy of Management Journal*, 39: 179–196.

Tang, C. S. K. and Wu, A. M. 2012. Gambling-related cognitive biases and pathological gambling among youths, young adults, and mature adults in Chinese societies. *Journal of Gambling Studies*, 28: 139–154.

Thagard, P. R. 1978. The best explanation: Criteria for theory choice. *Journal of Philosophy*, 75: 76–92.

Thomas, D. 2022. Theranos scandal: Who is Elizabeth Holmes and why was she on trial? *BBC News*, January 4. [www.bbc.com/news/business-58336998]

Thomas, D. C., Cuervo-Cazurra, A. and Brannen, M. Y. 2011. Explaining theoretical relationships in international business research: Focusing on the arrows, NOT the boxes. *Journal of International Business Studies*, 42: 1073–1078.

Tilly, C. 2001. Mechanisms in political processes. *Annual Review of Political Science*, 4: 21–41.

Toomer, G. J. 1984. *Ptolemy's Almagest*. London: Gerald Duckworth & Co.

Trout, J. D. 2002. Scientific explanation and the sense of understanding. *Philosophy of Science*, 69: 212–233.

Tsang, E. W. K. 1997. Organizational learning and the learning organization: A dichotomy between descriptive and prescriptive research. *Human Relations*, 50: 73–89.

1998. Can *guanxi* be a source of sustained competitive advantage for doing business in China? *Academy of Management Executive*, 12(2): 64–73.

2000. Transaction cost and resource-based explanations of joint ventures: A comparison and synthesis. *Organization Studies*, 21: 215–242.

2002. Self-serving attributions in corporate annual reports: A replicated study. *Journal of Management Studies*, 39: 51–65.

2004a. Toward a scientific inquiry into superstitious business decision-making. *Organization Studies*, 25: 923–946.

2004b. Superstition and decision-making: Contradiction or complement? *Academy of Management Executive*, 18(4): 92–104.

2006a. Economies of scale versus intellectual curiosity. *Asia Pacific Journal of Management*, 23: 157–165.

2006b. Behavioral assumptions and theory development: The case of transaction cost economics. *Strategic Management Journal*, 27: 999–1011.

2008. Transferring knowledge to acquisition joint ventures: An organizational unlearning perspective. *Management Learning*, 39: 5–20.

2013. Case study methodology: Causal explanation, contextualization, and theorizing. *Journal of International Management*, 19: 195–202.

2014a. Ensuring manuscript quality and preserving authorial voice: The balancing act of editors. *Management and Organization Review*, 10: 191–197.

2014b. Generalizing from research findings: The merits of case studies. *International Journal of Management Reviews*, 16: 369–383.

2016. How existing organizational practices affect the transfer of practices to international joint ventures. *Management International Review*, 56: 565–595.

2017. *The philosophy of management research*. New York: Routledge.

2022a. Alternative typologies of case study theorizing: Causal explanation versus theory development as a classification dimension. *Journal of International Business Studies*, 53: 53–63.

2022b. That's interesting! A flawed article has influenced generations of management researchers. *Journal of Management Inquiry*, 31: 150–164.

Tsang, E. W. K. and Blevins, D. P. 2015. A critique of the information asymmetry argument in the management and entrepreneurship underpricing literature. *Strategic Organization*, 13: 247–258.

Tsang, E. W. K. and Kwan, K.-M. 1999. Replication and theory development in organizational science: A critical realist perspective. *Academy of Management Review*, 24: 759–780.

Tsang, E. W. K. and Williams, J. N. 2012. Generalization and induction: Misconceptions, clarifications, and a classification of induction. *MIS Quarterly*, 36: 729–748.

Tsang, E. W. K. and Yamanoi, J. 2016. International expansion through start-up or acquisition: A replication. *Strategic Management Journal*, 37: 2291–2306.

Tsang, E. W. K. and Zahra, S. 2008. Organizational unlearning. *Human Relations*, 61: 1435–1462.

Tsilipakos, L. 2015. *Clarity and confusion: in social theory: Taking concepts seriously.* Farmham: Ashgate.

Tunçalp, D. 2016. Questioning the ontology of sociomateriality: A critical realist perspective. *Management Decision*, 54: 1073–1087.

Turner, J. H. and Maryanski, A. 1979. *Functionalism*. Menlo Park, CA: Benjamin/Cummings.

Udehn, L. 2002. The changing face of methodological individualism. *Annual Review of Sociology*, 28: 479–507.

Van de Ven, A. H. 1989. Nothing is quite so practical as a good theory. *Academy of Management Review*, 14: 486–489.

Van de Ven, A. H. and Engleman, R. M. 2004. Event-and outcome-driven explanations of entrepreneurship. *Journal of Business Venturing*, 19: 343–358.

Van de Ven, A. H. and Poole, M. S. 1995. Explaining development and change in organizations. *Academy of Management Review*, 20: 510–540.

Van Evera, S. 1997. *Guide to methods for students of political science*. Ithaca, NY: Cornell University Press.

van Fraassen, B. 1980. *The scientific image*. Oxford: Oxford University Press.

Van Lent, W. and Durepos, G. 2019. Nurturing the historic turn: "History as theory" versus "history as method". *Journal of Management History*, 25: 429–443.

von Mises, L. 1949. *Human action: A treatise on economics*. New Haven, CT: Yale University Press.

von Wright, G. H. 1971. *Explanation and understanding*. Ithaca, NY: Cornell University Press

Walton, D. 2007. Evaluating practical reasoning. *Synthese*, 157: 197–240.

Waskan, J. 2006. *Models and cognition*. Cambridge, MA: MIT Press.

Wathne, K. H. and Heide, J. B. 2000. Opportunism in interfirm relationships: Forms, outcomes, and solutions. *Journal of Marketing*, 64: 36–51.

Watkins, J. W. N. 1957. Historical explanation in the social sciences. *British Journal for the Philosophy of Science*, 8: 104–117.

Watson, J. D. 1968. *The double helix*. New York: Signet.

Watson, S. and Hewett, K. 2006. A multi-theoretical model of knowledge transfer in organizations: Determinants of knowledge contribution and knowledge reuse. *Journal of Management Studies*, 43: 141–173.

Weaver, G. R. and Gioia, D. A. 1994. Paradigms lost: Incommensurability vs structurationist inquiry. *Organization Studies*, 15: 565–590.

Weber, E., Van Bouwel, J. and De Vreese, L. 2013. *Scientific explanation*. New York: Springer.

Weber, M. 1922. *Economy and society*, reprinted by G. Roth and C. Wittich (Eds.). 1968. Berkeley, CA: University of California Press.

1958. *The Protestant ethic and the spirit of capitalism*. New York: Charles Scribner's Sons.

1962. *The sociology of religion*. Boston, MA: Beacon Press.

Weick, K. 2003. Theory and practice in the real world. In H. Tsoukas and C. Knudsen (Eds.), *The handbook of organization theory: Meta-theoretical perspectives*: 453–475. Oxford: Oxford University Press.

Weingartner, R. H. 1961. The quarrel about historical explanation. *Journal of Philosophy*, 58: 29–45.

Weissman, D. 2000. *A social ontology*. New Haven, CT: Yale University Press.

Welch, C., Paavilainen-Mäntymäki, E., Piekkari, R. and Plakoyiannaki, E. 2022. Reconciling theory and context: How the case study can set a new agenda for international business research. *Journal of International Business Studies*, 53: 4–26.

Welch, C., Piekkari, R., Plakoyiannaki, E. and Paavilainen-Mäntymäki, E., 2011. Theorising from case studies: Towards a pluralist future for international business research. *Journal of International Business Studies*, 42: 740–762.

Welch, H. 1957. *The parting of the Way: Lao Tzu and the Taoist movement*. Boston, MA: Beacon Hill Press.

Wensley, A. K. and Navarro, J. G. C. 2015. Overcoming knowledge loss through the utilization of an unlearning context. *Journal of Business Research*, 68: 1563–1569.

Weslake, B. 2010. Explanatory depth. *Philosophy of Science*, 77: 273–294.

Wilkenfeld, D. A. 2014. Functional explaining: A new approach to the philosophy of explanation. *Synthese*, 191: 3367–3391.

Williamson, O. E. 1975. *Markets and hierarchies: Analysis and antitrust implications*. New York: Free Press.

1985. *The economic institutions of capitalism: Firms, markets, relational contracting*. New York: Free Press.

1996. Economic organization: The case for candor. *Academy of Management Review*, 21: 48–57.

1997. Hierarchies, markets and power in the economy: An economic perspective. In C. Menard (Ed.), *Transaction cost economics: Recent developments*: 1–29. Brookfield, VT: Edward Elgar.

Wilson, G. M. 1985. Davidson on intentional action. In E. LePore and B. P. McLaughlin (Eds.), *Actions and events: Essays on the philosophy of Donald Davidson*: 29–43. Oxford: Basil Blackwell.

Wilson, R. A. and Keil, F. 1998. The shadows and shallows of explanation. *Minds and Machines*, 8: 137–159.

Wong, S. H. 2012. Does superstition help? A study of the role of superstitions and death beliefs on death anxiety amongst Chinese undergraduates in Hong Kong. *OMEGA – Journal of Death and Dying*, 65: 55–70.

Wong, W.-C. 2006. Understanding dialectical thinking from a cultural-historical perspective. *Philosophical Psychology*, 19: 239–260.

Wood, M. S. and McKinley, W. 2010. The production of entrepreneurial opportunity: A constructivist perspective. *Strategic Entrepreneurship Journal*, 4: 66–84.

Woodward, J. 2003. *Making things happen: A theory of causal explanation*. New York: Oxford University Press.

Wray, K. B. 2002. Social selection, agents' intentions, and functional explanation. *Analyse & Kritik*, 24: 72–86.

Wright, C. 2015. The ontic conception of scientific explanation. *Studies in History and Philosophy of Science*, 54: 20–30.

Wright, C. and van Eck, D. 2018. Ontic explanation is either ontic or explanatory, but not both. *Ergo*, 5: 997–1029.

Yaghmaie, A. 2017. How to characterise pure and applied science. *International Studies in the Philosophy of Science*, 31: 133–149.

Yan, A. and Gray, B. 1994. Bargaining power, management control, and performance in United States–China joint ventures: A comparative case study. *Academy of Management Journal*, 37: 1478–1517.

Yates, J. 2005. *Structuring the information age: Life insurance and technology in the 20th century*. Baltimore, MD: John Hopkins University Press.

Yin, R. K. 1984. *Case study research: Design and methods*. Beverly Hills, CA: Sage.

Ylikoski, P. 2007. The idea of contrastive explanandum. In J. Persson and P. Ylikoski (Eds.), *Rethinking explanation*: 27–42. Dordrecht: Springer.

2014. Rethinking micro-macro relations. In J. Zahle and F. Collin (Eds.), *Rethinking the individualism-holism debate*: 117–135. Cham: Springer.

Zajac, E. J. and Olsen, C. P. 1993. From transaction cost to transaction value analysis: Implications for the study of interorganizational strategies. *Journal of Management Studies*, 30: 131–145.

Zald, M. N. 1993. Organization studies as a scientific and humanistic enterprise: Toward a reconceptualization of the foundations of the field. *Organization Science*, 4: 513–528.

Zemla, J. C., Sloman, S., Bechlivanidis, C. and Lagnado, D. A. 2017. Evaluating everyday explanations. *Psychonomic Bulletin & Review*, 24: 1488–1500.

Zhang, F., Lyu, C. and Zhu, L. 2021. Organizational unlearning, knowledge generation strategies and radical innovation performance: Evidence from a transitional economy. *European Journal of Marketing*, 56: 133–158.

孟子《盡心上》Mencius. *Jin xin I*

莊子《養生主》Zhuangzi. *Nourishing the lord of life.*

Index

Printed in the United States
by Baker & Taylor Publisher Services